VOYAGES OF DISCOVERY

TimeFrame AD 1400-1500

CENTRAL AND SOUTH AMERICA

WESTERN EUROPE

TimeFrame AD 1400-1500

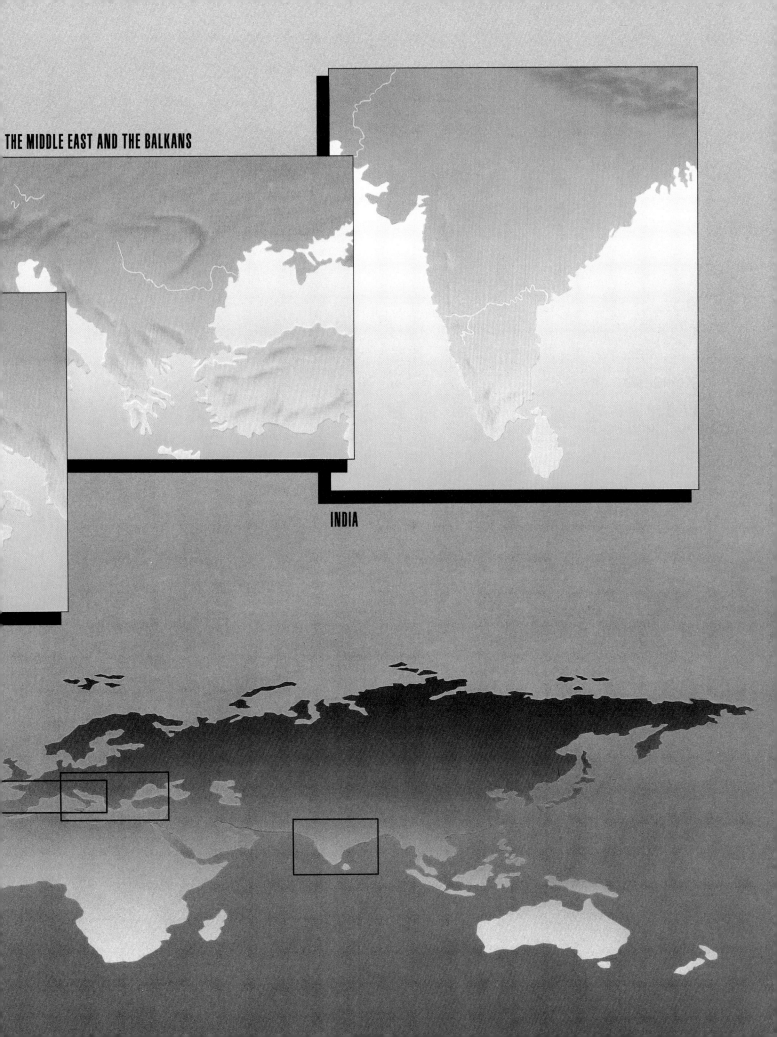

THE MIDDLE EAST AND THE BALKANS

INDIA

TIME®
LIFE
BOOKS

Other Publications:
AMERICAN COUNTRY
VOYAGE THROUGH THE UNIVERSE
THE THIRD REICH
THE TIME-LIFE GARDENER'S GUIDE
MYSTERIES OF THE UNKNOWN
FIX IT YOURSELF
FITNESS, HEALTH & NUTRITION
SUCCESSFUL PARENTING
HEALTHY HOME COOKING
UNDERSTANDING COMPUTERS
LIBRARY OF NATIONS
THE ENCHANTED WORLD
THE KODAK LIBRARY OF CREATIVE PHOTOGRAPHY
GREAT MEALS IN MINUTES
THE CIVIL WAR
PLANET EARTH
COLLECTOR'S LIBRARY OF THE CIVIL WAR
THE EPIC OF FLIGHT
THE GOOD COOK
WORLD WAR II
HOME REPAIR AND IMPROVEMENT
THE OLD WEST

For information on and a full description of
any of the Time-Life Books series listed above,
please call 1-800-621-7026 or write:
Reader Information
Time-Life Customer Service
P.O. Box C-32068
Richmond, Virginia 23261-2068

This volume is one in a series that tells the story
of humankind. Other books in the series include:
The Age of God-Kings
Barbarian Tides
A Soaring Spirit
Empires Ascendant
Empires Besieged
The March of Islam
Fury of the Northmen
Light in the East
The Divine Campaigns
The Mongol Conquests
The Age of Calamity

VOYAGES OF DISCOVERY

TimeFrame AD 1400-1500

BY THE EDITORS OF TIME-LIFE BOOKS

TIME-LIFE BOOKS, ALEXANDRIA, VIRGINIA

Time-Life Books Inc.
is a wholly owned subsidiary of
TIME INCORPORATED

FOUNDER: Henry R. Luce 1898-1967

Editor-in-Chief: Jason McManus
Chairman and Chief Executive Officer:
J. Richard Munro
President and Chief Operating Officer:
N. J. Nicholas, Jr.
Editorial Director: Richard B. Stolley
Executive Vice President, Books:
Kelso F. Sutton
Vice President, Books: Paul V.
McLaughlin

TIME-LIFE BOOKS INC.

EDITOR: George Constable
Executive Editor: Ellen Phillips
Director of Design: Louis Klein
Director of Editorial Resources:
Phyllis K. Wise
Editorial Board: Russell B. Adams, Jr.,
Dale M. Brown, Roberta Conlan,
Thomas H. Flaherty, Lee Hassig, Donia
Ann Steele, Rosalind Stubenberg
Director of Photography and Research:
John Conrad Weiser
Assistant Director of Editorial Resources:
Elise Ritter Gibson

EUROPEAN EDITOR: Sue Joiner
Executive Editor: Gillian Moore
Design Director: Ed Skyner
Assistant Design Director: Mary Staples
Chief of Research: Vanessa Kramer
Chief Sub-Editor: Ilse Gray

PRESIDENT: Christopher T. Linen
Chief Operating Officer: John M. Fahey, Jr.
Senior Vice Presidents: Robert M.
DeSena, James L. Mercer, Paul R.
Stewart
Vice Presidents: Stephen L. Bair, Ralph J.
Cuomo, Neal Goff, Stephen L. Goldstein,
Juanita T. James, Carol Kaplan, Susan J.
Maruyama, Robert H. Smith, Joseph J.
Ward
Director of Production Services:
Robert J. Passantino
Supervisor of Quality Control: James
King

Correspondents: Elisabeth Kraemer-Singh
(Bonn); Christina Lieberman (New York);
Maria Vincenza Aloisi (Paris); Ann Na-
tanson (Rome). Valuable assistance was
also provided by Elizabeth Brown (New
York); Josephine du Brusle (Paris);
Michael Donath (Prague); Ann Wise
(Rome); Traudl Lessing (Vienna).

TIME FRAME
(published in Britain as
TIME-LIFE HISTORY OF THE WORLD)

SERIES EDITOR: Tony Allan

Editorial Staff for *Voyages of Discovery:*
Designer: Mary Staples
Writer: Christopher Farman
Researchers: Louise Tucker (principal);
Marie-Louise Collard
Sub-Editor: Christine Noble
Design Assistant: Rachel Gibson
Editorial Assistant: Molly Sutherland
Picture Department: Patricia Murray
(administrator), Amanda Hindley (picture
coordinator)

Editorial Production
Chief: Maureen Kelly
Production Assistant: Samantha Hill
Editorial Department: Theresa John,
Debra Lelliott

U.S. EDITION

Assistant Editor: Barbara Fairchild
Quarmby
Copy Coordinator: Colette Stockum
Picture Coordinator: Robert H.
Wooldridge, Jr.

Editorial Operations
Copy Chief: Diane Ullius
Production: Celia Beattie
Library: Louise D. Forstall

Special Contributors: Iris Barry, John
Cottrell, Alan Lothian, John Man (text);
Sheila Corr, Timothy Fraser, Barbara
Moir Hicks, Linda Proud, Stephen Rogers
(research); Diane Kittower (copy); Roy
Nanovic (index).

CONSULTANTS

General:
GEOFFREY PARKER, Professor of Histo-
ry, University of Illinois, Urbana-
Champaign, Illinois

Ocean Voyages:
GEORGE WINIUS, Lecturer at the Center
for the Study of the Expansion of Europe,
Leiden State University, the Netherlands

Italy:
PETER BURKE, Reader in Cultural History, Emmanuel College, Cambridge University, Cambridge, England

Constantinople:
ROBERT IRWIN, Author of *The Middle
East in the Middle Ages*

The Hussite Wars:
MICHAEL MULLETT, Lecturer in History,
University of Lancaster, Lancaster,
England

General and India:
CHRISTOPHER BAYLY, Reader in Modern Indian History, St. Catharine's College, Cambridge University, Cambridge,
England

The Americas:
WARWICK BRAY, Reader in Latin-
American Archaeology, Institute of Ar-
chaeology, University College, London

**Library of Congress Cataloging in
Publication Data**
Voyages of discovery: time frame—AD 1400-
1500 / by the editors of Time-Life Books.
    p.   cm.—(Time frame)
    Bibliography: p.
    Includes index.
ISBN 0-8094-6445-4.—ISBN 0-8094-6446-2
(lib. bdg.)
    1. Discoveries (in geography) 2. Geography—
15th-16th cent.
I. Time-Life Books. II. Series.
G400.V69 1989
910'.9—dc20   89-4450
                                    CIP

Time-Life Books Inc. offers a wide range of fine
recordings, including a *Rock 'n' Roll Era* series.
For subscription information, call 1-800-621-
7026 or write Time-Life Music, P.O. Box C-
32068, Richmond, Virginia 23261-2068.

CONTENTS

THE OCEAN ADVENTURERS

1

"Said the mariners, this much is clear, that beyond this Cape, there is no race of men nor place of inhabitants, . . . while the currents are so terrible that no ship having once passed the Cape, will ever be able to return." So wrote the Portuguese historian Gomes Eanes de Zurara, describing the trepidation with which sailors in the early 1430s approached the southern limits of their world—Cape Bojador, a lonely, wind-whipped knob of sand and rock on the western bulge of Africa in the territory now known as Western Sahara. Travelers from Europe had journeyed east before, but not far south or west. In those directions lay lands and seas unknown and, according to some, unknowable.

Yet not much more than a century later, European navigators had seen and mapped a substantial part of the world. In a succession of pioneering voyages, explorers took their tough little wooden ships around the coastline of Africa to the islands of the Far East. Bravely setting out in the opposite direction, they charted the outline of much of the Americas. These navigators discovered, at hideous cost in human life, the unimagined vastness of the Pacific and completed the circuit of the world. The sea lanes they pioneered became highways for trade and plunder, ending forever the isolation of the world's major civilizations.

Their journeys were the keynote of a century of widening horizons, especially for Europeans. In fifteenth-century Italy, the flowering of art and learning known as the Renaissance began, setting man, rather than God, as the rightful focus of human endeavor. Elsewhere in Europe there were signs that the old feudal order, supported by the Church, was crumbling, threatened by men and women who in earlier times would have meekly accepted their lot. Nowhere was the new mood more keenly felt or more clearly evident than in Bohemia, where an unlikely group of peasant rebels took on and, for a time, held off the combined might of the Holy Roman Emperor's armies and a powerful papacy.

Moreover, the Christians of western Europe were dealt a major blow in the fifteenth century: Constantinople, capital of the 1,000-year-old Byzantine Empire, would collapse before the strength of the expanding Ottoman Empire. And there were parts of the world where Europe's new energies were not yet felt: In India and the Americas, great empires flourished in the calm before the storm that was to be whipped up by the unforeseen eruption of the Europeans.

There were many reasons why the great discoveries were European achievements. The Chinese and Arabs were good navigators, in some respects more advanced than the Europeans, and they had wealth enough to finance lengthy voyages away from coastal waters and across the open seas. China, indeed, made a series of extensive exploratory voyages at the start of the century, then decided on political grounds not to continue with the enterprise. It would be Europe's peculiar combination of reli-

Shown in a stained-glass window, a sturdy fifteenth-century cargo ship runs before the wind. The workhorses of Europe's Atlantic coastline, such boats contained features—notably square-rigging to catch following breezes—that were already proving vital to Portuguese sailors exploring the unknown coasts of Africa.

In less than forty years—between 1487 and 1522—explorers from Spain and Portugal, lured by dreams of wealth and inspired by crusading zeal, revealed in outline six of the seven major continental landmasses. Bartolomeu Dias's voyage around the Cape of Good Hope showed that Africa did not extend clear to the South Pole. Vasco da Gama became the first European to reach India by sea. Christopher Columbus, attempting to reach the Orient by sailing westward, unwittingly discovered a whole new world. And Ferdinand Magellan proved that North and South America were continents and revealed the vast extent of the Pacific.

Columbus's success impelled the rival exploring nations, Spain and Portugal, to divide the undiscovered world. By the Treaty of Tordesillas in 1494, Portugal agreed to restrict its claims to the east, and Spain to the west, of a line 370 leagues (about 1,250 miles) beyond the Cape Verde Islands. No one knew then that South America bulged east of the demarcation—a fact that later allowed Portugal to claim Brazil. No other country recognized the treaty, but the two nations' naval supremacy enabled them to enforce it for almost a century.

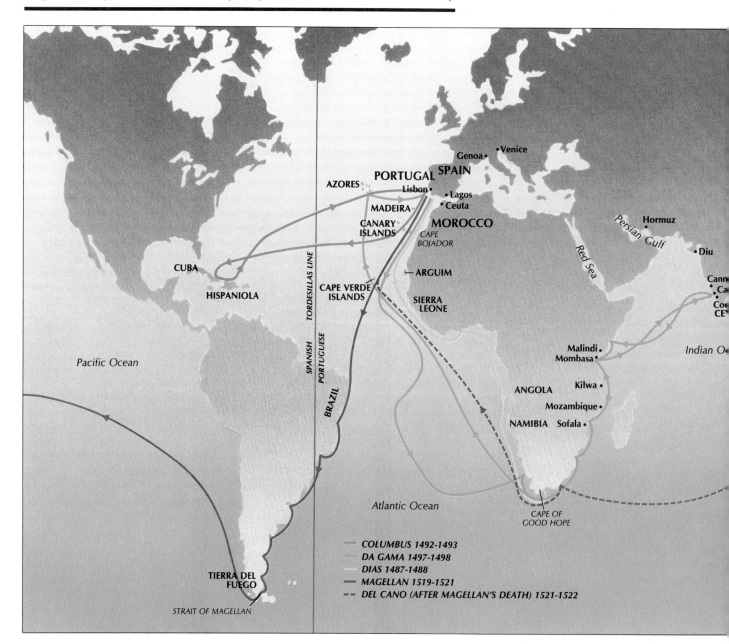

COLUMBUS 1492-1493
DA GAMA 1497-1498
DIAS 1487-1488
MAGELLAN 1519-1521
DEL CANO (AFTER MAGELLAN'S DEATH) 1521-1522

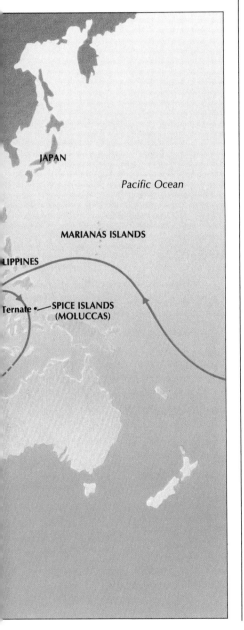

gious zeal, hardheaded acquisitiveness, and seafaring expertise that provided the necessary mixture of motivation and technical ability to realize the voyages. These qualities were common to several European nations, but because of geographical and historical factors, one country in particular pioneered the ocean routes—Portugal.

Europe in the early fifteenth century provided a good foundation for expansion. Commercially, it had motives for seeking new trade routes. Although it was a largely self-contained world, it had an appetite for certain luxury items that had been traded from the East since Roman times and for which demand far exceeded supply. For almost a century, from about 1250 on, several European explorers had trekked overland through central Asia, which was then unified under Mongol rule, searching for direct links with the suppliers; the best-known was the Venetian merchant Marco Polo. By the middle of the fourteenth century, however, the overland route had been cut off. In the East the Mongol Empire, which had guaranteed the peace that made such journeys possible, had collapsed. By the end of the fifteenth century, at the western limits of Asia, the Ottomans, who were fierce proponents of Islam, had carved out an expansionist and virulently anti-Christian nation from the ruins of the Byzantine Empire. The old channels of trade that passed from Asia to the Middle East and the eastern shores of the Mediterranean Sea were now firmly in the hands of Muslim intermediaries.

Although the Asia trade was quite small in comparison with the cargo-loads of grain, wool, and other essential commodities that made up the bulk of European commerce, it had always been associated with big profits. There was much money to be made from Eastern luxuries: silks from Persia and China, cotton from India, precious stones—Indian diamonds and emeralds, Burmese rubies, Ceylonese garnets, topazes, and sapphires—and, above all, spices.

Spices played a special role in the culinary, economic, and political life of Europe. Europeans were meat eaters by preference, but supply was seasonal. A shortage of winter fodder made it essential that many cattle be slaughtered in the autumn. The meat soon deteriorated, even when it was preserved by salting. Spices helped to make it palatable; in addition, they were reputed to be medicinal, many of them inspiring semimystical reverence.

Although the range of commodities handled by the spice merchants was huge—one popular handbook listed 288 substances, including sugar, waxes, gums, cosmetics, perfumes, drugs, and dyes—most in demand were pepper from India, cinnamon from Ceylon, and such exotic items as nutmeg, mace, and cloves from islands in the Moluccas, part of present-day Indonesia. By the middle of the fifteenth century, Europe had a growing population and thus an expanding market for most goods, including an almost insatiable demand for spices by those fortunate enough to be able to afford them.

Traditionally, trade goods were brought overland by pack animals to the Mediterranean and the Black Sea. As political change made these routes precarious, the goods came to be carried by boat—by Chinese junks to Malaya, and then by Arab ships to India, East Africa, Persia, and Arabia; next through the Red Sea and the Persian Gulf they made their way, with a short overland hop, to the great coastal ports of the Mediterranean. Only then did the commodities reach the hands of Europeans, via merchants from Genoa and Venice, who had dominated the trade for 500 years. At each stage, the price rose. Pepper bought for three ducats in India would cost sixty-eight in Cairo and nearly double that in Venice—almost a fiftyfold increase. Clearly, any trader who could deal directly with the source of the spices—for instance, by sailing there—would stand to make a fortune, as would the person or institution financing the voyage.

This idea, however, was only vaguely conceived in the early fifteenth century, when the limitations of geographical knowledge made any such venture a leap into the unknown. To those few interested in the matter, the world beyond the Black Sea, let alone beyond the Sahara or across the Atlantic horizon, was a mystery. It had been accepted by scholars since classical times that the earth was spherical. What it actually contained, however, was a subject of myth and speculation, based on ideas inherited from Aristotle and the ancient world as reflected through the prism of Christian orthodoxy. Commonly, medieval world maps showed a disk with Jerusalem at its center; radiating out from it were fanciful representations of the three known continents. The Garden of Eden and other locales from the Bible were then sketched in at appropriate points.

More accurate information, obtained by firsthand observation, was available: The book describing Marco Polo's journeys across Asia had been widely popular. But its very success had spawned apocryphal imitations, drawing on nothing more substantial than their authors' imaginations, and the reading public had no way of telling which were true. A book of pure fantasy, such as the popular and widely translated *Travels* of Sir John Mandeville, was quite as credible to people without additional evidence as Marco Polo's sober narrative, despite Mandeville's far-fetched accounts of headless peoples with eyes and mouths in their shoulders and men with ears hanging down to their knees.

However, the writings of the great Arab traveler ibn-Battuta, who journeyed from his home in Morocco via India to the Far East in the mid-fourteenth century, were totally unknown in Europe. Even the Arabs, though, had not probed the Atlantic. To them and to Europeans alike, the ocean beyond Gibraltar was a "green sea of darkness," an unnavigable, nightmarish world leading to zones that were cold enough to freeze the blood or hot enough to boil it.

But there was one recent source of more practical information. In 1406 or shortly after, a book appeared that started a revolution in knowledge and attitude. This was a translation into Latin, the language of all educated Europeans, of the *Geography* written by Claudius Ptolemaeus, or Ptolemy, in the second century AD. His text, summarizing the understanding of the earth at the height of the Roman Empire, contained a gazetteer of known places. In an important innovation, it also described a system of references based on a globe divided into a grid of two sets of circles marked off into degrees, the now-familiar coordinates of latitude and longitude. A map of the world as Ptolemy knew it accompanied the text. It showed the continents of Europe, Asia, and Africa with some accuracy, although they became increasingly distorted the farther they got from the Mediterranean region that Ptolemy, a Greek living in the North African city of Alexandria, had seen at first hand. The biggest mistake he made was to show Africa merging southward into a vast continent that enclosed the Indian Ocean and touched Asia—a reflection of Aristotle's flawed reasoning that the earth must consist of at least 51 percent land in order for it to stand clear of the surrounding ocean, and that the earth's northern landmass had to be balanced by a continent of the same size in the Southern Hemisphere.

Despite its errors, Ptolemy's map was nonetheless a huge improvement on anything else then available. It contained a wealth of detail, and it summarized the wisdom and knowledge of the classical world at a time when Europe was beginning to rediscover Greek and Roman literature. Perusing it, potential explorers not only saw the rest of the world as accessible but also had a model against which they could compare their discoveries.

Portugal was the first country in which the new spirit of inquisitiveness had practical results. In many ways, this coastal strip of fewer than a million people, most of them poor peasants, was an unlikely leader of commercial and geographical enterprise. But it had some advantages. Its position on the outer edge of Europe had given its sailors experience of navigation along the Atlantic coast as well as in the Mediterranean Sea. Trading wine, olive oil, and dried fruits with captains from northern Europe, Portugal's seafarers were safely removed from any direct threat from the Italians, who dominated the eastern Mediterranean.

The motives that drove the sailors and rulers of this hardscrabble little country to unprecedented feats of discovery were mixed. Certainly the desire for knowledge played a part. Of more immediate importance was the search for wealth through trade, although this in turn was imbued with a nobler purpose. As a matter of unquestioned dogma, kings and common sailors alike believed it to be their sacred duty to search out their coreligionists in foreign parts and to bring the word of God to the pagans of distant lands. When Vasco da Gama first arrived in India, one of his crew members was asked why the Europeans had journeyed so far. "We come," he said, "in search of Christians and spices."

The Portuguese brought to their self-elected task a jaunty ambition that was ideally suited to the risks involved in exploration. They were great individualists who were eager to make their mark on the world's stage. The Portuguese epic *The Lusiads,* written in the sixteenth century by Luis Vaz de Camões to honor his compatriots' achievements, recalls the spirit of braggadocio that accompanied their feats: "They were men of no ordinary stature, equally at home in war and in dangers of every kind . . . achieving immortality through their illustrious exploits."

Moreover, these were inhabitants of a proud, self-assertive nation only recently come to independence. Portugal traced its origins to 1140, when a Christian ruler first styled himself king following a victory over the Moors who then ruled most of the Iberian Peninsula. It

This intricate Portuguese astrolabe was a fifteenth-century marine adaptation of an ancient device used for measuring the angle of an object above the horizontal. With it, a mariner could discover his north-south position anywhere in the world, even in unknown waters. On one side *(left)* was a movable pointer. When the astrolabe was hung vertically from its ring, the navigator would aim the pointer at the sun or a known star to read off its elevation in degrees. The mariner could then refer to a set of tables—engraved on the reverse side *(below)* in this case—that related the angle of elevation to the date, time of day, and therefore the latitude.

PILLARS OF PORTUGUESE SOCIETY

Prince Henry the Navigator

White-robed Cistercian monks recall the zealous Christianity that infused Portuguese society and sanctified the aggressive business of exploration.

King Afonso kneels to Saint Vincent. Behind the king stands his uncle, Henry the Navigator, who died almost a decade before this portrait was painted.

Fishermen—one shown draped in a net—represent a seafaring tradition that stood the country in good stead when mariners tackled the unknown waters off Africa.

While his mariners reconnoitered the West African coastline, Afonso V, ruler of Portugal from 1438 to 1481, was also making more direct incursions into the continent by campaigning against the Muslim rulers of Morocco. His successes, which included the capture of Tangier in 1471, won him the nickname "the African." To give thanks for his victories, Afonso commissioned a new altarpiece for Lisbon Cathedral. The work of a local artist named Nuno Goncalves, its six panels show the king and representative groups of his compatriots in homage before twin images of Saint Vincent, patron saint of Lisbon. The groups chosen form a cross section of fifteenth-century Portuguese society, in particular those elements involved in the nation's overseas expansion.

Soldiers served as a reminder that Iberian kings had wrested their lands from the Moors and then honed their martial skills in factional wars.

Although the Jews were later to be persecuted by the Inquisition, they are here portrayed in obeisance to the Christian saint to recall their influence as bankers, artisans, and physicians.

Although the nobles were traditionally volatile, these aristocrats venerating a second image of Saint Vincent suggest a tough and battle-hardened class.

was not until 1249, however, that the last Moors were driven out and the nation was established in approximately its present boundaries. Even then, it remained under threat from the larger Christian kingdom of Castile to the east. A decisive victory at the Battle of Aljubarrota in 1385 confirmed the nation's separate existence, although skirmishing continued for some years. From that time onward, Portugal's position—facing the Atlantic and hemmed in by Castile—as well as patriotic and Christian fervor, directed attention outward, toward Muslim territory in North Africa and the unknown world beyond.

The outward urge was brought into sharp focus by one man: Prince Henry. Henry financed and inspired Portugal's explorers between 1419 and his death in 1460. His biographer Zurara, noting that "the noble spirit of this prince . . . was ever urging him both to begin and to carry out very great deeds," gave a number of reasons for his obsession. One was simple curiosity to find out what lay beyond Cape Bojador. Another was a desire to determine the exact extent of the Muslim domains in Africa and to find out whether lands inhabited by Christians or other well-disposed peoples lay beyond them; if so, it might be possible to trade with them or even to unite with them in a holy war against the infidel, "to make increase in the faith of our Lord Jesus Christ and to bring to him all the souls that should be saved."

This element in the prince's thinking was no doubt influenced by a popular legend of the time, the belief that a mighty priest-king called Prester (a corruption of the word "presbyter") John ruled a lost Christian kingdom somewhere beyond the Muslim lands. This kingdom—variously pointed out as being in Asia and Africa—was reputed to be large and wealthy, with neither poor nor thieves living there. Zurara, reflecting the superstitions of the age, added another reason to explain Henry's concerns: The prince's horoscope predicted that he would "attempt the discovery of things that were hidden from other men," and he was keen to fulfill the dictates of the stars.

Despite the nickname of "the Navigator" that was conferred on him by later historians, Henry never went exploring himself. He may, as has often been claimed, have run a navigation school in southern Portugal, but there is no direct evidence that he did any such thing. He was ascetic: He never married and always wore a hair shirt beneath his princely clothing in order to chastise the flesh. His portrait suggests a stern, withdrawn figure, with more talent for giving orders than inspiring people. In his bitter hostility toward the Muslim powers, he showed a crusading zeal more typically seen in rulers who lived in the twelfth century than in his own day.

While still a young man, Henry had acquired the power and opportunity to give expression to his ambitions. In 1411, Portugal finally made peace with Castile. With an army of knights now idle, Portugal looked toward its old enemy, the Moors, who were still entrenched not only in the caliphate of Granada on the nation's southeastern border but also across the Strait of Gibraltar on the North African coast. The Portuguese king set his sights on Ceuta, a rich port guarding the African side of the strait, and gave to Henry, his third son, the task of organizing the building and outfitting of the ships and crews needed for the expedition to take it. In this way the young prince gained firsthand experience of the practical business of organizing large-scale maritime enterprises. When the armada finally sailed in 1415, the port fell to its 200 ships in a single day.

Henry accompanied the fleet, and his valor in the ensuing action won him the governorship of the Algarve, Portugal's southern province. In 1420, when he was still only twenty-six, Henry was made grand master of a crusading body called the Order of Christ. It was thus as a governor and a crusader that he put into effect his grand plan—not only to confront the Moors in North Africa but also to outflank them by opening a sea route to sub-Saharan Africa.

In order to achieve his aims, Henry needed oceangoing ships, accurate charts, and men skilled in oceanic navigation. At first, these were all in short supply. There was, simply, no European tradition of open-water ocean sailing. A navigator had to that time been just a pilot, making his way along coastlines by the process known as "caping and kenning"—steering from cape to cape with the aid of the information his lookout could "ken" from the masthead. To aid him in his task, he might seek the help of charts known as portolans, which outlined the northern European and Mediterranean coasts in great detail and provided compass bearings to be followed from point to point. (It had been known for at least 400 years that a magnetized needle, pivoting freely, would point north.)

To leave sight of the coast, particularly in the stormy waters of the Atlantic, was to court danger. With all the familiar landmarks removed, navigation became largely a matter of guesswork. It was theoretically possible to get some idea of north-south position by gauging the angle of the North Star or midday sun against the horizon. But the tool for making such measurements, the astrolabe, was a complex piece of equipment that demanded considerable expertise if it was to provide accurate data. The angles changed slightly every day, making charts necessary, and an accurate measurement was hard to achieve on board a pitching ship, even if the weather was clear. Few captains were willing to bother. At best, they might simply use a hand to measure the angle: two degrees for a finger above the horizon, eight for a wrist, eighteen for a hand.

Even with a north-south reading, there was no way to tell one's longitude, or east-west location, by the sun or stars. A reading of longitude can be made by comparing local time with the time at some known point, and that in turn requires an accurate clock. No such reliable chronometer existed in the fifteenth century. The best any pilot could do was keep a careful account of his progress by dead reckoning—assessing the speed at which his ship sailed past flotsam and then trying to estimate sailing distances while allowing for the effects of currents and cross winds. (The open-sea technique of allowing a knotted rope to be pulled overboard by the pressure of water and measuring speed in "knots" would not emerge for another century.) In the fifteenth century, navigation was a rough-and-ready business in which experience was all.

Ships, too, were seaworthy on the open ocean. They had evolved solely to supply Mediterranean and Atlantic coastal needs, and each region had its own traditions. In the Mediterranean, besides the lightweight war galleys still powered by oarsmen as had been done in the days of ancient Rome, two types of sailing boat were used: huge merchantmen of up to 1,100 tons and smaller, two- or three-masted vessels of around 275 tons that were equipped with oars to help maneuver in and out of harbors. Both were cumbersome. Square sails, loosely hauled as they were at the time, forced sailors to be dependent on following winds. The curved keels demanded careful support when the ships were beached for overhauling. And with either side rudders or ungainly stern rudders curved to fit the shape of the hull, the vessels were slow to respond to steering.

The Atlantic coastal traders used tubby, buoyant "cogs," a style of vessel better suited to Atlantic swells. The keels and sterns were straight, allowing the use of a

When lateen-rigged, the caravel—up to sixty-five feet long with a 130-ton capacity—had its mainmast forward. The only cabin space was in the stern: The bow was kept clear to allow the heel of the spar to swing freely.

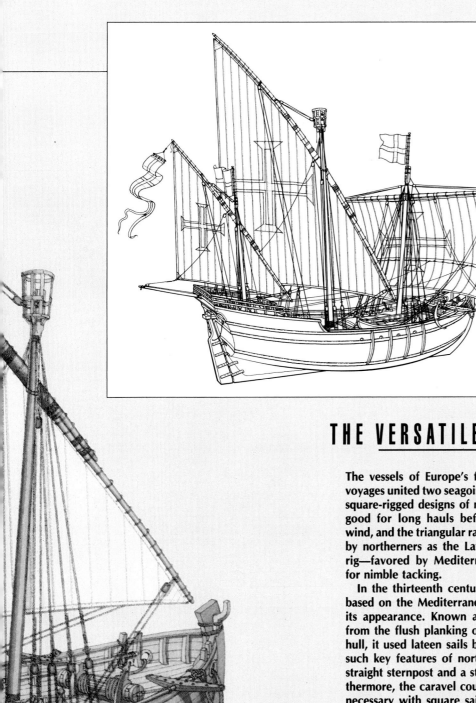

To refit their caravel with square-rigging—thus creating what was termed a *caravela redonda*—crewmen would restep the mainmast amidships and set a square sail on the foremast. If necessary, the mainmast could be reset with a square sail as well.

THE VERSATILE CARAVEL

The vessels of Europe's first great ocean voyages united two seagoing traditions: the square-rigged designs of northern Europe, good for long hauls before a following wind, and the triangular raked sail—known by northerners as the Latin, or "lateen," rig—favored by Mediterranean mariners for nimble tacking.

In the thirteenth century, a new vessel based on the Mediterranean model made its appearance. Known as the "caravel" from the flush planking of its carvel-built hull, it used lateen sails but also included such key features of northern boats as a straight sternpost and a stern rudder. Furthermore, the caravel could be rerigged if necessary with square sails to gain speed before a following wind and to provide improved handling in foul weather.

These boats were a natural choice for the first Portuguese explorers when they sailed southward to Africa in the 1440s. As journeys increased in length, however, disadvantages appeared. It took a crew of up to twenty-five to control the caravel's immense spars, and the open decks offered little protection to either crew or stores. After half a century of use, caravels were joined by larger, roomier vessels better suited to longer voyages.

straight stern rudder. The sail, which was set on a single mast, was easily furled or reefed in a wind. But because it was large, square, and loosely hauled, it still gave the ship little maneuverability.

There was, however, a third tradition of boatbuilding familiar, in concept at least, to European mariners. For 300 years, the Arabs had used a totally different rig, a triangular sail attached to a long yard set at an angle on the mast. This rig, named "lateen" by twelfth-century Crusaders who associated it with the Latin countries, had one great advantage over square-rigging: Because the yard could be moved and the sail's position changed, ships could sail close to the wind, enabling them to negotiate inland waters, slip in and out of harbors, and take direct routes over the open ocean without the need to wait for a favorable breeze. Though convenient for small vessels, the design had disadvantages. Reefing the sail to cope with a strong wind was difficult; and the ships could not come about easily, as modern yachts do, because the sail had to be taken down, stepped around the mast, and reset, a labor-intensive job that placed severe restraints on the size of vessels. A lateen-rigged vessel of any size needed a crew of fifteen just to handle the sails.

By the early fifteenth century, enterprising sailors—probably Spanish and Portuguese—had fitted the lateen rig to the Atlantic cog to produce versatile combination vessels known as caravels. These two- or three-masted ships, which were around sixty-five feet long and weighed approximately sixty-five to eighty tons, would become the workhorses of Portuguese exploration. The larger, more refined of them used a variable mix of lateen and square-rigged sails, allowing for an optimal use of following winds and also providing maneuverability for nosing in and out of unmapped bays and estuaries. Sometimes, too, the ships were rerigged from one style to the other in the course of voyages.

Though easier to handle than their predecessors, such ships were just as uncomfortable. Typically, they had one deck, cambered to allow breaking seas to run off. Although the captain often had the privilege of a minute cabin set at the stern, the rest of the crew of thirty or forty men had to sleep or relax wherever they could: on deck in warm weather, below deck with the cargo in rough and cold conditions. Not that they had much leisure for sleeping: Most of the crew's time was spent pumping out the bilges (all wooden ships leaked), dropping the lead-and-line to determine the ocean depth, and working the sails.

Such a life, though harsh and sometimes dangerous, was not particularly unhealthful. In the early decades of the age of exploration, voyages seldom lasted more than two months and usually still hugged the coasts, generally with several landings to replenish supplies. Barring tempest or war, crews could remain reasonably wellnourished, with fresh food and water regularly available. As the length of voyages increased, all that would change.

Encouraged by the knowledge that his sailors voyaged in increasingly sophisticated vessels, Prince Henry decided in 1433—after dispatching preliminary forays to Madeira and the Canary Islands, already known to mariners for some generations—to send out a ship under a captain named Gil Eanes with orders to proceed beyond Cape Bojador, the peninsula 200 miles to the south of the Canaries that was still the limit of the known world in that direction. Apparently, Eanes's courage failed him: He returned with the mission unachieved. He made excuses to his patron, citing the fearful perils he faced and no doubt recalling the "torrid zones" and Mandevillian monsters that supposedly lay ahead, ready to attack. Prince Henry had no patience with him or with the myths that he believed in. "In truth, I marvel at these imaginings that have possessed you all!" he said, and sent Eanes off again. "Strain every nerve to pass that cape!"

In the following year, Captain Eanes returned in triumph. He had skirted the shallows that reach 20 miles out from Bojador's wind-whipped barrens, landed almost 100 miles beyond, and even gathered a few plants to bring back with him. In reality, it had turned out to be an easy trip. The barrier of Cape Bojador had been less physical than psychological.

Now there was nothing to stop further exploration. Urged on by Henry, enterprising captains vied to travel farther with each passing year down the West African coastline. Soon there were indications that the enterprise could be economically worthwhile. In 1436, a captain named Afonso Baldaya landed near an inlet 125 miles beyond Bojador and found human footprints in the sand. The news excited Henry, who at once dispatched Baldaya on a second expedition. On his return voyage, the captain sent off two young members of the crew on horseback to reconnoiter for inhabitants. They found more than they bargained for, narrowly escaping with their lives from a band of spear-wielding warriors. Baldaya had better luck, however, in scouting the local fauna. He spotted some seals—"sea wolves," he called them—which he killed and skinned. His sealskins were the first commercial cargo to reach Portugal from the bulge of Africa.

Four years later, a two-vessel expedition returned to Portugal with a more sinister load—a dozen Africans. To Henry, the prisoners were merely a source of information, but others quickly saw that the discovery could be put to a different use: As slaves the Africans would solve a labor shortage that had been paralyzing the country since the devastating plague of the previous century. That was the start of a trade that was to be the economic backbone of the subsequent process of discovery. In 1448, the Portuguese established a fort on the island of Arguin, about 500 miles south of Bojador, and soon another 200 black captives appeared back in Portugal, where they were sold at a public auction.

Zurara described the ensuing scene in detail. "What heart could be so hard as not to be pierced with piteous feelings to see that company?" he asked. "For some kept their heads low and their faces bathed in tears, looking upon one another; others stood groaning very dolorously, looking up to the heights of heaven." The worst part was the division of families: "For as often as they had placed them in one part the sons, seeing their fathers in another, rose with great energy and rushed over to them; the mothers clasped their other children in their arms and threw themselves flat on the ground with them, receiving blows with little pity for their own flesh, if only they might not be torn from them." The trade in slaves, who were used in particular in the sugar plantations of Madeira, founded the Portuguese enterprise on a bedrock of suffering; slavery was to remain an essential part of Portugal's economy for the following 400 years.

In the next decade, two other explorers in Henry's service—a Venetian nobleman named Alvise Cadamosto and the native-born Diogo Gomes—edged farther around the bulge of Africa. By the time Henry died in 1460, the African coast was charted as far south as Sierra Leone (literally, "Lion Mountains," and so named because of the thunderstorms that grumbled like lions around the coastal heights).

With the death of its great patron, the task of financing and inspiring exploration

now devolved on the king of Portugal, Henry's nephew, Afonso V. Afonso was as ambitious as his uncle had been, but more wary of the economic risks he perceived as involved in such an uncertain enterprise. Accordingly, in 1469, he leased rights to the African trade to a certain Fernão Gomes on the condition that his mariners explore an additional 400 miles of coastline annually for the ensuing five years. This novel arrangement worked out well for both parties. Gomes grew rich, and Portugal acquired knowledge of almost 2,000 more miles of coastline, taking its sailors right around the bulge of western Africa. The eastward trend of the coast from Sierra Leone to the Bight of Biafra must have encouraged hopes that the way to the long-sought-after Indies might finally lie open.

The greater the hopes aroused by the newfound lands, the more jealously the sea routes were guarded. In 1480, King Afonso, embroiled in a bitter four-year dispute over the succession to the Spanish throne, gave stern orders that if any of his captains came across Spaniards "who are, or may be, on their way out to the said Guinea or on their way back, or who are in it . . . as soon as such persons shall have been seized, without any further order or course of law, all may be and shall be forthwith cast into the sea, so that they may then die a natural death."

Afonso himself died the following year, to be succeeded by his son John II, who proved to be an enthusiastic patron of the voyages. In the course of the 1480s, expeditions penetrated ever farther, to the barren shores of Angola and Namibia. To establish Portugal's territorial claims, John had his captains plant six-foot-high lime-stone pillars known as *padrões* (patrons) on newly discovered headlands. In the meantime, a fort was built in what is now Ghana, to act as a supply base for trade in gold and slaves as well as pepper (inferior in quality to the Far Eastern variety, but still marketable).

The southward turn of the coast beyond the Bight of Biafra had disappointed those seeking a path to India and resurrected old doubts about the shape of Africa; perhaps Ptolemy had been right after all, and it merged with some vast southern continent. The only way to settle the question once and for all would be to send an expedition to search out Africa's southern tip, if such a point existed. But such an enterprise would be more formidable than any of the voyages yet undertaken and would demand greater feats of seamanship.

As it happened, this task would be made easier because the means for improved navigation was at hand. In 1484, John was told that a table compiled by the Spanish astronomer Abraham Zacuto, listing the sun's midday position above the Iberian Peninsula for each day of the year, now made it possible to work out a ship's latitude accurately by simply measuring the angle of the noonday sun. Now a captain could ascertain how far south he had traveled even when sailing out of sight of land. When he reached the latitude of his destination, the mariner had only to turn toward the coast and use existing techniques of dead reckoning to make a straight line for shore. Encouraged by the new development, John determined that the time had come to settle the issue of the southern continent's existence: If there was indeed a southernmost tip of Africa, his ships would round it.

The person he chose to lead the quest was Bartolomeu Dias. Little is known of the man, but he must have been an experienced and reliable captain, for the expedition he

Two sixteenth-century ivory pieces from the powerful West African kingdom of Benin hint at the astonishment of Africans when they first saw Portuguese sailors—bearded, light-skinned men sailing ships of a type utterly unknown in Africa. On the left is a saltcellar topped by a bearded mariner peering from a crow's-nest. On the right is a mask, the braided hair formed into a row of bearded heads. Objects like this were often carved for Portuguese merchants, eager to trade their guns and other manufactured goods for slaves, palm oil, ivory, and pepper.

was put in charge of was planned on a large scale. In addition to getting two caravels, he was provided with a storeship to counter the difficulty of finding food and fuel on the southern African coast. When he set sail in August 1487, his mandate was unambiguous: to travel as far beyond previously mapped regions as necessary to find the southernmost point of the African continent.

It took Dias three months to reach the bay of Angra das Aldeias, on the coast of present-day Angola, where he restocked his caravels for a final thrust southward and left behind the storeship, guarded by nine of its crew. Then he set off past the last Portuguese padrão, which had been planted by the explorer Diogo Cão the previous year, into uncharted waters. For more than a month, his ships made slow progress down the coastline, sailing into headwinds of increasing strength. Finally, in early January, Dias made the decision to sail westward, out of sight of land, in search of more favorable sailing conditions. The gamble worked; for two weeks, rising winds drove his boats southward. When Dias finally decided to head back in the direction of the coast, he was swept eastward by winds of gale force. Where land should have been, according to his calculations, there was none. Dias turned north and duly sighted land, now tending eastward rather than southward. He must have guessed that he had rounded some sort of cape.

Determined to check, he pressed on for more than a month, despite increasing complaints from his crew. Eventually, Dias agreed to turn back, planting his furthermost padrão on a desolate promontory—possibly the one known today as Kwaaihoek, near South Africa's Great Fish River. Taking time to establish that the current was a warm tropical one coming from the northeast—sure evidence that he had rounded the tip of Africa—he headed back, according to the chronicler of the voyage, João de Barros, "with as much pain and sentiment as if he were leaving a beloved son in eternal exile."

On the return journey along the coast of southern Africa, Dias and his crew members spotted a "great and noble cape" with granite crags, behind which loomed a flat-topped mountain. There he placed a second padrão to mark what he mistakenly assumed was Africa's southern tip. (In fact, he had already missed the most southerly point, Cape Agulhas, which lay more than 120 miles to the southeast.) He named his discovery the Cape of Good Hope.

Working his way back up the coast, he relocated the storeship, only to find that most of the men he had left to guard it had been killed by local tribes. Of three survivors, one "was so

As revealed by a glazed earthenware bowl from Portugal *(below)* and the end of an oak bench from a chapel in King's Lynn, Norfolk, England *(right)*, the success of exploration by sea in the late fourteenth and early fifteenth centuries captured the popular imagination in countries across Europe. Both images are of high-decked carracks, or *naos*, as the Portuguese called them. Sturdier boats than caravels, naos were better suited to ocean voyages.

astonished with pleasure upon seeing his companions that he died shortly, being very thin from illness." Lacking men to crew the storeship, Dias took on provisions, then burned the ship before heading for home. He arrived to a hero's welcome at the end of 1488, having been away for sixteen months. The way to India was open at last.

Before the Portuguese could achieve the goal they had sought for so long, though, a new figure emerged on the scene to complicate their task. The interloper was a Genoese navigator—thirty-seven years old in the year of Dias's return—with a theory of the world and the determination necessary to put his ideas to the test. Cristoforo Colombo—the name was Latinized even in his lifetime to Columbus—had spent eight years in Portugal, from 1476 to 1484, trying to win royal backing for an expedition that would have marked a radical departure for the Portuguese monarch. For Columbus, while sharing the belief that there were fortunes to be made by trading directly with the Orient, was convinced that the fastest way to reach it was not by sailing south around Africa but by heading due west.

He drew his ideas from a variety of sources that included the *Travels* of Marco Polo and biblical texts. He had also corresponded with a Florentine cosmographer named Paolo Toscanelli dal Pozzo, who had studied Ptolemy, and was familiar with his theory that the Eurasian landmass stretched halfway around the world. From Toscanelli's calculations, Columbus deduced that the Indies lay less than 2,500 miles west of the Canary Islands. As it transpired, the figure was completely wrong for Asia, but by coincidence was almost exactly correct for the previously unknown and intervening continent of North America.

King John's experts turned down Columbus's scheme out of hand. John himself, who was by now too committed to the exploration of the Africa route to welcome Columbus's ideas, concurred; he dismissed the Genoese, whom he evaluated as "a big talker, full of fancy and imagination." Rebuffed, Columbus took his ideas to Spain, where after further agonizing years of rejection, he finally found an aristocratic backer and royal approval for an expedition.

Setting sail out of Palos in Spain's southern region of Andalusia with three ships—the *Niña*, the *Pinta*, and the *Santa María*—and approximately ninety crew members, he headed for the Canary Islands, where he restocked before setting sail again, this time due west, on September 6, 1492 (page 27). Thirty-three days later, his men sighted land: the island of San Salvador in the Bahamas. The three boats subsequently reached Cuba and Hispaniola, where the *Santa María* ran aground and had to be abandoned. The two other vessels then steered back to the Old World, bearing the momentous news of their discoveries.

On his return in March 1493, Columbus called in at Lisbon to effect repairs to his battered flagship, the *Niña*. The story he had to tell was, from the point of view of the Portuguese king, as unwelcome as it was sensational. If Columbus was to be believed, he had reached the very islands that the Portuguese had so long sought, but by a totally different route. Mocking the king for having thrown away a chance to claim such wealth, Columbus became boastful, "discourteous, and elated." John's initial reaction was to have him arrested, and several of his courtiers advised him to kill the upstart. To his credit, John swallowed his resentment and sent Columbus peacefully on his triumphant way to Spain.

The Portuguese monarch realized that Ferdinand and Isabella, Columbus's patrons and joint monarchs of a newly unified Spanish realm, would seek to exploit their protégé's discovery, and that Columbus would be dispatched again. There were now two accredited players in the exploration game, and Spain was in a position to lay claim to the very lands that Portugal had spent so much time and effort in seeking to reach. The possibilities of conflict were immense unless some mutually acceptable division of the spoils could be found.

There was at the time in Europe only one supranational power with the authority to arbitrate such matters, and that was the papacy. The Spanish monarchs duly turned to it for a ruling. As it happened, the Vatican's incumbent, Alexander VI, was a Spaniard who had been elected only the previous year with the backing of Isabella. It came as little surprise, then, that he proposed giving Spain rights to all discoveries made more than 100 leagues—nearly 350 miles—west of the Cape Verde Islands. The islands are located between 300 and 450 miles west of present-day Senegal.

The Portuguese were outraged. Not only was the suggested grant a threat to Portuguese control of the Indies, it also endangered further exploration: John's navigators were by now learning that to make optimum use of the route around Africa, they needed to head west in search of favorable winds and currents, into what would be Spanish waters.

John consequently opened discussions with Isabella and Ferdinand, spreading rumors of his intention to challenge the line with a great fleet if no agreement was reached. The Spaniards proved receptive to his claims, and after a year of negotiations at the little town of Tordesillas, more than ninety miles northwest of Madrid, a treaty was signed that shifted the line demarcating the frontier between the two nascent empires almost 1,000 miles to the west. At the time, the exact distance chosen seemed of limited significance. As it happened, however, it left the still-to-be discovered coast of Brazil jutting into the Portuguese sphere of influence, and as a result that nation was to become in later years a Portuguese enclave in an otherwise Spanish continent.

The Treaty of Tordesillas in effect divided the entire undiscovered world between Portugal and Spain. It was breathtaking in its scope, and the very width of its ambitions meant that it was bound to prove impractical in the long run. In the short term, however, it served its purpose well, leaving each nation free to pursue its own course of exploration unimpeded by the other. Spain proceeded to send Columbus on three more expeditions to America, while Portugal continued to concentrate on the route around the tip of Africa to India and beyond.

The hiatus between Dias's successful return in 1488 and the signing of the treaty of 1494 was perhaps filled by journeys that left no enduring record. One expedition still under way, however, was the extraordinary voyage of an explorer and spy named Pêro da Covilhã, the only great overland venture of a century of maritime enterprise. Covilhã was dispatched by John some months before the start of Dias's enterprise with instructions to make his way to India and report back on what he found; at the same time, a companion was sent out with him to travel into Africa in search of Prester John and his Christian kingdom.

Covilhã accomplished his mission by posing as an Arab merchant, traveling with a caravan from Cairo to Aden at the mouth of the Red Sea, and then on to the Indian port of Calicut by boat. Once in India he traveled up the coast, still in Arab disguise, reconnoitering the ports he encountered en route. He next crossed the Indian Ocean to East Africa on a dhow and made his way southward, visiting the prosperous Islamic trading towns that lined the shore. Bearing a plentiful store of information, he re-

UNWITTING DISCOVERER OF A NEW WORLD

At a time when most Portuguese thought the best route to the Indies was around the Cape, one man—Cristoforo Colombo—believed differently.

A Genoese by birth, Colombo—his name was Latinized as Columbus—arrived in Portugal in 1476, at the age of twenty-five, after a shipwreck. Like many others at the time, he was lured by the wealth of the Orient, but the route he proposed to take to reach it was unusual. Believing, along with several geographers of the day, that the world was much smaller than its true diameter of 7,900 miles and that after a mere 2,500 miles the Atlantic would lead to Japan and China, he claimed that the quickest way to the East lay westward.

Failing to win support in Portugal, Columbus eventually turned to the rulers of Spain, Ferdinand and Isabella. In 1492, with three small ships and 100 men, he sailed west into the unknown. Two months later, he sighted an island, one of the Bahamas. The naked inhabitants were clearly not Japanese, but, sure that this was part of an Eastern archipelago, Columbus called the people "Indians," and the name stuck.

Finding favorable trade winds, he arrived back in Spain, where he convinced his sovereigns that "Indian" gold would amply repay further trips. He captained three more voyages but died in 1506 still unaware that he had revealed a whole new continent. A year later, it was named—not after Columbus but after a fellow Italian explorer, Amerigo Vespucci.

Although no contemporary portraits of the burly, red-headed Columbus survive, this sixteenth-century picture hints at the obsessive determination that drove him to complete his quest in spite of repeated discouragements.

Part of the honors heaped on Columbus after his first transatlantic voyage, his coat of arms included royal symbols—a castle and lion for Isabella's realms of Castile and Leon—a scattering of islands representing his New World discoveries, and anchors symbolizing his title: Admiral of the Ocean Sea.

Two intricate wooden statuettes of Ferdinand and Isabella in prayer recall the piety that infused their collaborative efforts. They made an odd couple—she plump and chaste, he a sportsman and womanizer—but their marriage in 1469 laid the foundations of Spanish unity and overseas conquest.

turned to Cairo to rendezvous with his companion and to meet emissaries of the king.

The news he received there must have been unwelcome. He learned that his fellow explorer was dead, and the task of finding Prester John thereby devolved on him. No doubt weary from his many adventures, Covilhã cannot have relished the news, but he dutifully headed southward again. He duly found his way to Ethiopia, where he was obliged to remain, partly as a guest, partly as a prisoner, by the country's Christian ruler. Thirty years later, he was seen there by members of a Portuguese expedition. By then he was an old man, and he elected to stay where he was rather than return to his former home.

Covilhã presumably sent back to Portugal a report from Cairo on his earlier journeys, although no record of any such account has ever been found. If he did so, the information it contained may have proved useful in the process of planning the last great voyage of the fifteenth century, which was launched in 1497. By then King John was dead, but his successor, Manuel I, was happy to continue sponsoring the same work. Accordingly, the expedition he planned was equipped more ambitiously than any previous one, because its mission was to directly challenge the Arab monopoly of Indian Ocean trade.

Under Dias's experienced eye, four ships were fitted out. One was a small, lateen-rigged caravel of 55 tons for swift inshore sailing and scouting. Another was a storeship of more than 300 tons, to hold a three-year supply of food along with a cargo of the sort of knickknacks that had proved popular as trade goods and gifts in Africa—cotton, olive oil, sugar, coral, caps, beads, copper bowls, and the little round bells that falconers used to attach to their birds' legs. The last two ships, however, were something new: Sturdier than caravels, these square-rigged three-masters, known as *naos,* were mounted with ten guns each. The cannon afforded mute acknowledgment that this journey, unlike previous ones, might end in bloodshed.

Its leader, therefore, required boldness as well as seamanship among his attributes. In Vasco da Gama, Manuel found exactly the man he needed. Da Gama, who was then thirty-seven years old, came from a noble military family. He looked terrifying: His portrait reveals a huge nose and mouth, a black beard, a fearsome frown, and piercing eyes. He had a character to match: iron-willed, arrogant, ruthless, and quite capable of cruelty. (The story was told that he once extracted information from a captive by pouring boiling oil on the man's naked belly.) By way of compensation, he also had a reputation for fairness, honesty, and piety, as well as a good grounding in navigation and astronomy.

On July 8, 1497, priests led da Gama and his 170 men in solemn procession through the streets of Lisbon and blessed their departure. Da Gama took his little fleet past the Cape Verde Islands and then westward, sweeping out across the Atlantic in search of favorable winds for the long haul south. The route took the boats out of sight of land for three months—Columbus himself had gone just five weeks from the Canaries to his American landfall—but it paid off brilliantly. Knowing only the latitude of the Cape Verde Islands (sixteen degrees north) and the Cape of Good Hope itself (thirty-four degrees south), without charts or tables of winds and currents, da Gama brought his crew back to the African shore less than 125 miles north of his target, the Cape of Good Hope.

The next part of the journey could be taken in easier stages. For five months, da Gama probed around the tip of Africa, trading peacefully with the local Hottentot tribes. He passed Dias's last padrão and sailed almost 1,000 miles more, past unexplored coast to the edge of the Muslim world—the East African ports of Sofala and Mozambique, with their whitewashed houses, flowering vines, gleaming mosques, and sharp-sterned dhows. From there northward, the coast was divided among independent city-states, each ruled by a sultan protective of his own power. Here, the Portuguese were viewed not just as potential enemies, but, to their surprise, as barbarians. In one city, Kilwa, locals even tried a sneak attack, which was foiled by da Gama's cannon.

In Malindi, on the coast of present-day Kenya, however, da Gama was lucky enough to find a friendly sultan who saw him as a possible ally against his rivals and helped him to engage the services of an experienced navigator named Ahmed ibn-Majid for the next stage of the exploration—an eastward probe across the Indian Ocean to India. With ibn-Majid's guidance and good following winds, the 2,500-mile journey took just over a month. The fleet—the first European ships to reach India—anchored off the sweeping sands and waving palms of Calicut in mid-May.

Da Gama's stay in Calicut was not a happy one. His presence was resented by the Muslim merchants in whose hands the commerce of the port lay, and he was greeted with, at best, bare civility by the city's Hindu ruler. There was little demand for the goods the Portuguese had brought with them, and it was with the greatest difficulty that he and his men managed to gather a few packets of cloves, cinnamon, and jewels to show for their efforts.

Worse was to come. The navigator, ibn-Majid, disappeared during the crew's stay in Calicut, and it took da Gama's men three months to sail back against headwinds across the Indian Ocean. Low on stores during that voyage, the Portuguese mariners experienced for the first time all the horrors of long voyages over open sea. Rotting food and excrement gathered in the bilges to form a stinking slush breeding rats, lice, and maggots. The crew survived on freshly caught fish, salted pork heavily laced with garlic to disguise its tang of decay, and hardtack biscuits crawling with weevils. Deprived of fresh fruit and vegetables, the men eventually fell prey to scurvy. Gums swelled, bled, and decayed; joints became swollen; victims weakened into comas. By the time the crippled fleet finally succeeded in returning to Malindi, where the same friendly sultan saved their lives with supplies of oranges, eggs, meat, and poultry, thirty members of the crew were dead.

The troubles of the remainder were by no means over. Da Gama no longer had sufficient men to crew all three ships, and he therefore had to beach and burn one of the boats shortly after leaving Malindi on the voyage home. There were additional casualties in the course of the journey, including the leader's own brother, to whom he was apparently very attached. Nonetheless, the two surviving boats reached Lisbon, after six months' more sailing, in the late summer of 1499. Of the 170 men who had started the voyage, only 54 survived.

King Manuel was delighted by da Gama's achievement. He feted the survivors with an elaborate parade, struck a commemorative gold coin, and built a great memorial church and monastery near the mouth of the Tagus River to sanctify the land that was called "the shore of tears for those that go and the shore of pleasure for those that return." Although the human cost of the voyage had been great and the few trade goods brought back from India in no way covered the cost of the enterprise, the expedition had fulfilled its purpose. It had reached India—a fact that alone justified all the labors and costs of a century of endeavor.

Da Gama's voyage marked a watershed in the story of the age of exploration. The pace of discovery quickened in the early decades of the coming century as both Portugal and Spain, in their respective spheres, sought to turn the accumulated balance of knowledge acquired by their navigators into the hard cash of empire. Spain rapidly managed to acquire, through the exploits of the conquistadors, possessions in the Americas that were to make it the wealthiest and most powerful nation in the world; in the process it would destroy the sophisticated edifice built up by the native Aztec and Inca cultures.

Portugal's seafarers sought to build on da Gama's achievement, and the results were both speedy and spectacularly successful. Less than six months after da Gama's return, an armada of thirteen ships and 1,200 men was dispatched under the command of a thirty-two-year-old nobleman named Pedro Alvares Cabral. The expedition was a resounding success. On the outbound sweep into the Atlantic, the fleet traveled far enough west to touch the coast of Brazil, which Cabral duly claimed for Portugal. Coming eastward again and rounding the Cape of Good Hope, the boats made their way to Calicut, where they impressed the ruler with their gifts before engaging in—and bloodily winning—a trade war with the recalcitrant Muslim merchants. Cabral subsequently bombarded Calicut, accusing its ruler of siding with the Muslims against him, then moved on to trade peacefully with two other major ports, Cochin and Cannanore. He returned to Lisbon in June 1501 with only seven ships and half his men, but carrying cargoes of spices, porcelain, incense, and jewels that amply repaid the costs of the voyage.

The combination of trade and force was to bring rich rewards over the next few years. Annual expeditions were organized to India, and the Portuguese set up an exchange in the commercial center of Antwerp, in the Netherlands, from which to sell their spices to all of Europe. King Manuel appointed an official with the imposing title of viceroy to supervise the expansion of commerce in the Indian Ocean. The first such viceroy, Francisco de Almeida, led a force of twenty-two ships that, sailing in 1505, sacked Mombasa and captured the East African ports of Sofala and Kilwa, before winning a decisive victory in 1509 over an Egyptian fleet, sent to protect India's Muslim traders, in the port of Diu, north of Calicut. Almeida concluded a commercial treaty with Malacca, and his son explored new territory for Portugal.

With secure bases in the Indian Ocean and a confirmed mastery of the seas, the Portuguese were now free to fulfill the ambition that had driven them since Henry the Navigator's day: to reach the Spice Islands. A first fleet landed at Malacca, near present-day Singapore, in 1509, and by 1511, this important trading base was in Portuguese hands. It was only the first link in a chain of sites that eventually included Hormuz, at the mouth of the Persian Gulf; the islands of Ceylon and Ternate, a center of clove growing; and the ports of Diu and Goa in India and Macao in China. By 1520, Portugal dominated the seas of southern Asia. Muslim trade east of Aden declined drastically, as did the fortunes of the Venetian merchants who had acted as intermediaries receiving the goods in Europe. The balance of world trade shifted dramatically westward, and the ruler of Portugal would now style himself—rather optimistically, it is true—king "both on this side of the sea and beyond it in Africa, Lord of Guinea and of the Conquest, Navigation, and Commerce of Ethiopia, Arabia, Persia, and India."

One final achievement remained to complete the process of discovery set in motion by Prince Henry 100 years before: the circumnavigation of the world. That, too, was the act of a Portuguese seaman, although he did not live to complete the

EXPLORERS FROM THE EAST

When the Portuguese became the first Europeans to reach the Indian Ocean, they found themselves in waters already thoroughly explored by seafarers from Asian lands. A century before the Portuguese arrived, a Chinese commander named Zheng He had traversed the Indian Ocean in seven great naval expeditions that anticipated the later Portuguese efforts.

Zheng He was the chief eunuch of Emperor Yongle. The emperor, afraid that his deposed predecessor might be preparing an invasion fleet, commissioned Zheng He to track him down and at the same time to establish diplomatic and trade links in lands across the southern seas.

Of Mongolian origin and a Muslim, Zheng He proved a brilliant admiral. In 1405, he took a huge fleet comprising 62 large junks and more than 100 smaller ships, bearing in all some 30,000 crew members, as far as Calicut in southern India. Later expeditions, between 1407 and 1433, led to contacts with almost forty countries around the Indian Ocean *(map)*.

This giraffe, portrayed in a painting on silk, was a gift to the Chinese emperor Yongle from the sultan of Malindi, in present-day Kenya. It was collected on Zheng He's fourth journey, from 1416 to 1419, and received in person by the delighted emperor at the gate of his palace in Nanjing. The beast, placed in the imperial zoo, was termed a "celestial unicorn" and treated as an auspicious symbol.

•Nanjing

•Fuzhou

•Hormuz

Atlantic Ocean

•Jidda

Pacific Ocean

•Aden

•Qui Nhon

Calicut • CEYLON
Colombo •

Malacca
•

•Mogadishu
•Brava

SUMATRA

•Palembang

•Malindi

JAVA •Surabaya

•Kilwa

Indian Ocean

The vessels' cargo included tons of rice and other staples for consumption by the crew during the voyage. They also carried trade goods—silks, porcelain, barrels of peppers—to be exchanged or offered as gifts in the ports the fleet visited.

Chinese boats of Zheng He's day incorporated a structural feature unknown in the West at the time: the use of bulkheads to create watertight compartments belowdecks. As a result, if any one section of the hold sustained damage, only the cargo in that particular area was spoiled; the rest remained secure and dry.

Zheng He's Grand Treasure Ships

Zheng He's organizational skills must have been formidable: He controlled the Grand Treasure Fleets in the exploration of unknown oceans and coasts and transported soldiers for defense and enough wealth to impress foreign rulers.

His vessels were correspondingly massive. The largest, like the one shown at right, displaced more than 1,600 tons; almost 450 feet long, they were easily the largest ships built to that time. Up to 500 men crewed five masts with sails made rigid by bamboo stretchers, so they could be reefed in horizontal folds.

In such vessels, the Chinese could have ranged the world. In fact, exploration ceased abruptly. Even before Zheng He's last voyage, conservatives condemned his journeys as profligate and unnecessary, and Chinese society turned in upon itself.

The Chinese had some
knowledge of the impor-
tance of fresh foods in sus-
taining the health of their
sailors on long journeys.
Their boats were conse-
quently equipped with
tubs for growing vegeta-
bles and herbs, and with
pens for pigs that were
slaughtered and eaten in
the course of the voyage.

voyage, and he was sailing at the time under the flag of the king of Spain. Ferdinand Magellan had done honorable service for the Portuguese in the East Indies—where he saved the 1509 expedition to Malacca from disaster by giving warning of a surprise attack—and in North Africa, before false accusations of dishonesty by his rivals drove him to seek service with the neighboring power. He won the financial backing of an influential nobleman and the enthusiastic support of the Spanish king for his grand project, which was to seek a passage around the southern tip of the American continent to the recently discovered Pacific Ocean.

Magellan set sail in 1519 with five ships and approximately 260 men to crew them. Ruy Faleiro, his cocaptain-general, refused to leave Spain when his horoscope foretold that the trip would be the cause of his death. The ensuing voyage was an epic that took more than three years to complete and that cost not only the life of Magellan—who was cut down by native spears during a skirmish in the Philippines—but the lives of the vast majority of those sailors who set out to sea with him. The eighteen surviving crew members who eventually returned to Seville had horrifying tales to tell of mutiny, scurvy, and shipwreck, and the sale of the poor cargo of cloves aboard the one remaining boat provided insufficient profit to pay off in full even the sad remnants of the crew.

Yet as a pioneering enterprise, Magellan's voyage was priceless. Magellan achieved what had been suggested by Columbus: the connecting of western Europe with eastern Asia by sailing west. The last great unknown ocean had been crossed. The world itself stood revealed, even if only in the starkest outlines. Much remained to be mapped—Australia, New Zealand, and Antarctica, as well as the interiors of the newly found lands, were still undiscovered—but a framework had been established for future generations to fill in.

The explorers of the fifteenth and early sixteenth centuries did not set out to make a revolution in knowledge, but that is what they achieved—that and much more. The Portuguese not only ended the isolation of Europe; they also unwittingly set it on the path of worldwide expansion. Their voyages of discovery stand at the very beginning of the world's first global culture.

In the course of the fifteenth century, Europe's expanding knowledge of the world profoundly affected the art of mapmaking. In the late Middle Ages, most maps fell into one of two categories: Either they were schematic representations based primarily on the Scriptures, or they took the form of navigational charts, reflecting the practical experience of the sailors who plied the waters of the Mediterranean Sea and Europe's Atlantic shoreline. By 1500, however, the new knowledge brought back from the voyages of discovery and the old knowledge rediscovered in the renaissance of classical learning had each served in its own way to encourage the production of comparatively accurate and scholarly, though still incomplete, records of the world.

The scripturally inspired plans were known as *mappaemundi,* Latin for "maps of the world." Almost all represented the earth as a flat disk, rather than the orb that geographers had long known it to be. The aim of the mapmakers, however, was less to convey geographical information than to express biblical concepts in schematic form. One of the most popular versions was the *T-O* model, in which the *O* was formed by an ocean ring encircling the three known continents of the earth: Asia, Africa, and Europe. These in turn were associated in some of the maps, including the French example shown here, with the lands given to the three sons of Noah. The continents were shown separated by a *T* formed by waterways; the Mediterranean, dividing Europe from Africa, formed the upright, while Asia, depicted uppermost,

CHARTING A WIDENING WORLD

lay over a crossbar composed of the Don and Nile rivers.

The charts, which in contrast were surprisingly accurate, were known as portolans, from the Italian word for a pilot book describing navigational courses and anchorages. Drawn to scale, they were underpinned by a network of rhumb lines, from which a seaman could identify his chosen compass setting.

Not long into the fifteenth century, some cartographers began to draw world maps that, as far as possible, employed the principles of direct observation enshrined in the portolans. At the same time, others started producing maps that drew their inspiration from the *Geography* of Ptolemy, a second-century-AD Greek scholar whose works had been reintroduced to Europe from the Arab world. Ptolemy had shown how an accurate image of a round world could be projected onto a flat surface by dividing it into a grid of latitudes and longitudes. Although some of his measurements later proved to be wrong, his method created a sensation, and the influence of the *Geography* increased steadily throughout the century.

The most crucial contribution to people's expanding knowledge of the world, however, came not from scholars but from the explorers who charted the formerly unknown coasts of Africa and America. By the turn of the century, the news of their discoveries had found its way into the works of some cartographers to provide, for the first time, a reasonably accurate image of Africa and the first inklings of the Atlantic coastline of the Americas.

On this mid-fifteenth-century map, Majorca is drawn over a network of rhumb lines in the manner of a portolan. Using the latest available information, the map features an accurate outline of the Mediterranean and reflects the first discoveries of the Portuguese explorers in its rendering of Africa's northwest coastline. Inland, the mapmaker shows the Sahara and the Nile and Niger rivers. For the rest of the continent, however, the map is drawn based on hearsay; the sickle-shaped southern extension reflected a theory of the Greek philosopher Aristotle that somewhere in distant latitudes there existed *terra australis incognita*, an unknown southern land.

FIRST FRUITS OF THE JOURNEYS

This world map, drawn up with lines of latitude and longitude and surrounded by personifications of the winds, adorned an early printed edition of Ptolemy's *Geography*. Hand-colored, it was printed from a woodcut at Ulm in Germany in 1486. Ptolemaic maps of this kind generally remained faithful to the great geographer's world-view, perpetuating his errors as well as his insights. The most significant of the mistakes was a miscalculation of the length of a degree of longitude, which led Ptolemy to exaggerate the extent of the Eurasian landmass. This confusion led Columbus to conclude that the shortest sea route to China lay westward, and that he had arrived in the Orient when, in 1492, he landed in the West Indies.

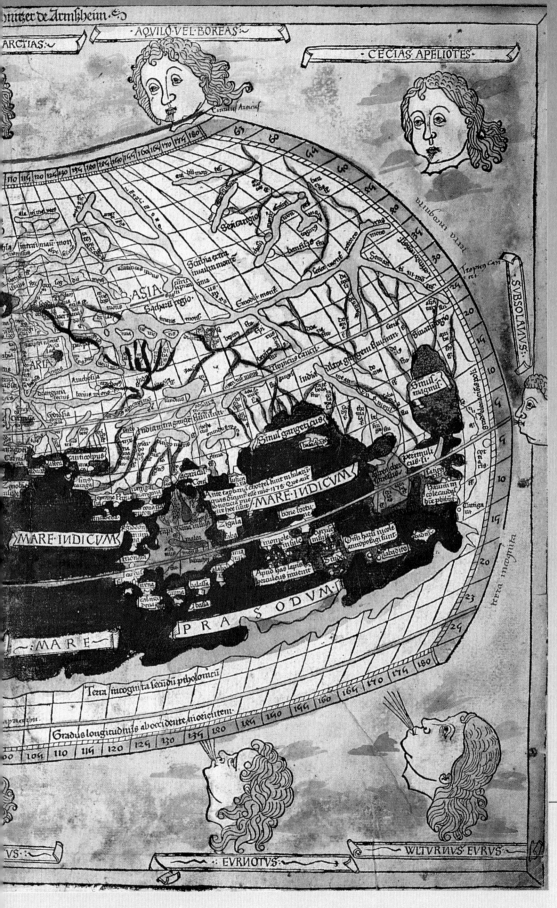

THE WORLD ACCORDING TO PTOLEMY

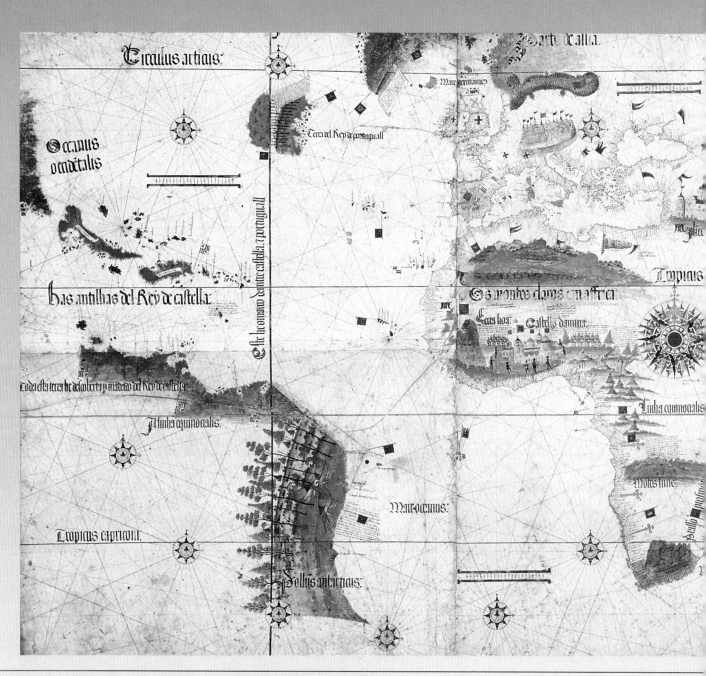

A SECRET RECORD OF DISCOVERIES

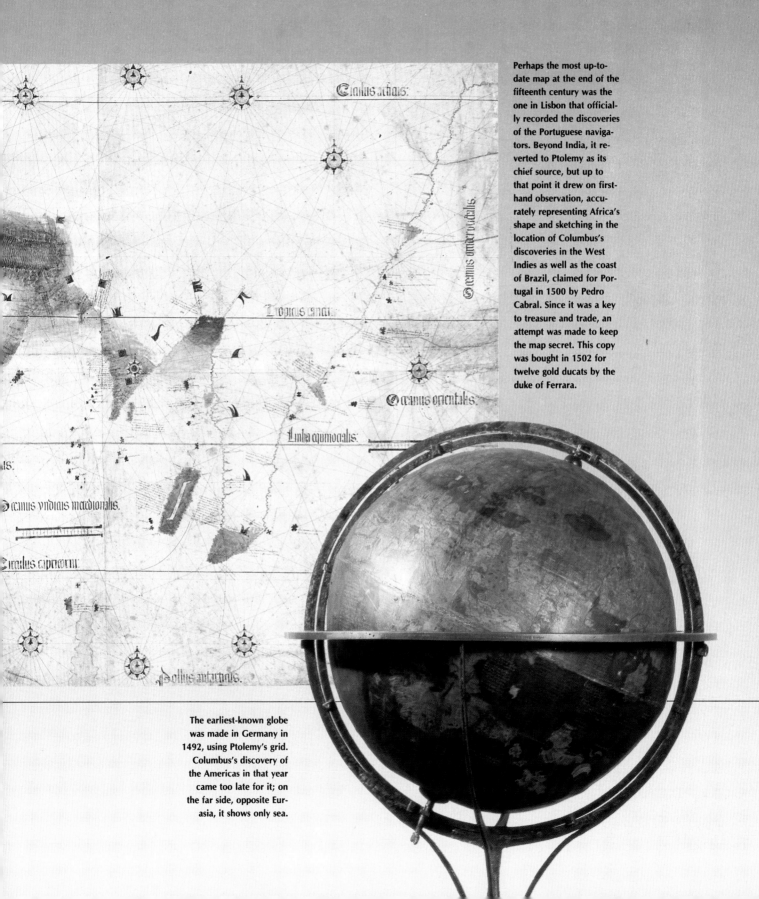

Circulus arcticus.

Oceanus amerouidalis.

Tropicus cancri.

Oceanus orientalis.

Linha equinocialis.

Oceanus yndicus meridionalis.

Circulus capricorni.

Polus antarticus.

Perhaps the most up-to-date map at the end of the fifteenth century was the one in Lisbon that officially recorded the discoveries of the Portuguese navigators. Beyond India, it reverted to Ptolemy as its chief source, but up to that point it drew on first-hand observation, accurately representing Africa's shape and sketching in the location of Columbus's discoveries in the West Indies as well as the coast of Brazil, claimed for Portugal in 1500 by Pedro Cabral. Since it was a key to treasure and trade, an attempt was made to keep the map secret. This copy was bought in 1502 for twelve gold ducats by the duke of Ferrara.

The earliest-known globe was made in Germany in 1492, using Ptolemy's grid. Columbus's discovery of the Americas in that year came too late for it; on the far side, opposite Eurasia, it shows only sea.

THE ITALIAN RENAISSANCE

2

"Thank God it has been permitted to us to be born in this new age, so full of hope and promise, which already rejoices in a greater array of nobly gifted souls than the world has seen in the thousand years that preceded it." So wrote Matteo Palmieri of Florence, an apothecary and scholar who described the world of fifteenth-century Italy in which he lived. His exhilaration reflected the mood of the period that was to become known, some four centuries later, as the Renaissance; the term acknowledged that Palmieri's generation of Italians witnessed the rebirth of knowledge shunned since the days of classical Greece and Rome.

With the diffusion of the long-forgotten learning came a novel way of thinking—Palmieri was one of its greatest exponents—based more on earthly wisdom than on the doctrines of the Church. Nor was the spirit of intellectual adventure confined to a few closeted scholars; it was carried far and wide by means of the printing press, a fifteenth-century invention. It reached the artist's studio as well as the library: This was the age of some of the greatest masters who ever lived, from Masaccio and Donatello as the century began to Botticelli and Leonardo toward its end.

Yet the new age so rapturously welcomed by Palmieri and his friends would have been difficult to predict when the century dawned. Italy had suffered a series of shocks in the preceding 200 years that would hardly seem to have prepared it for a golden age. In the thirteenth century, the land had been devastated by wars between the Holy Roman Empire and the papacy, a contest that had ended in the defeat and eventual extinction of the emperor's house, Hohenstaufen. The popes had been unable to fill the ensuing power vacuum, for they too had been gravely weakened, both morally and politically, by the struggle. And during the fourteenth century, a combination of internal squabbling and international power politics had torn the Church apart in the shameful agony of the Great Schism, which set rival popes in Rome and the French city of Avignon competing for the devotion of the faithful.

Without a single, dominant power to unite it, the Italian peninsula had fragmented politically. At the start of the fifteenth century, five major powers vied for supremacy. The kingdom of Naples, despite the corrupt torpidity of the Spanish overlords who had won it in the wake of the Hohenstaufen debacle, ruled the fertile island of Sicily and the mainland south of Rome, and it stretched northward along the Adriatic through the mountains of Abruzzi almost as far as Ancona. Squarely across its northern border lay the Papal States, a substantial belt of territory that included not only the traditional Patrimony of Peter—the former province of Latium that engirdled Rome itself—but also the northeastern plain of Romagna and the old imperial city of Ravenna. In addition, the various lords of the central regions of Umbria and The Marches owed the pope an allegiance that was rarely more than nominal.

To the north and east of the pope's principality lay the republic of Venice, secure

Shown in a colored woodcut, architect Filippo Brunelleschi's cathedral dome dominates the skyline of fifteenth-century Florence. Protected by encircling walls, the city streets, radiating out on both banks of the Arno River, were lined with the houses of the merchants whose wealth helped make the Tuscan capital a showplace of the Renaissance. This flowering of art and scholarship, stimulated by the rediscovery of classical learning largely lost to western Europe since the fall of the Roman Empire 1,000 years before, began in northern Italy and then spread out across Europe in the course of the succeeding century.

in its inviolable lagoon, and the mainland territories on which it depended for its food supply. The duchy of Milan filled the Lombard plain as far as the Alps to the north, bordering on Venice to the east and the ailing state of Genoa to the southwest. Squeezed dangerously between Milan and the Papal States, the republic of Florence dominated Italy's Tuscan center.

These five intrigued ceaselessly with and against one another; a host of lesser players—the Gonzaga rulers of Mantua, for instance, and the Este dukes in Ferrara—existed in the shrinking space between the great five and lived or died according to their skill in an endless, unscrupulous game of alliance and counteralliance in which bribery, assassination, and coup d'état were the maneuvers of everyday politics.

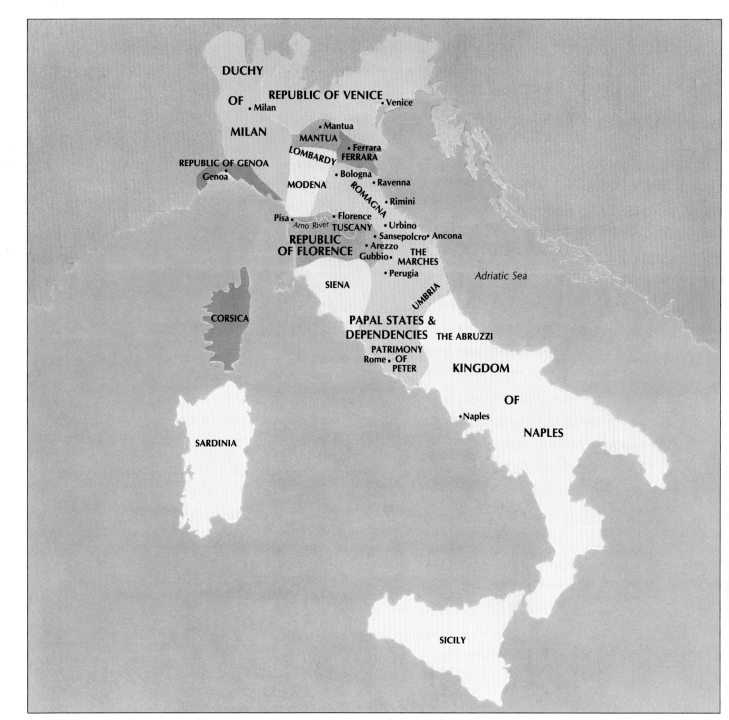

Fairly typical of the tough, talented men who thrived in this competitive world was Federigo Montefeltro, from 1444 duke of the small state of Urbino, set amid the rugged hills of The Marches. Since the thirteenth century, the Montefeltro family domain had consisted of the hill towns of Urbino and Gubbio and the few hundred villages that surrounded them. Federigo's profession was war. There was little wealth in The Marches, and soldiering was as good a livelihood as any for the men his modest dukedom's rocky land could not support. He was good at it, too: Among his clients he counted Florence, Milan, Naples, and the papacy, and his income regularly exceeded 100,000 ducats a year.

Federigo spent his money lavishly. He converted the old Gothic fortress from which his ancestors had dominated their little capital into an elegant ducal palace, furnished with the best antique art that could be found, as well as the best modern work he could commission from the talented artists who regularly graced his brilliant court. Between campaigns, he planned policy in an atmosphere as cultivated as any in Italy. He was admired and loved by his people, who had not always been so favorably disposed toward their rulers; they had dealt with the lustful brutality of his predecessor and half brother by the simple expedient of murdering him.

Federigo's Urbino was by no means unique. Throughout Italy there was a vitality that seemed to feed on chaos, a creative vigor that gave the age its astonishing style. The paradox of the Renaissance was that the very conditions of disunity that should, according to usually accepted ideas, have bred weakness, apathy, and decline, in fact stimulated a great outpouring of creative endeavor. The reasons are to be found in the wealth that trade had brought to the peninsula, and the competitive drive of the various, mainly northern Italian cities that fought to control and channel the riches— and, gloriously, to spend them.

The rise of civic power, which had gotten under way as early as the eleventh century, reached its apogee in fifteenth-century Italy. In Flanders and the Netherlands, too, there were thriving towns with similar traditions of commerce and independence, and around the shores of the Baltic Sea, the ports of the Hanseatic League were a force to be reckoned with. But only in Italy were such communities to be found in large numbers. Not since Greek and Roman times had so many men and women lived an urban existence.

Florence was perhaps the most glittering example of civic success. At almost any time during the fifteenth century, a stroll around Palmieri's hometown would have convinced anyone that his marvelous new age was no fantasy. Inside its stout, protecting wall, Florence was thriving, brimming with wealth and art, and bustling with the commerce and industry that had provided them.

A congested town of dank and ill-constructed tenements had given way, during the previous century, to a well-built city—brick and rubble were the main materials, faced with good local stone—amply provided with open spaces. The wall, built in 1299, enclosed farms and gardens as well as the populated center, still less than a mile square, and the remaining tenements were steadily being replaced by neat three-story houses of the merchant class, soberly ornamented without and lavishly decorated within. Most had their own wells; an effective sewage system drained into the Arno River, and an increasing number of houses possessed the remarkable luxury of an inside toilet. (Disputes over cesspit emptying were a frequent cause of lawsuits.) Fireplaces were becoming commonplace; torches outside the houses of wealthier

The First Family of Florence

For much of the fifteenth century, the Medici family were in effect the rulers of Florence, although in name they remained mere private citizens. Their fortunes derived in large part from the banking activities of Cosimo de' Medici, the first of the clan to dominate the city. He was succeeded by his son Piero, whose ill health won him the nickname "the Gouty."

Perhaps the most gifted of the line was Piero's heir, Lorenzo, whose astute statesmanship, athletic prowess, and intellectual flair made him the archetypal Renaissance man. His only weakness was in financial matters; lavish patronage of such artists as Botticelli and Michelangelo, together with the extravagant spectacles that he staged to entertain and impress the citizens of Florence, drained the family's resources.

He passed on a diminished treasury to his son Piero di Lorenzo who, confronted by an invasion from France, signed a treaty with the foreign power. The unpopularity of this move led to his expulsion in 1494 and an eclipse in the fortunes of Renaissance Italy's most distinguished dynasty.

inhabitants provided a primitive form of street lighting, and the streets themselves, to the amazement of visitors both at the time and for centuries afterward, were paved with even slabs of stone.

But something more than urban renewal was taking place. In the first thirty years of the century alone, thirty-four statues of saints and prophets, all larger than life and executed with a skill and talent not seen for a millennium, had been erected in the new squares and public buildings—all within a few paces of the thirteenth-century Palazzo della Signoria, the grim fortress-palace where Florence's rulers took time off from the city's tempestuous politics to commission more and greater works of beauty. In the same period, the great bronze doors of the baptistery, the city's oldest building, had been decorated with unsurpassed metalwork. Nearby, the cathedral itself, begun in 1296, was completed in 1436 by the architect Filippo Brunelleschi with a majestic dome that vaulted high above the busy streets and struck a chord in the hearts of his fellow townspeople: "Dome-sickness" was ever after their word for the pangs of nostalgia they endured when they were absent from their native city.

These gleaming new works were signs of political as well as artistic self-confidence. Commissioned in the course of a prolonged struggle with the Visconti dukes of Milan, they were a declaration of the city's faith in its own future. Art, just as much as the gold in Florence's thirty-three banking houses, was a clear demonstration of civic power.

Since at least the early thirteenth century, the city had been the focal point of a far-flung trading empire: According to one medieval pope, its merchants were so widely scattered around the known world that after earth, air, fire, and water they had to be accounted "the fifth element." And Florence's wealth and power were just as apparent nearer home: By the 1420s, the city controlled two-thirds of the encircling province of Tuscany.

The city needed its surrounding countryside not only for its food supply—some agricultural commodities, notably olive oil, also featured in Florence's international trade—but for its people. By the 1400s, Florence, with about 40,000 inhabitants, was

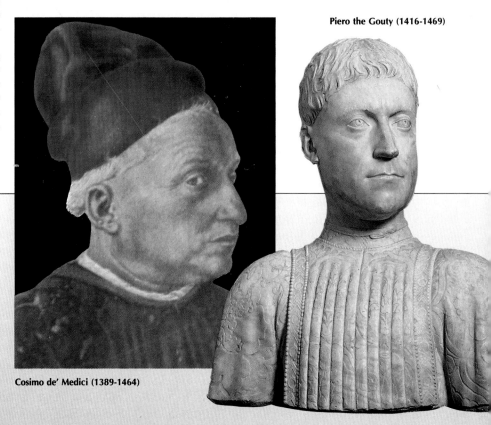

Piero the Gouty (1416-1469)

Cosimo de' Medici (1389-1464)

a metropolis by medieval standards, and no urban population of the time could maintain itself without regular immigration. Given the general crowding, the low standards of contemporary public health (even though Florence was better provided with water and drainage than most cities) guaranteed that people died at a younger age in town. The price for urban opportunity was paid, especially by the lower classes, in life expectancy.

For those farther up the social ladder, however, the prospects were inviting. Lucrative possibilities existed in banking, insurance, trade, and most of the other activities that would come to be associated with a modern economy. Foreign travel was common, since most enterprises—which ranged from simple family businesses to partnerships and carefully constructed holding companies, both recent Italian inventions—had offices throughout Europe's commercial centers and beyond, wherever a florin (the city's prized golden coin, first minted in the thirteenth century) might be earned. More than fifty Florentine concerns even had branches in the alien and ostensibly hostile Ottoman Empire. There were also diplomatic and government posts that could be used not only to the general benefit of Florence but also to the specific advantage of their holders.

This new style of existence was far removed from the life of the itinerant merchants of the early Middle Ages, traveling peddlers who simply toted their goods from fair to fair, and it made different demands upon those who practiced it. Above all, it required education—and education directed toward secular ends, not in the service of the Church, to which almost all academic pursuit had been dedicated for a thousand years. The ability to read, write, and do arithmetic was now essential: It was no use controlling a business by means of an advanced system of double-entry bookkeeping—a recent Italian innovation—if no clerks could be found to understand it. But the real driving force behind the growth of secular learning was the demand for trained lawyers created by the sheer complexity of the new society. The study of the law, in turn, revived interest in and enthusiasm for Latin and Greek and the authors of classical times. The result was the remarkable phenomenon that came to be known as humanism.

The word was derived from the Latin *studia humanitatis,* "studies of mankind," as opposed to the Church-directed scholastic theology that had hitherto dominated the intellectual life of Christendom. Humanism still had the enormous respect for ancient authority, rather than for original thought, that had distinguished all medieval philosophy. But in the works of Plato, Aristotle, Cicero, and Quintilian, humanists discovered, in place of the Church's old, monolithic certainty, ancient authorities who actually disagreed among themselves. It was both shocking and invigorating. Moreover, thoroughgoing classical studies required intelligence and dedication, not noble birth. With a little good fortune, bright young men of relatively humble background could find themselves a place in the new, self-conscious humanist elite.

One fourteenth-century figure who had personified the new virtues was to serve as a model to his fifteenth-century successors. Francesco Petrarca—known to posterity as Petrarch—was born in 1304 in Arezzo, then still independent, where his lawyer father was a political exile from Florence. He spent part of his youth at the papal court in Avignon and later at the University of Bologna, where he showed himself to be a brilliant classical scholar as well as a great poetic talent. Rapidly establishing his reputation, he traveled widely, collecting a great quantity of ancient

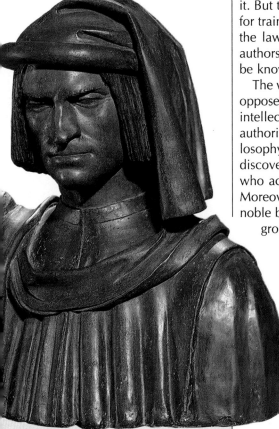

Lorenzo the Magnificent (1449-1492)

manuscripts. Petrarch was welcomed by most of the royal courts of Europe for his ideas as well as his lyrics: It was time, he declared, to dispel "this slumber of forgetfulness" and to "walk forward in the pure radiance of the past." His Italian poetry had an individual flavor rare in the Middle Ages, although it was little read at the time in comparison with his Latin works, which were popular with scholars all over Europe. Petrarch had an immense following during his lifetime; in the fifteenth century, his works would have a place in the library of any educated household worthy of the name.

Thus the groundwork, intellectual as well as economic, had been laid for the creative powerhouse that was fifteenth-century Florence. But there were other factors, too, and the most powerful of them had nothing of Petrarch's "radiance" surrounding it. In 1347, a new and invisible immigrant had arrived in Europe: the bacillus of bubonic plague. Brought by trading ships from Asia, it was carried in the bloodstream of infected rats and transmitted by fleabites to the bodies of human beings. The Black Death, it was called, and with good reason. By 1353, it had killed an estimated one-third of the European population, and the plague returned at regular intervals to terrify the survivors for another 300 years.

In crowded cities such as Florence, the impact was at its most devastating, and the closely settled Tuscan countryside was almost as vulnerable as the town itself. Exact statistics are hard to come by, but such figures as exist are chilling enough. Florence had almost 100,000 people on the eve of the Black Death; not until the sixteenth century was the population to edge beyond the 50,000 mark again. Other Italian cities suffered a similar fate: Milan, for instance, lost almost half its inhabitants, and Pisa lost three-quarters.

Clearly, no community could sustain losses on such a scale without serious economic dislocation. For those who lived through the disaster, however, the net effects were not all bad. If markets both at home and abroad had shrunk, so had the numbers who had to make their living from them. And the plague had destroyed humans, not things. Real assets—land and buildings, ships, whatever primitive machinery existed, and of course the gold that nestled in Florentine vaults—were untouched, but they were shared by far fewer people. In fact, the Black Death had created a cash surplus that could not easily be spent in the ordinary fashion, for the means of production, being almost exclusively based on human labor, had decreased with the population. But the money could always be spent, given sufficient ingenuity. In a very real sense, the plague dead's share of the wealth would finance the expensive artistic display of the Renaissance.

Neither before nor after the Black Death were Florentine assets shared even remotely equally. The fortunes of the various social groupings in the city had ebbed and flowed, but one or another had always been dominant. Back in the thirteenth century, during the pope-emperor conflict, the city's great merchants had triumphed over the old, proimperial nobility. A century later, power had spread downward: The lower-middle classes, even the artisans, shared in the city's government by means of the great guilds to which most of them belonged. But the mass of ordinary workers, most employed in the wool industry, remained excluded from both civic politics and civic prosperity. In 1378, there was a great revolt, arguably the Western world's first proletarian revolution. The revolt failed: The outcome was not only savage repression but also a drift away from limited democracy toward a narrow oligarchy, while wealth became increasingly concentrated in the hands of fewer and richer families.

Wealthiest of all were members of a house whose name was to become almost synonymous with Renaissance Florence. They were called Medici, and several times they came close to losing everything in the risky business of civic politics. But by the 1430s, the head of the clan, Cosimo, had firmly established himself as the city's leading powerbroker.

Cosimo de' Medici was the archetypal merchant prince of the period. He was no prince by blood, although well-planned marriages would later bring authentic royalty into his family, but in his own way he was as great a genius as Leonardo or Michelangelo. A lean, ascetic-looking man, he was almost proverbially shrewd, a far-sighted politician who was publicly genial and approachable—he knew hundreds of his fellow citizens by name—and privately ruthless. He was a uniquely discerning patron of the arts and an intellectual in his own right: He died (peacefully and in extreme old age, to his enemies' chagrin) while listening to a reading from his beloved Plato. But first and foremost, he was a businessman, and his life's obsession was the Medici family firm.

In essence, it was a holding company whose board of directors, some of them minority shareholders from outside the family, supervised controlling interests in a major bank, local industries, and a range of trading enterprises handling commodities as diverse as English wool, olive oil, horses, paintings, and even slaves. Of the three, industry was the least important, yielding only 10 percent of the company's profits. It included some mining but was primarily a matter of miserably paid laborers who worked in their own homes producing finished goods from Medici wool and silks.

Banking made up the most profitable column in the family balance sheet. The best moneymaker was in Rome: Cosimo's excellent relations with the Church guaranteed the firm a lucrative slice of the Vatican's financial dealings. As the century progressed, one of the biggest losers was the office in London, whose main purpose was to buy English wool. Its failure exemplified the risks and difficulties the Medici and their like faced: England's own merchants constantly agitated for laws to restrict the more efficient foreign competition, and as his price for ignoring their protests, their king extracted large loans from the Italians. The cash, as well as any prospect for its repayment, vanished in the civil conflict known as the Wars of the Roses, and the Medici London branch went bankrupt in 1472. The office in Brugge, across the Channel in Flanders, went the same way for similar reasons: Despite stern warnings from Florence, the local agent allowed himself to be pressured into providing credit for the ruling duke, Charles of Burgundy.

That was long after Cosimo's death, however. He never contented himself with issuing directives: At the cost of lengthy absences from Florence, the old fox kept the family's overseas operations under close personal supervision. Government loans were, in fact, something of a specialty of his: He furnished or denied them as required by his foreign policy, in which Florentine and family interests were inextricably and advantageously mixed. Venice and the kingdom of Naples, for example, both suffered military defeats after Cosimo judiciously refused to advance the funds needed to finance their armies.

Medici profits were immense, at least during Cosimo's lifetime. A healthy percentage was plowed back into the business. A great deal was also spent on political patronage and straightforward bribery in Florence itself. Unlike the Visconti dukes of Milan, the doges of Venice, and other city-state rulers, the Medici had no official title, and their power depended on the skillful management of a clique of self-interested supporters. But Cosimo's lasting fame, and the indelible association of the Medici with the Florentine Renaissance, came from another kind of patronage: the largesse with which he supported culture and the arts.

Cosimo founded an academy devoted to Platonic studies, which became a discussion group for new ideas where the brightest spirits of the age were welcome, and around the informal, unofficial Medici court there revolved a galaxy of Italy's humanist writers. Greater renown, however, was to come from another group, of whom Cosimo once tolerantly remarked, "One must treat these people of extraordinary genius as if they were celestial spirits, and not like beasts of burden." These were the artists—the sculptors, painters, and architects whose work was to provide the century's lasting memorial.

The social background of the Renaissance artists was, as a rule, fairly lowly—most came from the artisan class—and a majority lacked formal education. Generally, they had had no time to acquire any: Their careers almost inevitably began with apprenticeships at an early age in the workshops of masters, who were quite likely to be relatives. They were heirs not so much to the rediscovered learning of Greece and Rome as to the long and versatile tradition of medieval craftsmanship, of highly skilled work performed anonymously and for small reward.

The best surviving examples in Florence of the old ways were the dozens of workshops engaged in producing decorative and charming *cassoni nuziali,* the nuptial chests, intended to hold bedding and clothes, that were an essential gift for every wellborn bride. Their makers were not exactly specialists: A good worker was expected to turn his hand to painting, sculpture, even goldsmithing, as his clients demanded, and indeed a first-class chest might include a little of all three.

Such versatility was a valuable asset, although the medieval tradition did not place much premium upon originality. But by the 1400s, artists were also heirs to a newer tradition, already more than a century old. It had begun with the work of Giotto, a peasant's son from the Florence area, one of the earliest artists to leave behind him not only his works but also his name. Before Giotto's time, painting and sculpture had tended to follow the rigidly conventional lines established long before, in the Greek-speaking Byzantine Empire. This style had its virtues—the eleventh-century Saint Mark's Cathedral in Venice, with its marvelous mosaics, represented a high point—but its formality left little room for artists to use their own powers of observation to re-create what they could see.

Giotto broke new ground in realism and in sheer technique, including the first use of foreshortening. According to the sixteenth-century artist and biographer Giorgio Vasari, whose *Lives of the Painters* followed years of collecting both pictures and anecdotes, "A very great miracle was at work in Giotto, for even in those coarse and careless times his skill had the power to revive the whole art of drawing, of which his contemporaries knew little or nothing."

By the 1400s, there were many painters and sculptors following in his formidable footsteps. The old traditions continued: There were plenty of cassoni nuziali in production. But the idea of the artist as an individual creative force had taken firm root, as evidenced by the fact that from this time onward many painters signed their works, and the artist's social standing grew from that of a craftsman who delivered his work at the trade entrance to the position of a respected genius, welcome any-

Two Florentine moneylenders carry out transactions at a counter decorated with an embroidered cloth. Known as *banchi* in Italian, such work surfaces were to give their name to banks—the institutions that developed from the activities of the city's financial markets. The local coinage, the gold *fiorino,* or florin, weighing seventy-two grains of gold, was the most stable money of its day and the benchmark against which other states' currencies were measured—a status reflecting Florence's position as the most prosperous trading state of fifteenth-century Europe.

where. The artists' expectations rose as the century progressed. In the early decades, Donatello, the sculptor who did so much to adorn Florence, felt too embarrassed to wear the fine clothes Cosimo de' Medici had given him. Fifty years later, as Vasari observed, Luca Signorelli "always lived more like a lord or an honored gentleman than a painter"; and his behavior was not atypical.

Despite improved status, though, the artists were first and foremost a confraternity of working professionals. The names by which many of them have been remembered give a clue to their own attitudes toward one another: Most are casual sobriquets bestowed by colleagues. Botticelli, for example, means no more than "little barrels"—a nickname bestowed on the creator of the *Primavera* and the *Birth of Venus* because his forebears were coopers. Andrea del Verrocchio, Leonardo's first teacher, was so called because of his "true eye." Pietro Vannucci, who gave Raphael his early training, was known then and later simply as il Perugino—the man from Perugia, the Umbrian city near which he was born. And for all the respect that came to be granted to individual genius, there was still a collective element to production; a successful artist's studio would employ many men of lesser talents as well as student apprentices. Some specialized in detail—hands or feet, for example—while others

Surrounded by inattentive classmates, young Massimiliano Sforza, son of the duke of Milan, tries to concentrate on his teacher's words. The expanding economic and social horizons of Renaissance Italy increased the demand for secular, as well as religious, knowledge.

NURSERIES OF THE NOBLE SPIRIT

Education played a crucial part in the development and spread of the Renaissance. Whereas medieval universities had primarily prepared students for the priesthood and had heavily relied on theological studies, teachers in fifteenth-century Italy were increasingly required to train future lawyers, merchants, and courtiers. The emphasis of the curriculum consequently shifted toward grammar and rhetoric, designed to enable pupils to speak and write well.

Classes were still conducted in Latin, but lectures were concerned with a wider range of classical texts than had been the case in the Middle Ages. Another new development was an emphasis on sports and physical education in some establishments: One of the great teachers of the era, Vittorino da Feltre, included swimming and riding among the activities of his school in Mantua. Families from all over Italy competed to send their sons there.

The very image of the
Renaissance scholar-
soldier, an armor-clad Federigo Montefeltro, duke
of Urbino, reads from a
bound volume in the pres-
ence of his son in this
painting attributed to the
Spaniard Pedro Berrugue-
te. A captain of mercenaries as well as one of the
most effective rulers of his
day, the duke was also a
discerning patron of the
arts who is said to have
prized his library above all
his other possessions.

made a meager living as little more than common laborers, performing such menial tasks as preparing pigments.

Throughout most of the century, there was plenty of work for all. Commissions were numerous; it was a time when every important family—and not just in Florence—was engaged in the politics of conspicuous display. Fine art enhanced prestige. When in the years after 1436 Cosimo de' Medici spent lavishly on the restoration and reconstruction of churches and other buildings, it was a not-so-subtle assertion of Medici power that was well understood by his fellow citizens, some of whom responded with commissions of their own. The city's great guilds all contributed, too, and even ordinary, reasonably well-off merchants found that judiciously exercised patronage could draw favorable attention to themselves in the city's ruling circles. The combination of sophisticated taste and civic ostentation was an unprecedented gift for the epoch's artists.

They went about their work in their own way. Like the humanists, the artists were learning from the classic examples of Greece and Rome. Whereas the humanists scoured ancient manuscripts for ideas, the artists searched the statuary and architecture that had survived the centuries for techniques, in some ways a more difficult task: There were many exemplars of the triumphs of the past to be studied, but most of the methods by which they had been produced had to be rediscovered from scratch, usually by trial and error.

More important, the Renaissance artists were also learning from one another and from nature. They showed an investigative thoroughness and a self-confident dedication that later eras would come to recognize as "Renaissance" qualities.

Take, for example, the painter Piero della Francesca, born in Sansepolcro around 1410. A surviving self-portrait shows a heavyset, scholarly man with the works of Euclid and Archimedes close at hand. It is captioned like a calling card with a list of his skills and accomplishments: "Piero . . . of the noble house of the Francesca, Painter, Mathematician, Geometer, and Surveyor." He exaggerated his lineage somewhat—he came from a respectable merchant family, not the nobility—but the rest of the description was true enough. He had indeed studied the classical mathematical texts, being one of the few artists with a Latin education, and his work was distinguished by an exquisite sense of interrelated form, in which exactness of observation was presented with mathematical precision.

As a young man, he worked and studied in Florence. His career subsequently took him to the court of the princely Este family in Ferrara, where he came in contact with at least one of the leading Dutch painters of the day, artistic skill and development not being confined to Italy. Later he received commissions in the eastern Italian towns of Urbino and Rimini.

Piero was much admired by his colleagues for his skill, and he was well aware of the impor-

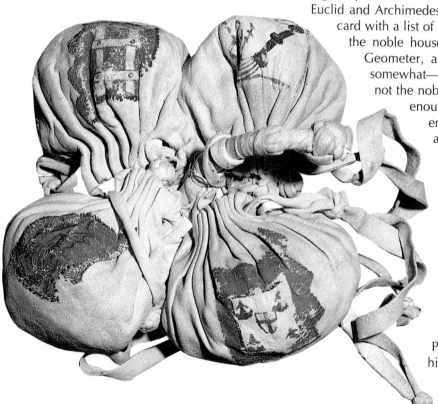

To Florentines, these electoral ballot pouches represented a buffer against despotism. In them were placed the names of citizens seeking election to public office; a random draw then determined the successful candidates. The purpose of this lottery was to prevent any one faction from gaining political ascendancy. It failed to achieve its aim, however, because of a built-in imbalance in the system: Three-quarters of the available posts were reserved for members of the seven principal merchant guilds, which were dominated by the city's most powerful families, notably the Medici.

tance of the discoveries he had made in the art of naturalistic depiction. As his eyesight failed toward the end of his life, he spent years writing, in Latin, the first scientific study of perspective. In another book he described the rules of proportion that create harmony in solid geometry. And he had respect from more than his fellow artists: When he returned to Sansepolcro, his own merits as well as his family position won him a place on the town council.

Piero was already well established by 1452, when Leonardo, the greatest all-around genius of the period, perhaps in all history, was born in the little village of Vinci, outside Florence. The illegitimate son of a moderately successful lawyer, he was apprenticed to Andrea del Verrocchio (with his father's approval, for by the 1460s, even lawyers considered art a respectable occupation) and by his early twenties was producing his first masterpieces.

While Piero had perfected linear perspective, Leonardo invented what came to be called aerial perspective, the use of multiple layers of translucent paint to create a gentle softening of detail that gave a picture an astonishing illusion of depth. Leonardo's drawings had an inspired exactitude unequaled before or since—as a young man, he used to follow his subjects around the streets of Florence for hours until he had captured them to perfection. He drew maps of a quality not seen for centuries afterward, and in what amounted to his spare time, he tossed off designs, often workable, for ingenious machines that ranged from submarines and helicopters to a mass-production plant for pins, which he calculated could earn 60,000 ducats a year. He worked as a military engineer and town planner, and he even wrote to the Ottoman sultan in Constantinople, offering to build a bridge across the Golden Horn.

Leonardo had one governing quality: his burning desire for knowledge. He wanted to know everything. Never a Latinist, he devoured such classics as were available in Italian translation, especially Pliny the Elder's *Natural History*. But he was by no means in awe of books. "Anyone who in an argument appeals to authority," he once wrote, "uses not his intelligence, but his memory." Leonardo, who often signed himself "disciple of experience," preferred to trust his own observations, and there had never been an observer quite like him. The drawings in his *Codex on the Flight of Birds,* to give only one example, revealed details that no one else saw until the discovery of high-speed photography. And in his remorseless study of human anatomy, he ignored contemporary theories and believed only what his scalpel and his eyesight revealed. "I have dissected more than ten human bodies, destroying all the various members," he wrote, a grim labor of which he was understandably proud. "You might be restrained by the fear of living through the night hours in the company of these corpses, quartered and flayed and horrible to behold."

Leonardo's career had its failures. In painting, especially, he was always searching for new techniques to replace the time-honored fresco method, in which pigment was applied to wet lime-plaster and became permanently bonded as the plaster dried. Leonardo preferred to work more slowly than the traditional procedure allowed, but the alternative approaches he developed were unsuccessful, and many of what were considered his best works peeled off from their walls within a few years. Yet his genius continued to be respected, and he was welcome anywhere he cared to travel.

In fact, genius was a far more reliable safe-conduct than any signed by an Italian ruler. Italian politics had always been complex and often villainous, but as the century progressed, corruption, opportunism, and ruthlessness became dangerously endemic. Florence remained probably the best-governed of Italian states, but it, too,

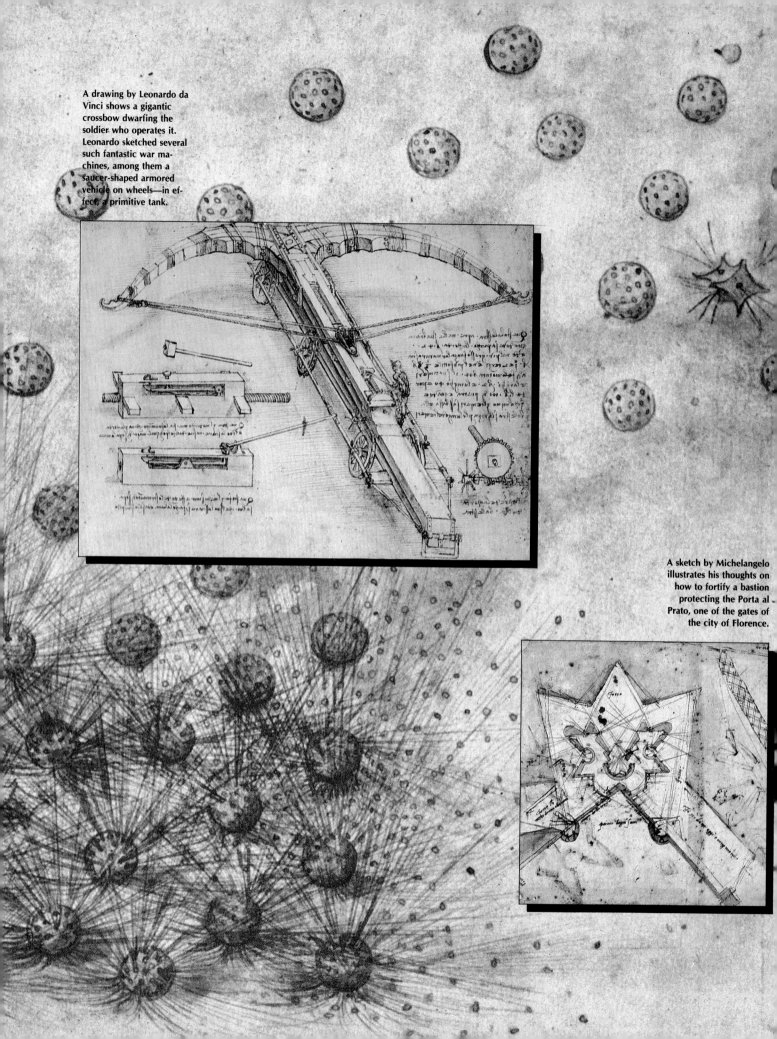

A drawing by Leonardo da Vinci shows a gigantic crossbow dwarfing the soldier who operates it. Leonardo sketched several such fantastic war machines, among them a saucer-shaped armored vehicle on wheels—in effect, a primitive tank.

A sketch by Michelangelo illustrates his thoughts on how to fortify a bastion protecting the Porta al Prato, one of the gates of the city of Florence.

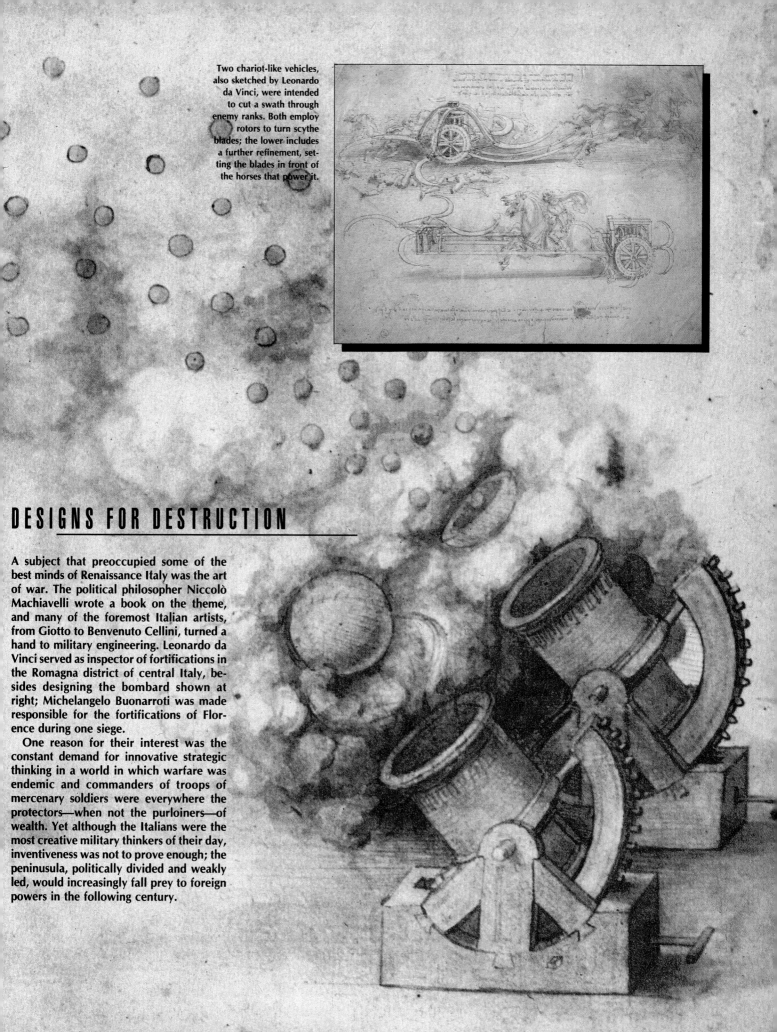

Two chariot-like vehicles, also sketched by Leonardo da Vinci, were intended to cut a swath through enemy ranks. Both employ rotors to turn scythe blades; the lower includes a further refinement, setting the blades in front of the horses that power it.

DESIGNS FOR DESTRUCTION

A subject that preoccupied some of the best minds of Renaissance Italy was the art of war. The political philosopher Niccolò Machiavelli wrote a book on the theme, and many of the foremost Italian artists, from Giotto to Benvenuto Cellini, turned a hand to military engineering. Leonardo da Vinci served as inspector of fortifications in the Romagna district of central Italy, besides designing the bombard shown at right; Michelangelo Buonarroti was made responsible for the fortifications of Florence during one siege.

One reason for their interest was the constant demand for innovative strategic thinking in a world in which warfare was endemic and commanders of troops of mercenary soldiers were everywhere the protectors—when not the purloiners—of wealth. Yet although the Italians were the most creative military thinkers of their day, inventiveness was not to prove enough; the peninusula, politically divided and weakly led, would increasingly fall prey to foreign powers in the following century.

had its troubles. Cosimo was succeeded briefly by his son Piero "the Gouty" and then in 1469 by his grandson Lorenzo, who set about earning the more appealing title of "the Magnificent." Lorenzo—who initially shared power with his younger brother Guiliano—was a man of refined tastes and great personal charm. He was a politician first and a businessman second, and since he spent lavishly, it was natural that under his control the family fortunes declined. Judicious tapping of public funds maintained the Medici lifestyle, but steadily increasing taxes caused friction (tax evasion became rife), and although Lorenzo generally ruled with skillful benevolence, he made more enemies than his grandfather had.

There were limits to his goodwill. In 1478, the rival Pazzi family and their allies tried to assassinate him at High Mass beneath Brunelleschi's cathedral dome. His young brother Giuliano fell to their daggers, but Lorenzo escaped. Within hours, several of the conspirators were hanging from the windows of the Palazzo della Signoria; Botticelli was commissioned to depict the dangling bodies. And over the next few years, those who had escaped were hunted down remorselessly. (One was even dragged home from Constantinople, and the young Leonardo sketched his execution.) The first victims, though, had included an archbishop and a teenage cardinal, and Lorenzo's revenge brought war with the boy's infuriated uncle, Pope Sixtus IV, in alliance with King Ferdinand of Naples.

Like almost all Italian warfare, the fighting was conducted by mercenary soldiers led by the *condottieri* each side had hired. Literally, condottiere meant "contractor"; such men were less military chieftains than the managing directors of commercial enterprises, often of many years' standing. They were understandably reluctant to risk their expensively trained employees and their even more costly equipment to the fortunes of battle, and campaigns were generally decided by subtle tactical maneuvering rather than a straightforward clash of arms. Lorenzo's war was no different. His mercenaries gradually retreated to Florence; the enemy's mercenaries slowly advanced, and any real suffering was endured by the people in the rural areas through which the armies passed.

Two Tuscan villas belonging to the Medici family illustrate the changing social climate of Renaissance Italy. The fortress-like dwelling at Trebbio *(left)*, twelve miles north of Florence, dates from the late Middle Ages, when the countryside was a dangerous place in which to live. In the course of the fifteenth century, however, the better-governed city-states managed to impose the rule of law throughout their territories by using forces of mercenary soldiers. It thus became possible to build graceful, relatively unprotected properties of the type of the estate at Poggio a Caiano *(right)*, rebuilt in the 1480s, where Lorenzo de' Medici went to relax, personally supervising the raising of Sicilian pheasants.

But subtle maneuvering was not confined to the battlefield: Faced with the prospect of a long siege, Lorenzo set off on a secret journey to Naples, where a generous outpouring of Florentine gold caused a sudden change in Ferdinand's allegiance. Deprived of his ally, Sixtus abandoned the struggle.

The conflict was of no lasting importance, but it was typical of its time. Palace murders, a corrupt and aggressive Church, condottieri avoiding pitched battle while they ravaged the countryside, and allies waiting only for a suitable bribe in order to break faith: These were all regular elements in late-fifteenth-century Italian quarrels. They marked the age with a brutal shortsightedness that in the end was self-defeating. The papacy, for instance, in the closing decades of the fifteenth century, was the plaything of a few families who milked it ruthlessly for what it was worth. Popes were chosen from among like-minded cardinals, who schemed endlessly against one another but were cut from the same far-from-holy cloth.

Innocent VIII, Sixtus's successor, raised huge sums from the sale of indulgences and pardons, much of which were spent on his acknowledged son. When the youth married a daughter of Lorenzo the Magnificent in 1486, the cost of the celebrations obliged the pontiff to mortgage his papal tiara and other regalia. The money spilled with such profusion was good news for the artists and intellectuals who enjoyed papal patronage, yet almost the only seriously "religious" act of Innocent's pontificate was the promulgation in the year of his son's wedding of the bull *Summus desiderantes,* authorizing the first large-scale persecution of witches in centuries.

Innocent was greatly helped by his chancellor, Cardinal Rodrigo Borgia, who blandly justified the sale of pardons for capital crimes that might even include murder: "The Lord desireth not the death of a sinner, but rather that he should live and pay." In the long run, though, it was the Church that paid, for in a few decades, the hot wind of scandal from Rome had fanned the flames of the Reformation.

In the meantime, though, the popes indulged themselves. Borgia had his turn on Innocent VIII's death—his election as Alexander VI in 1492 was a triumph of wholesale bribery—and promptly set about using papal power to carve out a new territory

THE PURSUIT OF BEAUTY

The Renaissance worship of beauty extended to the world of fashion as well as to art. Ignoring laws intended to curb excessive spending, wealthy Italians relentlessly sought out the latest and most luxurious styles of adornment. They were assisted in this pursuit by the growing availability of silk, well adapted to the contemporary taste for bright colors, and by elegant and expensive accessories such as the comb of inlaid ivory shown at far right.

A concern with personal adornment was by no means limited to such professional temptresses as the two courtesans shown in this painting by the Venetian Vittore Carpaccio *(right)*. Books of etiquette stressed the importance of an elegant wardrobe, as well as courtesy and good breeding, among the accouterments of every ambitious young man and woman. In the words of one such work: "Everyone should dress well, according to his age and his position in society. If he does not, it will be taken as a mark of contempt for other people."

Among the more bizarre fashion accessories in fifteenth-century Italy were clogs with four-inch soles. This apparently extravagant style in fact had a practical purpose; the footwear kept the hems of the ankle-length dresses favored at the time safely above the mud that covered city streets.

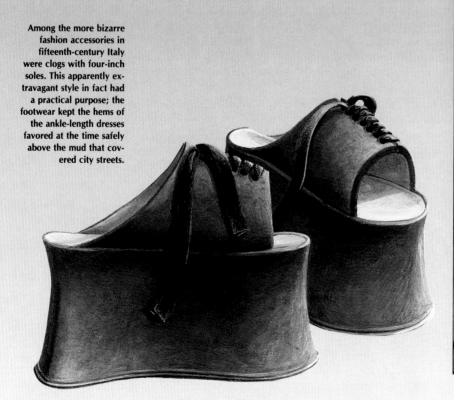

Piero di Cosimo painted this portrait of the Florentine beauty Simonetta Vespucci after she died of consumption at the age of twenty-three. The snake entwined in her necklace may have been intended as a symbolic reference to the disease that killed her.

not for the papacy itself but for his son Cesare. Between them, they almost succeeded. For unlike Innocent's foolish and forgotten child, Cesare Borgia was something of a political and military genius, as charming as he was ruthless.

His father made him a cardinal at the age of seventeen. Shortly afterward, an elder brother died of a mysterious ailment that left Cesare the unchallenged heir—if not to his father's papal throne, then certainly to his family ambitions. An adroit military campaign made Cesare master of central Italy; among his staff, as "our exceedingly eminent and much beloved architect and engineer," was Leonardo da Vinci. It only remained for him to secure the election of a friend as pope on his father's death to ensure that the conquered territory would stay in his control. But before Cesare did so, Alexander died (of fever, the host declared; many suspected poison) and Cesare was taken grievously ill after a banquet on the eve of a new campaign. While he slowly recovered, Saint Peter's See passed to a Borgia enemy, and all Cesare's plans came to nothing. A few years later he was dead himself, killed in a skirmish during a siege in faraway Navarre.

But times were changing. Even before Cesare Borgia's near-triumph, a stern reaction to the age's excesses had begun in Florence, of all places. Lorenzo died in 1492, the same year that Columbus discovered the Americas and Cardinal Borgia succeeded Innocent. Two years later, in a fit of civic revulsion, the Florentines drove the Medici family from the city and entrusted its governance to a pietistic monk called Girolamo Savonarola. For four years, he and his bands of armed disciples purged the city, ignoring Pope Alexander's bulls of excommunication and building a huge "Bonfire of the Vanities" to destroy such irreligious paintings as they could find. It was a brief repentance: The Florentines came to their senses in 1498 and, weary of fanatic virtue, burned Savonarola himself.

By then, the fifteenth-century Renaissance as a distinctive and exciting period was over. It was brought to an end not by debased religion but by corrupt politics. In 1494, during a trivial war with Naples, Duke Ludovico Sforza of Milan enlisted the aid of Charles VIII of France, whose family had a claim to the southern kingdom. Unfortunately for Ludovico, Charles also had and lay claim to Milan. And Charles was no Italian princeling: He was king of a great nation-state, with a frighteningly large army in which cavalry and artillery were shrewdly combined for the first time in history with a well-trained infantry equipped with pikes and harquebuses.

Despite his marvelous new army, Charles was a poor strategist, and for a few years an improbable alliance between Naples and Milan kept the French at bay. But in 1498, Charles died and was succeeded by the soldier-king Louis XII. Even while Cesare Borgia planned and executed his campaigns, a new French invasion swept across the Alps and seized Milan. Worse followed. As the new century got under way, the Spaniards, too, became interested in Italian adventures. Italian independence was effectively at an end, and the price for its loss came high. Italy's popes and princes had been murderous, but their murders had been on a limited scale. By the 1520s, thanks to their blunders, Italy's former rulers were forced to look on almost powerless as famine stalked a ruined land in the wake of mighty armies whose clashes killed more men in a single afternoon than the condottieri had lost in half a century.

It is fitting that, apart from its miraculous profusion of great art, the age left behind the work of a leading political thinker. Niccolò Machiavelli was born in Florence in 1469 and came of age during the terrifying days of Savonarola. He accompanied

Cesare Borgia during his campaigns and lived to see Italy laid waste by foreign invaders. In his way, he was as acute an observer as any painter, and he had no time for the kind of idealized city-state the humanists enthused over. Like Leonardo dissecting his corpses—the two men, in fact, became acquainted during their time with Cesare Borgia—he was interested in what he saw, not what he would have liked to see. Thus a key chapter in his best-known book, *The Prince*—in effect, a ruler's workshop manual—is entitled "On Cruelty and Mercy, and whether it is better to be loved than feared, or rather feared than loved." The chapter draws precise examples from Machiavelli's experience: "Cesare Borgia was held to be a cruel man, yet thanks to his cruelty he pacified the province of Romagna, united it, and kept it peaceful and loyal"; it goes on to describe how elsewhere he had seen the policies of less "cruel" rulers lead to massacre and destruction. His conclusion: Fear is more effective than love, but a wise ruler will take care not to be hated.

With the passing of time, Machiavelli's name became a byword for deviousness and betrayal. Yet no one ever wrote more clearly of the naked realities of power, and his central idea, that only "the Prince"—that is, the state itself—can be the judge of what is right and wrong in statecraft, was never seriously challenged in practice. In other works, he elaborated surprisingly modern ideas of constitutional checks and balances, and a theme of all his writing was the disastrous consequences to his beloved Italy of the disunity created by princely incompetence. As Machiavelli noted, Italian rulers did not recognize any law but their own self-interest. The problem was that they acted without his cool, penetrating intelligence. Few had the sense to realize where self-interest truly lay.

Machiavelli thought the age was one of lost opportunity, and he was probably right. Although the art was incomparable, the immediate consequences of Renaissance Italy's travail amounted to far less than national rebirth. Unstable politics, foreign invasion, and the terrible moral ruin of the Church all served to undermine what had been achieved. The sad futility of Leonardo's last days summed up the failure of the age: A pensioner of the king of France, one of the greatest minds in history spent his final years puttering around the French court at Amboise, arranging fireworks displays and conjuring tricks for children. The fate of some of the master's greatest work, too, was a lesson in futility. For centuries after his death, many of his drawings and almost all of his brilliant anatomical studies moldered in an attic in Rome. They did not play the part they could have in the great intellectual and scientific advances that were to come.

The fifteenth century in Italy was not the beginning of the modern world, in which new ways of thinking matched with continually developing technology would grant Europeans brief but near-absolute sovereignty over the planet. But there had at least been an essential change, and by 1500, the old Europe of the Middle Ages seemed, in Italy at least, as far off as the Greece and Rome so beloved of the humanists. The Italian Renaissance, stormy, contradictory, sometimes futile, and often breathtakingly exciting, had shown what was possible.

A REVOLUTION IN ART

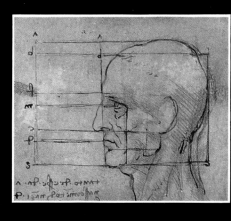

The fifteenth century was a period of intense exploration and innovation for painters, sculptors, and architects. The pioneering efforts of these artists in aesthetic theory and practice marked a turning point in the course and character of art throughout the Western world.

The flowering of Renaissance art was the culmination of an intellectual revival inspired by the gradual rediscovery of the learning of ancient Greece and Rome. Plato's speculations about the essence of reality and Aristotle's example of scientific investigation into nature were particularly powerful inspirations. The newly acquired knowledge spread throughout the courts and universities of Europe, stimulating a mood of rational inquiry. Philosophers began to explore the implications of humanism—the study of humanity for its own sake—rather than the relationship of humanity to the works of God.

The first breakthroughs of the new art were made in Italy, where relics of the past glories of the classical world lay close at hand. It was here, in the flourishing city of Florence in the 1420s, that a small group of uniquely gifted individuals set out deliberately to create a new art. Under the lavish patronage of Florence's merchant princes, who welcomed the importance that humanism gave to lay individuals, the great architect Filippo Brunelleschi and his circle together began to elaborate and apply a set of linked ideas that were to give Renaissance art its character.

Among the group's tenets was a belief in the unsurpassed virtue of classical models, especially in the fields of sculpture and architecture. Equally significant was a newly direct and detailed observation of reality. In addition, these artists gave a prominent role to mathematical calculation as a key to the understanding of the world. Many artists undertook exhaustive measurements—such as those noted in the sketch of a head *(above)* by Leonardo da Vinci—in their attempt to explain beauty by the concept of perfect proportion.

Of all the innovations of the Italian Renaissance, however, perhaps the most important was the discovery of perspective—the product of artists' preoccupation with mathematics and with the immediate appearances of reality. Brunelleschi was the first to propound the laws of perspective, which were later spelled out in greater detail by his followers.

THE SIGNIFICANCE OF BALANCE

For the artists of the Renaissance, beauty was a consequence of harmonious proportion. The aesthetic appeal of any entity, natural or manmade—a building, a flower, a human body—could, they believed, be traced to the perfect balance among its constituent parts. Many theorists sought to establish a universal formula that could be applied to all forms of creation.

These men also believed that the ancients had possessed the secrets of true proportional harmony; and since its rules were specifiable mathematically, they sought to elicit the truth by studying, measuring, and analyzing the surviving buildings of ancient Rome, as well as by combing the works of the Roman writer Vitruvius on the theory of architecture.

Brunelleschi, the Florentine architect and engineer who inspired and led this great undertaking, was revered as the rediscoverer of the secrets of Roman architecture. His successors, especially the architects Leon Battista Alberti and Francesco di Giorgio, put his findings into practice and developed his theories in treatises of their own.

Such theorizing was typical of the Renaissance. Whereas, during the Middle Ages, architects and artists had been anonymous craftworkers offering up their skills for the glory of God, artists now came to be seen as individuals with a mind and style of their own, who took pride in signing their works. The artists of Florence, in particular, showed a bent for exploration and experiment that sometimes brought their work close to a spirit of scientific inquiry.

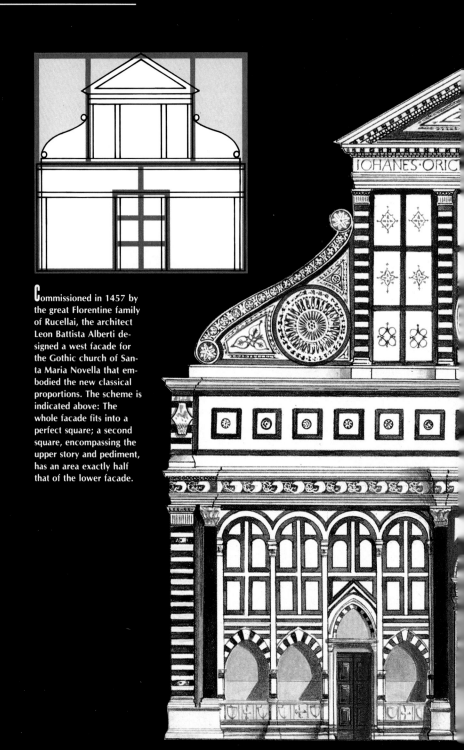

Commissioned in 1457 by the great Florentine family of Rucellai, the architect Leon Battista Alberti designed a west facade for the Gothic church of Santa Maria Novella that embodied the new classical proportions. The scheme is indicated above: The whole facade fits into a perfect square; a second square, encompassing the upper story and pediment, has an area exactly half that of the lower facade.

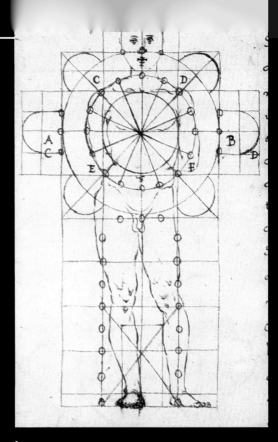

In a study from his manuscript treatise on architecture written in the 1480s, the architect Francesco di Giorgio uses a human figure as the basis of a design for a geometrically perfect church building, a complex arrangement of circles and squares.

THE ILLUSION OF DEPTH

The discovery of the laws of linear perspective brought a quantum leap forward in the depiction of reality on a flat painted surface. It was Brunelleschi—an engineer by training, and deeply interested in mathematics—who undertook optical experiments to demonstrate why objects close to the spectator appear larger than distant ones. His follower Alberti recorded and amplified these discoveries in his treatise *On Painting* of 1436, explaining how to calculate the proportionate difference in size according to the distance from the person viewing the painting and how to make the horizontal planes of the picture converge at a point deep within the scene. Every major painter of the early Renaissance became obsessed by the manipulation of perspective effects.

The possibilities opened up by the use of perspective were intensely exciting to the Renaissance mind. By enhancing the impression of three-dimensional reality in a painting, the use of perspective aided the artist in the quest to show the world as it really was. Furthermore, the new technique chimed perfectly with the humanist emphasis of Renaissance thought: By drawing spectators into the picture and giving them an indispensable role as representatives of the point of view on which the perspective depended, the individual's position of central importance in the world was confirmed.

Piero della Francesca's cool and eerie *Flagellation of Christ,* painted about 1450, constitutes a complete lesson in perspective. The rectilinear composition of the portico and columns combines with the tiling on the floor to define a three-dimensional grid on which the heights of figures at different distances from the observer can easily be calculated. The horizontals—made explicit in the diagram above—all converge at a point two-thirds from the top of the painting and equidistant from each side.

OBSERVING FROM LIFE

The realism that was so marked a feature of Renaissance drawing and painting stemmed from a desire to understand at first hand every aspect of creation. Such an ambition was relatively new in the fifteenth century; in the past, artists had on the whole been content to absorb in their apprenticeships a time-honored repertoire of skills to be used for the celebration of eternal holy truths.

Renaissance painters tried to understand nature's workings rather than simply to worship God through his sacred creation. The results of their curiosity were displayed in lively studies of animals and plants, psychologically penetrating portraits, and an increasing accuracy and sensitivity in representing landscape.

Figures of dogs on a page from a sketchbook of the Veronese artist Antonio Pisanello, who died about 1455, show an accuracy and lively delicacy that bespeak direct observation. Renowned as a medalist as well as a painter, Pisanello worked for patrons throughout Italy.

A vivid sketch of a rearing horse—a study for an equestrian monument—eloquently reveals Leonardo da Vinci's interest in movement and how to capture it on paper. Leonardo's restless curiosity led him to make detailed anatomical studies of the human and animal forms he constantly drew.

In an unflinchingly realistic portrait traditionally attributed to the Florentine painter Domenico Ghirlandaio, an old man with a misshapen nose exchanges a look of grave affection with his grandchild. Glimpsed through the window of their chamber is a recognizably Tuscan landscape, flooded with tranquil light.

GLORIFYING THE HUMAN FORM

Sculptors felt the influence of classical ideals of beauty even more immediately than painters, since enough antique statuary had survived to provide plentiful models of style and subject matter. Abandoning the medieval practice of using sculptures almost exclusively to adorn churches with figures of the saints, Renaissance artists brought the human figure into the center of their work and began to treat it in a less stylized manner than their Gothic predecessors had done.

In order to be able to represent this most complex and beautiful of forms with a true understanding of its structure, sculptors made the study of anatomy a priority. Besides studying the available texts and making detailed sketches of the body in action, some—Antonio Pollaiuolo, Leonardo da Vinci, and Michelangelo among them—dissected corpses to advance their knowledge.

The life-size bronze *David* that Donatello produced in about 1440 was revolutionary: the first Renaissance sculpture of the naked human body that was freestanding and liberated from any architectural context. Donatello, a friend of Brunelleschi and one of the original Florentine circle of artists, was inspired by classical models; he had visited Rome between 1431 and 1433 to study the antiquities.

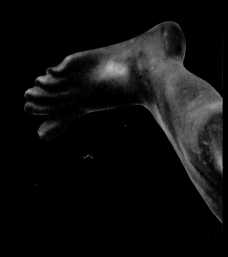

The contours of the straining muscles in Pollaiuolo's statuette (less than eighteen inches high) of the Greek hero Hercules wrestling with the giant Antaeus show a detailed anatomical knowledge and a satisfaction in representing it. Small bronzes, especially of classical subjects, were popular among the wealthy patrons of fifteenth-century Florence.

THE FALL OF CONSTANTINOPLE

On December 10, 1399, Manuel II Palaeologus, emperor of Byzantium, sailed out of the besieged city of Constantinople on a mission to the rulers of Western Christendom. He planned to appeal to them as fellow Christians to save his empire from the Muslim forces that were blockading his capital and threatening to destroy the eastern bulwark of the faith.

The emperor cut an imposing figure. Fifty years old and always dressed in flowing white robes, he was a handsome, bearded man of commanding presence, great scholarship, and unswerving religious convictions. He attracted huge crowds on his arrival in Venice, Padua, Vicenza, Pavia, and Milan. In London, he was lavishly entertained by King Henry IV, who staged a tournament and a masquerade in his honor. In Paris, he was the guest of King Charles VI, with his own suite in the Louvre.

On the surface, the emperor's mission was a triumph. All the Western powers were sympathetic to his cause. The pope called for a crusade to rescue Byzantium. Henry talked of raising an army and a fleet; Charles promised to supply an expeditionary force. The Venetians—eager to protect their commercial interests—declared themselves ready to fight, though only if an international force strong enough to ensure victory could be mounted.

Manuel was sufficiently encouraged to send messages to Constantinople, reassuring his beleaguered people that help would soon be on its way. But more than a year went by without any sign of action. Gradually, the emperor came to recognize the bitter truth: Western Europe was too preoccupied with its own affairs to act with urgency on behalf of a distant city surrounded by the Turks.

The fact was that the 1,000-year-old Byzantine Empire, inheritor of the eastern realms of imperial Rome, had by now lost much of its political importance. At its height, under Justinian in the sixth century AD, it had ruled almost the entire Mediterranean world; by the start of the fifteenth century, it had dwindled into a petty principality on the borders of Europe and Asia. Its territory was now confined to Constantinople itself, part of the peninsula of the Peloponnese, a few towns strung along the Marmara and Black Sea coasts, and a handful of islands in the Aegean Sea.

In religious affairs as well, Byzantium and the West had become isolated from each other. The eastern empire had embraced the Orthodox branch of Christianity, which over the centuries had become increasingly different in custom and ceremony from the Catholic faith of Rome. Although the doctrinal differences between the two churches were limited, they were disputed with all the bitterness that medieval theologians could muster.

Hostility between East and West had come to a head in 1204, when Constantinople was captured and savagely sacked, not by Muslims but by the Christian soldiers of the Fourth Crusade. The city was won back for Orthodox Christianity only after half

The army of the Ottoman sultan Mehmet II lies encamped outside the walls of Constantinople in this contemporary French manuscript illumination depicting the siege of the city in 1453. The Byzantine capital finally surrendered to the Turks after an epic fifty-four-day ordeal. The fall of Constantinople marked the end of more than 1,000 years of imperial rule and helped consolidate the position of the Ottomans as the dominant power in the Middle East.

a century of Catholic rule. Although scholarship and the arts had flourished anew under the native Greek dynasty restored at that time, the empire's political and economic base could not be rebuilt. Indeed, by the mid-fourteenth century, the state was so impoverished that its crown jewels had been pawned to the republic of Venice for 30,000 ducats. They were never to be redeemed.

In the course of the fourteenth century, the empire had suffered a host of disasters that ranged from invasion and plague to a series of dynastic civil wars. None, however, was as devastating in its long-term implications as the rise on its borders of a new, aggressive Muslim power: the Ottomans.

At the start of the fourteenth century, the Ottomans had been an obscure Turkish clan occupying land near the Byzantine frontier, across the Bosporus and about sixty miles from Constantinople. Several such small emirates had been established in the area by ghazi warriors, Turks dedicated to holy war against the infidel. Then, on July 27, 1302, under the command of their emir, Osman, they had achieved an important victory over a Byzantine army at Bapheus, near the seaport of Nicomedia (now Izmit). Subsequently, ghazis throughout the part of Turkey known as Anatolia flocked to the Ottoman banner; and Osman's ever-swelling forces campaigned north toward the Black Sea and southwest to the Sea of Marmara.

By 1389, under the command of Osman's grandson Murad I, the small border emirate had become the dominant Turkish state in Asia Minor. Murad made a vassal of Byzantine Emperor John V Palaeologus. Worse still for the Byzantines, the Ottomans had crossed the Dardanelles into Europe, where they had overrun Thrace and

When the last Byzantine ruler, Constantine XI, was crowned in Constantinople in 1449, the empire he inherited consisted of nothing more than the underpopulated city itself, the distant and beleaguered Peloponnese peninsula, and a scattering of isolated ports and islands. In contrast, Mehmet II inherited extensive territories in Asia Minor and the Balkans *(shaded yellow on the map)*. The continued Christian presence in Constantinople not only hindered the easy passage of Turkish ships and soldiers from one frontier to another but also posed a constant threat to the security of the Ottoman domains. Strategic necessity dictated that Mehmet should seek to capture it.

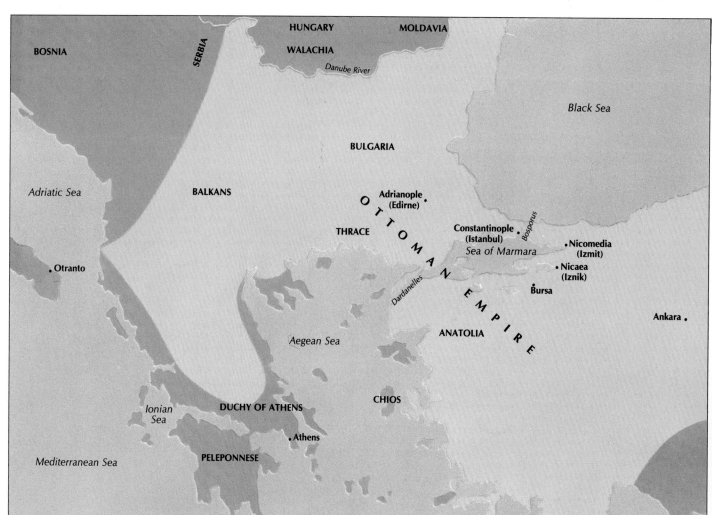

had defeated Serbia, Bulgaria, and Bosnia to establish their mastery of the Balkans. In that year, the Turkish victory of Kosovo confirmed their dominance and completed the isolation of Constantinople, which was now surrounded by Turkish-held lands.

The city's fortunes, meanwhile, had declined with its political importance; the population had shrunk from more than one million in the twelfth century to perhaps 100,000, and the various urban districts were now separated by areas of farmland and dereliction. Although commerce still flourished, it was largely dominated by foreign traders. The Venetians had their own prosperous quarter on the south bank of the harbor inlet known as the Golden Horn. The suburb of Pera, on the north bank, was in the hands of the Genoese, to whom it had been ceded in 1267.

Constantinople itself was still a formidable stronghold, and as such was a thorn in the side of the Ottomans, since it occupied a strategic location at the very heart of their empire. They had compelling reasons for wishing to eliminate this enclave, which, though harmless in itself, could at any time become a threat by way of some foreign alliance.

It came as little surprise, then, when in 1396, Sultan Bajazet I sent an army to starve its citizens into submission. Six years later, in the spring of 1402, the sultan formally demanded the surrender of the city—a traditional "courtesy" that, if unheeded, was regarded as justification for launching an all-out military assault.

Since Manuel II had failed to stir the Western powers into action, the fall of Constantinople now seemed imminent. But at the eleventh hour, the sultan was forced to withdraw to counter an invasion that came, ironically, not from the Christian West but from the Islamic East. His empire was in danger of being overrun by the hordes of Timur the Lame. Better known as Tamerlane, the Turkish-Mongol potentate had, from his base in Samarkand in what is now Soviet Central Asia, expanded his dominions in all directions to become the scourge of the Orient.

The city had won a reprieve, which was handsomely extended when Tamerlane went on to crush the Ottoman army and capture the sultan. For two decades, the pressure was off Byzantium, which was even able to regain some of its former territories in Thrace. By the 1420s, however, the Turks had regathered their forces; and when, in 1422, the ruler of Byzantium unwisely supported a pretender to the Ottoman throne, another army, 10,000 strong, was dispatched to besiege the city.

On August 24, Sultan Murad II ordered an all-out assault: A revered Islamic religious leader had foretold that the Christian capital would fall on that date. But after hours of bitter fighting along the land walls, the Turks had still not breached the Byzantine defenses. A retreat was ordered, and soon after, the siege was abandoned.

The sultan, it transpired, had been forced to divert his troops to put down a revolt in Anatolia. But the Greeks saw the withdrawal as another example of divine intervention. Constantinople had received its second respite.

No one, however, was so foolish as to believe that the threat looming over the city had been permanently lifted. Byzantium needed allies, and to find them it once again turned westward. Emperor John VIII, who had succeeded Manuel II, convinced himself that the lack of enthusiasm shown earlier by the Western powers for the Byzantine cause had its roots in the religious differences separating the Catholic and Orthodox faiths. In a desperate bid for security, he proposed the convening of a council to resolve the centuries-old rift between the Eastern and Western Churches.

The council assembled at Ferrara in Italy in 1438; following an outbreak of bubonic plague, it transferred to Florence. For sixteen months, the issues dividing the churches were debated until at last, on July 5, 1439, agreement was reached and a document of union was signed.

Implementing the agreement proved a different matter. It aroused bitterness throughout the Orthodox world; the attitude of its more extreme opponents was summed up in the saying, "Better the sultan's turban than the cardinal's hat." A leader of opposition to the union soon arose in the person of a brilliant Greek scholar named Gennadius, who won huge popular support. Ironically, the Union of Florence achieved the opposite of what was intended: Constantinople became the more insecure because its populace was divided. In addition, the alliance of the Greeks and the Western Church increased Ottoman apprehensions of the threat the city could pose to their power.

There was, therefore, little mourning, when Emperor John VIII died in October 1448. His reign had been undistinguished. In his last years, however, he had made at least two wise moves. He had allotted a large part of the state's financial resources to the repair of the great land walls of Constantinople, and, being childless, he had chosen as his successor his brother Constantine.

Constantine XI was nearly forty-five years old when he entered Constantinople as the newly crowned emperor in March 1449. He had fought heroically but unsuccessfully against the Turks in defense of the Peloponnese, Byzantium's last remaining province, and was respected as a soldier, administrator, and man of honor. He commanded the support of lay officials and scholars, and the affection of many of his subjects. But he also faced stern opposition from the clergy because, as a political realist, he accepted the necessity for union with Rome.

The fact was that Constantine soon needed the support of Western Christendom more than ever. In February 1451, Sultan Murad II died at Adrianople, his European capital in Thrace, to be succeeded by his only surviving son, Mehmet—a determined young man eager to make his mark on the world.

The new sultan—just nineteen years old on his accession—was well tutored in the sciences and philosophy. He was also a man of iron will and innate shrewdness. He started his reign on a pacific note by confirming existing treaties and swearing on the Koran that he would not violate Byzantine territory. The more optimistic Byzantine counselors convinced themselves that the empire was at no immediate risk.

Some such reading of the situation led Emperor Constantine, in the autumn of 1451, to make a dangerous diplomatic blunder. He sent envoys to remind the sultan that a pretender to the Ottoman throne—an obscure prince named Orkhan—was living in Constantinople, and that under a longstanding agreement, the Turks were bound to pay an annuity for his maintenance. The payment was badly in arrears. If it was not paid, Constantine stated, the Byzantines could no longer guarantee that the pretender would remain in their safekeeping.

This veiled threat infuriated the sultan, who regarded it as just cause for breaking his promise not to intrude on Byzantine territory. Perhaps he had had designs on the capital from the beginning. He took a first, major step toward open hostilities by ordering the construction of a huge fortress on the European shore of the Bosporus, on a ridge about five miles north of Constantinople. In April 1452, more than a thousand masons, together with thousands of laborers, began to build the castle on what was officially Byzantine soil. Constantine sent envoys to seek assurances that his capital would not be attacked. Mehmet promptly had them decapitated—an act tantamount to a declaration of war.

The sultan was convinced that the key to Constantinople was command of the sea approaches: Past sieges had been prolonged because the Byzantines had been relieved by supply ships. This time, the blockade would be complete. His new fortress, constructed in four and a half months and armed with three great cannon, was at the Bosporus's narrowest point, directly across from the existing Turkish castle of Anadolu-Hisar, less than a mile away on the Asian bank. Together, they effectively secured the sea lanes from the Black Sea.

At the same time, the sultan blocked the western end of the Bosporus by assembling a huge fleet in the Dardanelles. His armada comprised at least 125 vessels, large and small, including 16 warships (triremes and biremes, powered by both oars and sails) and an assortment of galleys, longboats, sailing barges, sloops, and cutters. In late March, it moved into the Sea of Marmara.

Meanwhile, a huge army, drawn from every corner of the Ottoman Empire, was gathering in Thrace. Eventually it was to number about 100,000. Roughly one-fifth were irregulars, including not only Turks but also adventurers from Christian countries—Hungarians, Germans, Italians, Slavs, and even some renegade Greeks. These mercenaries were poorly equipped, relatively ill-disciplined, and not totally reliable, since they were motivated only by the prospect of booty. But they were the exception. The rest of the force, some 80,000 Turkish regulars, were well disciplined; well armed with javelins, swords, and bows; armored with chain mail, breastplates, helmets, and shields; and driven by religious fervor. They were dedicated to holy war; and it was generally believed that a special place in paradise was reserved for the first soldier of the Prophet to penetrate the Christian capital.

The force that was to besiege Constantinople was possibly the most formidable army of the fifteenth century. Certainly, there were no finer soldiers than the 12,000 who made up its janissary regiments. They were the elite of the sultan's troops—men of Christian birth who, after being captured or recruited under duress as boys, had been brought up as Muslims. They were superfit gladiators trained only for war, to the extent that they were forbidden even to marry. The regiment was their only family, and the sultan was their father as well as their commander in chief.

Mehmet's preparations for war had been meticulous and lavish. Now, in the late summer of 1452, his arsenal was further strengthened by the fortuitous arrival of a Hungarian engineer who specialized in the making of heavy artillery. This stranger, named Urban, had already offered his services to the Byzantines, who could not afford his fees. The sultan had larger resources and was more than willing to pay the asking price for the weapons Urban promised to deliver: cannon powerful enough to devastate the land walls of Constantinople.

A few months later, the first of Urban's cannon was installed on the ramparts of the newly built fortress overlooking the Bosporus. The castle, now known as Rumeli Hisari (European Fortress), was then called Boghanskesen, mean-

When the Florentine painter Benozzo Gozzoli was commissioned in the mid-fifteenth century to paint the *Journey of the Magi,* his model for one of the kings was the Byzantine emperor John VIII, who had visited Italy and neighboring lands in 1439. Confronted with growing Ottoman pressure on his capital, John saw no alternative but to turn to the West for aid. Help was duly promised, but at a price. John was told that the Orthodox church—the state religion of his empire—must admit its doctrinal errors and accept the supremacy of the pope in Rome. Although John was willing to accept this condition, and even attended the council held at Florence to negotiate a settlement, he thereby compromised his popularity among his subjects and in fact received little practical assistance in exchange.

A Turkish artist, Sinan Bey, painted this portrait of Sultan Mehmet II sniffing a rose. The likeness tallies with a word picture given by an Italian soldier captured after the fall of Constantinople, who described him as "of medium height, fat and fleshy; he had a wide forehead, large eyes with thick lashes, an aquiline nose, a small mouth with a round, copious, reddish-tinged beard."

ing the "Cutter of the Strait." Its name defined its purpose: All passing ships, by order of the sultan, were required to anchor nearby for inspection. In November, a Venetian ship defied the command. Urban's cannon blasted it out of the water. The survivors were executed, and their captain was impaled on a stake and displayed close to the fortress as a warning to would-be transgressors.

Mehmet II now ordered the construction of a larger cannon. Urban obliged; he cast a whole battery of weapons, including one twice as large as the great gun of Rumeli-Hisar. This monster had a barrel twenty-six feet long and was reportedly capable of propelling a 1,500-pound stone ball more than half a mile. Built at Adrianople, it was carried toward Constantinople on a cart drawn by sixty oxen, with an escort of 200 men to strengthen bridges and help steady the gun carriage along the way. By early April, the enormous cannon was within range of the Byzantine capital's land walls, as was the bulk of the Turkish army under the sultan's command. The siege of Constantinople was about to begin.

April 1, 1453, was Easter, normally the most joyful day in the Orthodox calendar—the time when the long fast of Lent ended in feasts and festivities, and the traditional call of *Christos anesti,* "Christ is risen," rang around the city. But that day the celebrations were muted. From the city's heights, the Greeks had seen the Turkish fleet cruising in the Marmara and the cannon of Urban lumbering toward their land walls. Now was a time for continued prayer. They needed another miracle.

Strategically, the Byzantine defenses comprised two principal elements. One was a great chain, floated on wooden pontoons, which on Easter Monday was stretched as a boom across the mouth of the Golden Horn, denying access from the Bosporus to the city's harbor and northern boundary. The other was the twelve miles of sturdy land and sea walls enclosing the city.

The walls of Constantinople were arguably the most formidable defenses in the world at the time. On the Marmara side alone they were studded with 188 towers; attack there was made all the more hazardous by treacherous currents, shoals, and reefs. The sea walls along the Golden Horn had proved vulnerable when stormed by the soldiers of the Fourth Crusade in 1204, but that approach was now barred by the boom. Consequently, the main Turkish assault had to come

opened there in the outer wall. A tense competition then began. Each night, defenders would slip out from the city to repair the damage with improvised stockades of wooden planks on which they piled earth-filled sacks and barrels. The following day, the sultan's guns would blast open the breach once more.

Early on, the defenders gained two morale-boosting successes. On April 12, a Turkish fleet, under the command of the Bulgarian-born Suleiman Baltoghlu, tried to break through the boom across the Golden Horn. Though armed with cannon, his ships were repelled by the tall Christian sailing boats, which had the advantage of higher decks for raining down a hail of arrows, javelins, and stones on the foe. Then, on April 18, the sultan's infantry launched an attack against the damaged land wall in the Lycus valley. Superior in numbers, but less well-protected by body armor, they were driven back, after four hours of fighting, by Greeks and Italians under the inspired leadership of Giustiniani.

Two days later, the Byzantines gained further encouragement. From the sea walls on the Marmara, they sighted the three long-awaited supply ships from Genoa, along with a Greek boat carrying grain from Sicily. They had been able to reach the Marmara because the sultan had left the Dardanelles unguarded while deploying his fleet for the siege.

Now a vast array of Turkish ships closed in to prevent the relief boats from reaching the Golden Horn. Again the fleet commander was Baltoghlu; again he found that the firepower of the enemy was superior because it was delivered from higher decks. This time, moreover, his sailors confronted not only a hail of arrows, javelins, and stones but also the deadliest weapon in the Byzantine arsenal: Greek fire. For hundreds of years, the defenders of Constantinople had successfully employed this mysterious flammable substance (possibly consisting of saltpeter, quicklime, or petroleum) that had only to be moistened to make it blaze up uncontrollably. The emperor's cargo ship carried barrels of the substance, which were emptied on any Turkish vessels that drew alongside it.

Following a drop in the wind, the Christian ships were inexorably drawn by the prevailing currents toward the western shore of the Bosporus. There, beyond the walls of Pera, Sultan Mehmet watched the battle on horseback, urging on his men with growing impatience. He could not comprehend how four ships—lashed together now so as to pool their defensive resources—could survive for hours against scores of hostile vessels challenging them from all sides.

By late afternoon, the tide of battle seemed finally to be turning in favor of the Turks, who were on the point of boarding the Christian ships. But suddenly the wind whipped up anew; with their great sails billowing, the relief boats managed to force their way through the blockade. Baltoghlu ordered a withdrawal to regather his scattered fleet; as darkness fell, the boom was lifted and, to the frenzied acclamation of the defenders on the walls, the relief boats reached safe harbor in the Golden Horn.

The next day, the sultan publicly disgraced the unfortunate Baltoghlu. The admiral, who had been injured in the fighting, was bastinadoed, stripped of rank and offices, and deprived of his possessions, which were divided among the janissaries.

The engagement gave fresh heart to the Byzantines and provided valuable supplies of armaments and food. But the respite was short-lived. A brilliant strategic stroke by the sultan and his planners was quickly to restore the initiative to the Turks in the battle of the boats.

On April 22, more than seventy Ottoman ships began to advance on the Golden

A late-fifteenth-century Turkish miniature shows a legendary hero slaying a dragon in a style that suggests the artist was familiar with images of the Christian dragon-killer, Saint George. Mehmet allowed his Christian subjects to continue practicing their religion. A certain amount of cultural cross-fertilization ensued—in part because Mehmet, unlike many of his Muslim subjects, was not opposed to the portrayal of living things in art.

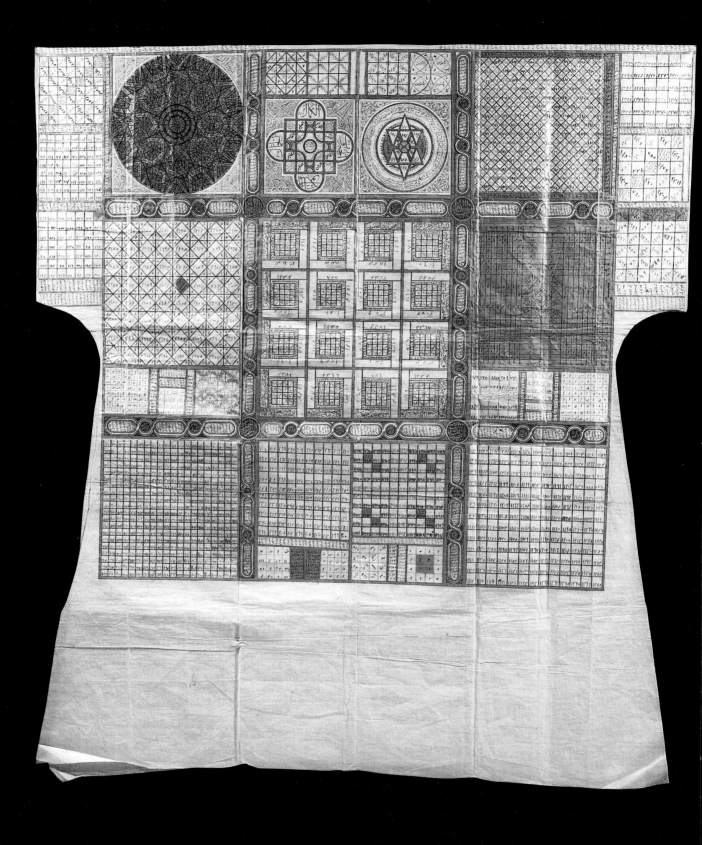

Horn, but not by sea. Instead the boats moved overland, breasting the ridge that rose steeply behind the neutral colony of Pera. Their sails were hoisted and their oars were manned, although the oarsmen were beating ceremoniously against empty air. The ships were actually powered by teams of oxen, which hauled them on sledge-shaped cradles over a slipway of greased logs laid uphill from the Bosporus to bypass the Byzantine boom.

The defenders of the city could only watch as the sultan's fleet descended into the Golden Horn. From there the ships could bombard the harbor walls, occupying the Byzantines on an additional front. To further complicate the defenders' task, the sultan had wine barrels lashed together to form a pontoon bridge across the upper waters of the harbor, just above the city walls. Timber platforms, each carrying a cannon, were roped to the far sides of the bridge, providing a base for bombardment from yet another angle.

Realizing the severity of the threat, the Byzantines tried to take counteraction. On the night of April 28, a Christian raiding party sailed across the Golden Horn to attack the Ottoman ships. But, forewarned by spies, the Turks were waiting for them. Many sailors and small boats were lost. The following day, Mehmet had 40 of the raiders executed in view of the city. The Byzantines replied by beheading 260 Turkish prisoners on the harbor walls.

Now Constantinople was under daily bombardment on two fronts; every night its citizens toiled to repair the damage. Although their manpower resources were stretched, the Byzantines still had some successes. On May 7, they held off an attack by Turkish infantry on the breach in the Lycus valley. Later, the Turks attempted to launch an assault from a huge siege tower, which they wheeled up to the outer walls. In a night raid, defenders destroyed the machine before it could be used.

They also successfully countered Turkish attempts to mine the walls. Under the direction of a Scottish engineer who had come in Giustiniani's company, the Greeks dug countermines to drive out the underground attackers by fire or flood. On one such sortie, they captured a Turkish officer involved in the operations, who revealed, under torture, the location of undetected tunnels.

Despite these small victories, the siege was taking its toll. The citizens of Constantinople were weary of war in body and spirit and desperately short of food. The Venetian and Genoese contingents were split by petty squabbles. Hopes still centered on the Venetian relief force, but there were growing apprehensions that it would not arrive in time to help the city.

Driving himself to near-exhaustion, the emperor convened councils of war, organized food rationing, and rode to every sector of the city to rally his troops. But even he could not counter the dismay provoked by certain events generally interpreted as portents of doom. On the night of May 24, there was an eclipse of the moon; citizens recalled an ancient prophecy that their city would stand as long as the moon waxed in the sky. The next day, during a religious procession, one of the city's most hallowed icons of the Virgin Mary, borne shoulder-high on a wooden frame, slipped and fell to the ground. Almost at once, a thunderstorm brought torrential rain and hail, flooding the streets and forcing the faithful to run for cover.

After seven weeks of siege, the sultan was winning the war of attrition. Yet he, too, had problems to confront. The cost of keeping 100,000 men in the field was phenomenal, and it was mounting daily. And there were important officials in his camp who regarded the whole campaign as misconceived. They were disturbed by the

The inscriptions on this shirt indicate not merely when it was begun and finished (March 30, 1477, and March 29, 1480) but also what the presiding astrological influences were on those days, since this was a magical shirt, decorated with cabalistic letters and occult signs to protect its owner from misfortune and death. The garment was made for Jem, youngest son of Mehmet, but the unlucky prince never wore it. Defeated in a bid for the throne in 1481, he fled to the West, where he is said to have owned such exotica as a chess-playing ape and a magic goblet, but apparently not the shirt, which remained in Constantinople. Jem died, probably of a slow-acting poison, in Naples in 1495.

losses suffered, the lack of real progress, and the possibility of reinforcement coming from the West. At their urging, the young sultan offered terms to the besieged. He would spare the lives of all Christians, he said, in exchange for unconditional surrender. Alternatively, he informed the emperor, he was prepared to lift the siege if the Byzantines would agree to pay an annual tribute of 100,000 gold bezants. It was a sum that the impoverished city could never hope to raise.

Constantine rejected the offers, and Mehmet decided on an all-out attack to force the issue. Mehmet condemned the fainthearted among his advisers; and, to encourage his flagging soldiers, he promised them three days' looting if their assault on the city succeeded. To refresh them for the coming struggle, the following day, May 28, was declared a day of rest. After weeks of cannon fire and the incessant blaring of military bands, an eerie silence fell over the Ottoman camp. In response, the emperor gave the order for church bells to sound throughout Constantinople. The Greeks knew the supreme test was at hand.

The climax came in the early hours of May 29. Shortly after one o'clock in the morning, Mehmet launched an assault against the entire four-mile length of the land walls, with the main thrust concentrated in the Lycus valley. Screaming war cries, and spurred on by beating drums and blaring trumpets, thousands of irregular troops hurled themselves against the outer walls in the first wave of the onslaught. These were the expendable pawns of the sultan's army; behind them stood a line of military police to urge them on and strike down any who attempted to turn back before the order was given.

Most of the mercenaries fought with their own weapons, primarily scimitars, bows, and slings; many had been provided with scaling ladders. They were no match for defenders protected by body armor and, in some cases, armed with muskets. Nor was their numerical superiority of any real advantage. As they crowded into the valley, they impeded one another's movements and made an easy target for defending musketeers, archers, and stone throwers, who could see them by the light of flares and the occasional glow of the moon between scudding clouds.

For nearly two hours, the irregulars sought unsuccessfully to scale the stockade, which was defended by Greeks and Italians under the command of Giustiniani. At last, the sultan gave the order for them to retreat. Their losses had been heavy, but they had tired the defenders, who now had to face the assault of the more-disciplined and better-armed regular troops.

Under the command of Ishak Pasha, governor of Anatolia, the sultan's regiments fought tenaciously in the face of a determined defense. Another two hours passed without a breakthrough; then the attackers fell back to allow the great cannon of Urban to blast a gap in the stockade. Shouting triumphantly, the Turkish infantry charged into the breach, but once more the defenders stood firm. Led by the emperor himself, they formed a human chain across the gap, driving back the enemy until the defenses could be repaired.

The Christians had now been fighting for more than four hours, and they desperately needed rest. But no respite was to be given. The sultan chose this moment to display his strength. He ordered the janissaries into combat. Re-

Even after Constantinople became the political and commercial capital of the Ottoman Empire, Iznik—a town in northwest Asia Minor—remained the center for the manufacture of porcelain and tiles. The town straddled major trade routes and had access to adequate deposits of suitable clay. At first, Iznik's kilns produced peasant goods, but by the late fifteenth century, its potters—taking their inspiration partly from Chinese models—were creating distinctive, high-quality blue-and-white pieces with a clear glaze.

splendent in their coats of mail, with plumed helmets strapped over their turbans, they quickly advanced in successive groups, each soldier hacking at the wooden supports of the stockade and positioning ladders before retiring to make way for the one behind. The fate of the entire campaign was about to be decided.

Encouraged by the tolling of church bells from the city behind them, the defenders rallied once more. For a time, it seemed that they might triumph against the odds. After an hour of hand-to-hand combat, the janissaries had still not been able to breach the stockade.

A simple human error finally tipped the scales. About half a mile to the north of the Lycus, a defender returning from a sortie failed to bar securely a gateway in the single Blachernae wall. Members of an Ottoman detachment noticed the lapse, forced a passage through the gate, and fought their way into the space between the inner and outer walls. The presence of the Turks caused consternation, but even so, the Greeks might have managed to repel them if their entry had not coincided with an even greater disaster: While defending the stockade, Giustiniani was shot through the breastplate and wounded.

For fifty-four days, the Genoese warrior had commanded the land-wall defenses with exemplary vigor and courage. Now his strength failed him. Although the emperor personally pleaded with him to stay, he insisted on being carried off to a Genoese ship waiting in the Golden Horn. The sight of his departure, coupled with the news that the Turks had entered the city to the north, spread panic among his Genoese compatriots, who abandoned their positions, leaving the Greeks and Venetians to fight on alone.

Emperor Constantine did what he could to rally the defenders at the Blachernae wall, then rode back to the Lycus valley to join his men in the breach. He arrived just in time to face a fresh onslaught by the janissaries. This time their impact was decisive. Soon Turks were swarming through breaches in the blockade and slaughtering the many Greeks trapped between the inner and outer walls. Constantine realized the implications. Seeing that the battle was all but lost, he flung off his imperial insignia and, sword in hand, plunged into the oncoming horde. The emperor was never seen again.

The defenses of Constantinople swiftly crumbled. Greeks ran to their homes to protect their families. Venetians fled to their ships in the Golden Horn. The land-wall gates were flung open and through them, like locusts, surged Turks and foreign mercenaries by tens of thousands to strip the city bare. Turkish sailors, deserting their ships in the Golden Horn, also joined in the rush for booty. As a result, the Venetian fleet, plus some Genoese ships and a few of the emperor's galleys, were able to break through the boom and sail to freedom. All the ships were crowded with refugees who had swum out from the shore.

But there was no escape for the citizens who remained within the walls. The narrow streets ran with blood as the conquerors rampaged through the capital in a daylong orgy of looting, rape, and murder. Men, women, and children were slaughtered indiscriminately as Turkish soldiers fought to eliminate isolated pockets of resistance. The Imperial Palace at Blachernae was stripped of its treasures; churches were desecrated, monasteries and convents gutted, precious libraries burned. After several hours, the city was dotted with myriad small flags, each denoting a house that had been ransacked.

At dawn, the great cathedral of Hagia Sophia had been packed with worshipers praying behind barred doors for deliverance. Soldiers forced an entry, smashed the holy icons, and tore down all the gold and silver ornaments. A few members of the congregation were killed; the women, including nuns, were bound together by their veils or scarves and dragged away to be shared among the troops.

Sultan Mehmet II—henceforth to be known as Fatih (the Conqueror)—delayed his entry into the city until the afternoon. Then, in grand procession, he rode to the cathedral, which he commanded to be rededicated as a mosque. Despite the promise he had made to his troops of three days of plundering—the same length of time, as chance would have it, that had been granted to the Christian soldiers of the Fourth Crusade—the sultan found the city already so devastated that he ordered an immediate end to the looting.

Prominent among the spoils was the human booty: some 50,000 captives, including perhaps 500 soldiers. Among the Greek prisoners, the Turks soon identified ten of the emperor's ministers. The highest-ranking was Grand Duke Loukas Notaras, who had commanded the defenses along the Golden Horn. At first the young sultan treated him and his colleagues with courtesy. But five days after the conquest, while drunk at a banquet, he demanded that the grand duke's son, a handsome boy of fourteen, be sent to him for his pleasure. Notaras, who had already lost two sons in the battle, refused. The sultan retaliated by ordering the decapitation of Notaras and both his surviving children; the other ministers later shared his fate.

Mehmet, in general, felt it necessary to eliminate the male Byzantine aristocrats, although ladies of noble family were allowed to go free. A number of the emperor's male relatives nonetheless managed to survive, either by remaining unidentified in captivity or by escaping on the last ships out of the Golden Horn. Giustiniani, the military commander, escaped only to die of his wounds soon after reaching the Aegean island of Chios. Most remarkable, the papal legate, Cardinal Isidore, evaded capture by exchanging his red vestments for the rags of a beggar. The beggar was subsequently executed; the cardinal, though arrested, was sold for a pittance to a knowing Genoese merchant in Pera, who later helped him to escape back to Rome.

News of the fall of Constantinople soon reached the West, sending shock waves throughout Christendom. The effect was the greater because the outcome was unexpected; most foreign observers had been convinced that the legendary fortifications of the city would stand firm until the arrival of the Venetian relief force. In fact, that armada had gotten no farther than Chios, where it lay awaiting a favorable wind when news of the city's fall arrived.

The rulers of the Western nations duly expressed their horror at the catastrophe, and there was talk of organizing a crusade to win back what had been lost. Yet no country was immediately willing to take up arms. Indeed, the Venetians hastened to pay their respects to the city's new Turkish ruler, hoping thus to retain their commercial privileges. The Genoese also negotiated, in order to keep their trading colony at Pera, and were allowed to do so on condition that its inhabitants surrender their arms, demolish their fortifications, pay a poll tax, and be subject to Ottoman law.

Pera subsequently was as much under Turkish rule as was the city of Constantinople itself, just across the Golden Horn. There, the conquered Byzantines were organized into a *milet,* a self-governing community that was to operate within the Ottoman Empire under a religious leader held responsible for its civil obedience. To this end, Mehmet II shrewdly persuaded Gennadius, head of the party that opposed the Orthodox–Roman Catholic Union, to accept the patriarchate. After election by a newly formed general synod, the scholar-monk was formally enthroned in the cathedral of the Holy Apostles, the city's second-largest church. Apart from the loss of Hagia Sophia, the religious life of the Orthodox community quickly returned to normal. Indeed, the Greek Church was more influential than ever; it now had secular as well as ecclesiastical power.

At the same time, the authority of the young sultan remained absolute. Soldier, statesman, poet, voluptuary, and tyrant, Mehmet II proved to be a vigorous ruler of strangely mixed character. He was a man of great culture, who founded colleges and promoted the advance of mathematics, astronomy, and Muslim theology. He showed a degree of tolerance unusual for his time, welcoming Italian humanists and Greek scholars to his court and often engaging in friendly theological debates with Patriarch

Gennadius. But he was also an autocrat who enforced his laws and decrees with the utmost severity. Indeed, as the conqueror of Constantinople, he saw himself as the legitimate heir of the Caesars. He assumed the title of Kayser-i Rum (Roman Caesar), and he set himself the task of restoring the eastern Roman Empire to its former dimensions. By the time he died, in 1481, he had gone a long way toward success.

Within eight years of the fall of Constantinople, virtually all of the Greek world was under Mehmet's domination: The lands he annexed included the Peloponnese, the duchy of Athens, numerous Greek islands, and all the Christian settlements strung along the coasts of the Black Sea. He also conquered all of Serbia except Belgrade, and in later years overran the kingdom of Bosnia, besides campaigning in Hungary, Walachia, Moldavia, and the Crimea. In 1480, he even gained a temporary toehold in Italy by conquering Otranto in the southeast extremity of the Italian peninsula.

By then the new Caesar had returned Constantinople to much of its former glory. Its great walls had been repaired, its architectural grandeur restored, its population increased fourfold by the encouragement of immigration and by the forced resettlement of entire Muslim and Christian communities from Anatolia, the Balkans, and the Crimea. Once again the city was the spectacular capital of an empire, a prosperous metropolis in which the sultan's disparate subjects—Turks, Greeks, Armenians, Genoese, and Jews—could live, for the time being, in peace and relative harmony.

The elongated faces and stylized clothing of the figures in this fresco of the Last Supper, painted in Cyprus in the early sixteenth century, show that Byzantine styles in art outlived the empire that had given them birth. After the fall of Constantinople, many refugees fled to the Venetian-held islands of Cyprus, Crete, and Corfu, where Greeks had always formed the majority of the population. Others, particularly scholars and clergy, made their way to the West, where some were to play a significant role in the spreading of the Renaissance.

But this city of mosques and minarets was no longer identifiable with the Byzantium of old. Its new architecture and character reflected the imperial might of the Ottomans and the glory of Islam. The Greeks, cast in a subservient role, had become aliens in their own city, and the fall of the great capital had finally extinguished the unique civilization that had preserved the heritage of the classical world for more than a millennium.

BOHEMIA'S HOLY WARS

The dawn of July 14, 1420, found Holy Roman Emperor Sigismund I in a rare good humor. For almost a year, his realm of Bohemia had been in turmoil, with many areas, including even the capital, Prague, under the sway of heretical priests and rebellious commoners. But the situation, it seemed, was about to change. After finally prevailing on Pope Martin V to proclaim a crusade against the heretics, Sigismund now stood with an army of 80,000 before the walls of Prague, determined to win back the city's inhabitants to the true faith.

The emperor had good reason for feeling confident. His troops controlled all approaches to the city except the one to the east; once that route was severed, the upstart citizens of Prague could be starved into submission. The eastern road was protected by a rebel garrison positioned on the crest of the Vitkov, a small hill less than a mile beyond the city gates. But this seemed of little consequence to the emperor, who felt sure that his professional soldiers would easily seize the Vitkov from its tatterdemalion defenders. Such was the objective that he had set for July 14.

Already five weeks old, the siege had settled into a routine, and the day began with crusaders shouting to the defenders of the city across the Vltava River, "Ha, ha! Hus, Hus! Heretic, heretic!" taunting them with the name of their religious leader, who had been burned at the stake five years earlier with the emperor's knowledge. While the main body of the imperial army was thus engaged, a force of several thousand, having crossed the river at its easternmost point, climbed the Vitkov to seize the outpost at its summit.

The action that followed was described by the Hussite chronicler Lawrence of Brezova: "When they tried to scale the wall erected from earth and stone, two women and one girl, together with about twenty-six men who still held the bulwark, defended themselves manfully, hurling stones and lances, for they had neither arrows nor guns." Despite all their courage, these poorly armed defenders were no match for the imperial troops, and their defeat seemed imminent. As the crusaders were preparing to launch a final assault, however, the sound of singing rose up behind them. A relief column had made its way out of the city gates and was mounting the hill. At its head marched a priest holding aloft a chalice, the symbol of the Hussite movement; behind him were ranks of soldiers wielding flails and pikes and roaring out the Hussite battle hymn, "Ye Warriors of God." Their fighting proved no less fervent than their singing, and the crusaders were soon in headlong retreat. In the scramble to get away, many of them tumbled down the slopes and broke their necks. Others, unable to outrun their lightly armed opponents, were cut down as they fled.

Although the crusaders' losses were far from heavy—one report puts them at 500—the realization that some of his best troops had broken before a handful of impudent rustics was a severe blow to the emperor's pride. Having learned of the

Charging into battle under a banner depicting a chalice, the symbol of the popular religious movement inspired by the reformist Czech preacher Jan Hus, Hussite warriors seize a standard of Holy Roman Emperor Sigismund I. The dead infant *(foreground)* in this sixteenth-century Hussite manuscript illustration represents the atrocities that were attributed to the emperor's soldiers, shown here supported by black-robed clerics *(lower right-hand corner)*. The Hussite army was primarily made up of ill-equipped Bohemian peasants, not the fully armored cavalry portrayed here; their religious fervor—and the brilliant leadership of their blind general, Jan Žižka—enabled them to win many victories against vastly superior forces.

defeat, Lawrence writes, "he returned quietly to his encampment with his whole army, filled with fury, disgust, grief, and bitterness." The Hussites, on the other hand, were jubilant. Gathering in a field below the Vitkov, they "fell down on their knees and, to render thanks to God, sang with loud voices the Te Deum. For they were conscious that not by their prowess but by a miracle God had given the few of them victory over their enemies."

Central Europe was to witness many more such apparent miracles in the course of the next eleven years, for the Bohemian rebels were to beat back five crusades called against them by the pope and the emperor. Although their cause was ultimately doomed to fail, the Hussites introduced a new element into the history of medieval Europe—that of a small, beleaguered people unified by their religion in a revolt against the established powers of church and state. And in military terms, the peasant forces, under the leadership of a blind genius named Jan Žižka, were to pioneer an improvised method of fighting that was eventually to revolutionize the art of war.

Jan Hus, the initiator of the struggle, was born of poor peasants in southern Bohemia around 1370, while the kingdom, consisting approximately of the western half of present-day Czechoslovakia, was still basking in a golden age presided over by Sigismund's father, Emperor Charles IV. Assuming the Bohemian crown in 1346 and the imperial crown in 1355, Charles proved to be a ruler of outstanding ability. Shrewd, cultivated, and conscientious, he transformed his realm into one of the most peaceful and prosperous in Europe. He curbed the feuding of Bohemia's unruly nobles and cleared the roads of brigands, making it safe for merchants to go about their business; he reorganized the judicial system and saw to it that the law was strictly and impartially enforced. (At the execution of one convicted robber, a no-

Landlocked in the heart of Europe *(inset map),* the wealthy kingdom of Bohemia was ravaged in the fifteenth century by warfare between supporters of the Hussite movement and the forces of its powerful neighbors. Prague, capital of the Holy Roman Empire for much of the fourteenth century, was often threatened by armies dispatched against the Bohemians by the pope and the emperor. Tabor in the south was the center of the most radical of the Hussites, while Kutná Hora in the east was a stronghold of the emperor's cause.

bleman to whom he had once given a gold chain for bravery, the emperor arranged the hangman's noose himself, remarking that "it was not only golden chains that he had to give to his friends.")

Along with his secular reforms, Charles helped foster a religious awakening. Churches and monasteries were founded, and under Charles's patronage a major spiritual revival, linked to vernacular preaching and moral reform, swept the nation.

Energetic and creative, Charles was a patron of the arts and a great builder. He founded, for instance, the city of Carlsbad (modern Karlovy Vary), about sixty miles west of Prague, which was to become famous for its springs. However, the main object of the emperor's attention was Prague itself, the place of his birth and the city that he had chosen to be his imperial capital. He adorned it with much fine construction, including the Gothic Cathedral of Saint Vitus and the fortified Charles Bridge, which linked the two parts of Prague separated by the Vltava. He also gave it a university, the first such institution in central Europe. His foundation quickly acquired a reputation for scholarship that attracted not only Czechs but also scholars from Germany, Poland, France, Italy, and even England.

Charles died in 1378 and was succeeded by the eldest of his three sons, seventeen-year-old Wenceslaus. Though not without charm or intelligence, the young monarch was hardly in the mold of his illustrious father, preferring the pleasures of the chase, the cup, and the flesh to the less exciting day-to-day routine of government. He was soon embroiled in conflicts with the Bohemian nobles, who twice went so far as to imprison him. Eventually, he was stripped of the imperial crown, which passed to a German prince in 1400. Although Wenceslaus managed to retain the Bohemian throne, the continuing struggle for power with the nobles sapped his energy and undermined his authority.

While the king was thus preoccupied, a second and more dangerous conflict cast its shadow over the realm. Ever since the eleventh century, German immigrants had been moving eastward into Bohemia, drawn by its virgin lands and untapped mineral wealth. Bohemian rulers encouraged the newcomers, since their hard work, technical skills, and commercial expertise contributed greatly to the country's prosperity. But as German influence grew, so did the resentment of the native inhabitants.

Discontent was focused mainly in the towns, which the Germans came to dominate politically as well as commercially. In Prague, for example, the Old Town was run by a municipal council made up almost entirely of Germans, even though a majority of the city's inhabitants were Czech.

Another source of disaffection among the Czech community was the Bohemian church, whose opulent style and prodigious wealth—it owned at least half the land—increasingly aroused the hostility of nobles and peasants alike. A large part of its riches was derived from the extortionate taxes and tithes with which it burdened the faithful; there was no religious ministration, from baptism to burial, for which some sort of a fee was not charged.

The Church's coffers were further swollen by the sale of indulgences—remissions of punishment for sin—and by the practice of simony, the buying and selling of ecclesiastical offices. The prevailing preoccupation with the worldly and the venal was reflected in the personal behavior of the clergy, many of whom were more devoted to hunting, drinking, and gambling than to the saving of souls. It was not uncommon for priests to become the proprietors of inns and brothels and to parade through their parishes arm in arm with their concubines.

Such abuses drew forth indignant calls for reform from a succession of evangelical preachers in Prague. Their appeals went unheeded, however; the Catholic Church was at the time distracted by internecine power struggles that culminated, in 1378, in the Great Schism. There were then two popes—one in Rome and one in Avignon—each claiming universal authority and denouncing the supporters of the other as servants of the Antichrist. (Eventually there were three papal claimants. The rulers and prelates of Bohemia were loyal to the pontiff in Rome.)

The Bohemian reformers were not alone in speaking out against the moral decline, of which this latest catastrophe was a symptom. Similar sentiments were echoed throughout Europe—especially in England, where the Oxford theologian John Wycliffe denounced the Church's shortcomings. But in Bohemia, the religious controversy was complicated by the conflict between Czechs and Germans, with most of the former supporting reform and a majority of the latter, who provided the Church with many of its prelates, opposing it.

Nowhere was this chronic antagonism more acute than at Charles University in Prague. Under the constitution of its founder, the professors were divided into four "nations"—Czech, Saxon, Bavarian, and Polish, the last being dominated by Germans from Silesia. Each of these was entitled to one vote in the election of officials and the formulation of policy. Since the Polish "nation" was effectively German in composition, ethnic Germans had an automatic three-quarter preponderance in voting, and the Czechs were condemned to be a permanent minority in what they had come to regard as their own university—a state of affairs that did little to ease their resentment or their radicalism.

It was into this ideological whirlpool that the young Jan Hus was plunged when he arrived in the capital as a student in 1390. He graduated in 1393, and three years later, having received his master's degree, he was appointed a philosophy lecturer at the university. His interests began to turn increasingly to religious affairs, partly under the inspiration of Wycliffe, whose writings were a powerful influence on the Czech reform movement. An outspoken critic of ecclesiastical shortcomings, Wycliffe had challenged the right of an unworthy priest or bishop to administer the sacraments. He also encouraged individuals to seek guidance directly from the words of the Bible and to act on what they found there even if it conflicted with pronouncements of the Roman Catholic Church.

Certainly, Hus did not accept all of Wycliffe's teachings—a point he was to argue one day in defense of his life—but in 1398, having lectured for two years on Greek philosophy, he decided to expound the ideas of the English doctor instead. He copied for his own use four of the doctor's treatises, writing in the margin of one, "Wycliffe, Wycliffe, you will unsettle many a man's mind."

He was ordained in 1401, and in 1402, he was appointed rector of Prague's Bethlehem Chapel, founded a few years earlier to provide a pulpit for preaching exclusively in the vernacular and housed in an austere, cavernous building with room for 3,000 people. While he was at the Bethlehem Chapel, Hus began a reform of the national written language, introducing a simplified spelling system that enabled syllables to be expressed by one letter instead of a combination of letters. The system gradually came into common use and remains the basis of written Czech today.

But it was Hus's passionate preaching that made the greater impact on his fellow citizens at the time. He quickly became the spokesman for a new generation of educationally emancipated Czech-speaking youth. His admirers were drawn from all sections of Czech society, including the royal court: Queen Sophia herself regularly attended the Bethlehem Chapel. Indeed, so impressed was she by Hus's fiery eloquence that she made him her confessor.

Besides carrying out his duties at the Bethlehem Chapel, Hus continued to teach at the university. Here, in 1403, political and religious tensions heightened when the German-controlled administration banned the teaching of forty-five propositions extracted from Wycliffe's works. The Czech professors, including Hus, at first simply ignored the ban, and the authorities turned a blind eye to their noncompliance. Not until 1409 did a crisis come, precipitated by King Wenceslaus, who had decided to give his backing to a new, audacious scheme for ending the Great Schism.

Proposed by a powerful group of cardinals from both Rome and Avignon, the plan was for a general council of Christians to depose the two existing popes and elect a new one. For Wenceslaus, the restoration of Christian unity was of only secondary importance; his main intention was to secure the installation of a pontiff who would help him regain the title of Holy Roman Emperor. However, when the plan was put before Prague's Charles University, as the highest authority in ecclesiastical law, only the Czech "nation" voted in favor. The three foreign "nations," unwilling to renounce their allegiance to the Roman pope, voted against the plan.

So incensed was the king at this rebuff that he promptly reversed the voting procedure, giving the Czech "nation" three votes and the other three one vote among them. The Czechs were, naturally, delighted, since they had been long campaigning for just such a change. The Germans, on the other hand, were bitterly angry; in June 1409, led by the head of the university, Henning von Baltenhagen, they made a mass exodus to Saxony, where they founded the University of Leipzig.

From now on, Charles University was to be a purely national institution, dedicated to the twin ideals of political independence and religious reform. Although Hus had played no direct part in the voting drama, he was chosen to succeed Baltenhagen as university head. This dangerous honor placed him at the forefront of the reform movement and guaranteed him the implacable hostility of the departed Germans, who spread stories of a heretical Bohemia turning its back on ecclesiastical orthodoxy.

Partly as a result of this hostile publicity, the papacy demonstrated a growing concern with the activities of the Bohemian reformers. In a bull issued in December 1409, Alexander V instructed Archbishop Zbyněk of Prague to prevent preaching in private places—a move that was obviously intended to disrupt Hus's well-known ministry at the Bethlehem Chapel. The pope also encouraged Archbishop Zbyněk to denounce the writings of Wycliffe, which the archbishop in due course had burned publicly. When Hus protested the destruction of the books and defiantly continued to preach, the archbishop excommunicated him. Hus was then summoned to the papal court. Upon Hus's refusal, because he feared an attempt might be made on his life, Cardinal Odo

This silver bust of Wenceslaus I, who ruled Bohemia in the tenth century and was venerated as the country's patron saint after his death, was commissioned by Vladislav Jagiello, who assumed the Bohemian throne in 1471. Coming to power in the turbulent aftermath of the Hussite wars, Vladislav—a Polish Catholic—sought to restore public faith in the monarchy by identifying himself with the spirit of Bohemian nationalism.

Colonna, the papal official in charge of the case, confirmed his excommunication.

Undaunted, Hus continued with his evangelical activities. At this stage, he not only enjoyed massive popular support but also benefited from the protection of King Wenceslaus, who wrote personally to the papal authorities, suggesting that "if any-one wishes to accuse Hus of anything, let him do so in our kingdom before our university of Prague or other competent judge. For our kingdom does not see fit to expose so useful a preacher to the discrimination of his enemies and to the distur-bance of the whole population."

It was not long, however, before Hus became embroiled in a new and much more dangerous conflict that was to lose him Wenceslaus's backing. It was sparked by the dispatch of a large number of indulgence sellers to Bohemia by the pope in Rome, who needed money to fund his struggle against rival claimants to the papal throne. Hus bitterly condemned the trade on the grounds that it amounted to "trafficking in sacred things."

Hus's protests were echoed by the people of Prague, who mounted rowdy, sometimes violent, demonstrations against the indulgence vendors. During one such clash, three young men were seized by the city authorities and summarily executed. Rioting broke out all over the city, and the three corpses were carried in procession to the Bethlehem Chapel, where Hus conducted a Martyrs' Mass before a huge congregation.

These events did not go unnoticed by the Roman papacy, which in July 1412 renewed the excommunication decree against Hus and again summoned him to appear before the papal court. If he continued to ignore the summons, Prague or any other city where he dwelt was to be placed under interdict, which meant the suspension of all religious ceremonies and church services.

Now, Hus could no longer count on Wenceslaus's support, because a large share of the proceeds from the sale of indulgences went into royal coffers. The fact was that Hus had become an embarrassment to the king, who, in October 1412, ordered the vexatious priest to leave Prague for the relative obscurity of the coun-tryside. Hus found refuge in southern Bohemia, where, in the next two years, he produced some of his most important works. Besides writing, he continued to preach, although his congregations now consisted largely of peasants, and his sermons were often delivered under the open skies. Nonetheless, the appeal of his oratory was as great as in the Bethlehem Chapel, and the rural areas would subsequently become the chief recruiting grounds for the Hussite armies.

The final confrontation between Hus and the papacy began in 1414, when he accepted an invitation to attend the church council that had been convened at the lakeside town of Constance, in southern Germany. The council's primary task was to devise a formula to end the Great Schism. But Wenceslaus's younger brother, the newly elected Holy Roman Emperor, Sigismund—the title had again eluded Wence-slaus—was anxious for the council to also settle the long-drawn-out dispute with Hus and the national reform movement he led.

Hus's first response was to reject the invitation. But after receiving the emperor's promise of safe-conduct, a fair hearing, and a free and unhindered return to Bohemia irrespective of the council's decisions, he decided to make the journey. His trust soon turned out to be misplaced. Less than a month after his arrival, he was arrested by papal officials and—despite the promised safe-conduct—imprisoned in the dungeon

Depicted in a late-fifteenth-century tract, Satan dressed as a prelate personifies the Hussite conviction that the corrupt hierarchy of the Roman Catholic Church rep-resented the forces of the Antichrist. Such images were frequently painted on placards and carried through the streets to spread the message. The belief of Jan Hus and other theologians that the wealth of the Church and many of its practices—especially simony, the buying and selling of ecclesiastical office—were contrary to the teachings of Jesus found favor with both common-ers and nobles in Bohemia, to whom corruption among the clergy had long been evident.

of the local Dominican priory. For the next seven months, he was held prisoner in a succession of jails, kept in fetters by day and chained to a wall at night.

Throughout this time, a panel of judges appointed by the council interrogated him on a range of charges, most arising out of his alleged adherence to Wycliffe's forty-five heretical articles. Hus was accused, for example, of challenging the power of a priest in mortal sin to administer the sacraments and of denying the doctrine of transubstantiation, which declares that the bread and wine used in Holy Communion are converted by the words of consecration into the Body and Blood of Christ. Hus, for his part, strenuously denied the charges, insisting that all his beliefs were in accordance with both Church practice and scriptural authority.

But the judges had already made up their minds, and Hus was given no opportunity to explain what his beliefs really were. Instead, the panel chose to accept the lies and distortions of his detractors, and it was made clear that he could hope to save himself only by recanting the views ascribed to him. He replied that he was unable to renounce beliefs he had never held, "fearing to offend God and fall into perjury."

The climax of his ordeal came on July 6, 1415. Condemned, cursed, and defrocked, he was led through the streets of Constance wearing a tall paper crown upon which were painted three devils fighting for possession of a soul. When the procession reached a meadow outside the city, he was stripped and chained to a wooden stake. Bundles of wood and straw were piled up to his chin. Before the order to apply the torch was given, he was offered a final chance to recant, which he refused.

As the pyre was lit, Hus began singing prayers to Christ. One of those who witnessed his agony wrote that "when he began to sing the third time, the wind blew the flame into his face. And thus praying within himself and moving his lips and the head, he expired in the Lord." His clothing was burned and his ashes thrown into the Rhine River, so that no relics might remain. Ten months later, Jerome of Prague, a disciple of Hus's who had gone to Constance to testify on his master's behalf, was similarly condemned and executed. (Wycliffe himself had been dead for more than thirty years, so the council had to content itself with giving orders that his remains be disinterred and removed from consecrated ground; they were then burned and flung into an English river.)

The council's main task was not completed until November 1417, when, having persuaded one papal incumbent to resign and deposed the other two, it chose a new pontiff, Martin V. One of the deposed aspirants, Benedict XIII of Avignon, clung to his claim, but for all practical purposes, the Great Schism was over. Yet even as one breach was being healed, another was opening up—this time, between the papacy and the outraged supporters of Jan Hus.

When the news of the reformer's death reached Bohemia, it ignited fury throughout the country. In September 1415, an assembly of Czech and Moravian nobles, meeting in Prague, addressed an outspoken and indignant rebuke to the council, protesting Hus's innocence, pledging their support for his cause, and declaring that anyone who claimed that there was heresy in Bohemia "speaketh lies as a treacherous enemy of our kingdom and our nation."

Popular anger showed itself in a number of attacks against monasteries, and in several towns, the administrations were taken over by armed insurgents. But opposition to ecclesiastical authority was most clearly reflected in the growing number of ordinary worshipers who received Communion "in both kinds"—receiving, in addition to the bread offered to all communicants, wine from the chalice, a privilege that the Roman Catholic Church previously accorded only to priests. From this time on, the taking of the wine, which the reformers called indispensable to salvation, was the theological bedrock of the Hussite cause, and the chalice was its symbol.

Open conflict did not come until 1419, when Wenceslaus, fearing the possibility of an invasion by his Roman Catholic neighbors for reasons of religion, made a belated attempt to stem the reformist tide. He restricted Hussite services to only three churches in Prague, and he dismissed the Hussite members of Prague's New Town council, selecting reliable Roman Catholics to take their place. On July 30, the storm broke: A mob led by the inflammatory Hussite orator Jan Zelivsky smashed its way into the New Town Hall, seized a number of Catholic councilors and magistrates—whom they denounced as "enemies of God"—and flung them from the upper window onto the pikes of those below.

The incident was to become known as the First Defenestration of Prague. It so infuriated the king that he suffered a series of strokes, the last of which, on August 16, proved fatal. The reformers now faced their greatest challenge, for Wenceslaus's heir was none other than Emperor Sigismund, whom they saw as the betrayer of Jan Hus and who had pledged himself to sweep Bohemia free of heresy.

Despite the contempt in which he was held by most Czechs, Sigismund was not without support. His main allies were the German settlers, but even among the Czech nobility, especially in Moravia, there were those who accepted him as their rightful sovereign, no matter how he had behaved toward Jan Hus. At the same time, there was serious disunity within the ranks of Sigismund's Hussite opponents. On one side stood the moderates, or Utraquists (from the Latin for "in both kinds"). Composed largely of the nobility, the Prague burghers, and the professors of the university, this group differed from orthodox Roman Catholics principally in its demand for lay access to the chalice; its ardent hope was for a reconciliation with both Sigismund and the Church of Rome. On the other side stood the radicals, drawing their strength from elements of the priesthood, disaffected country squires, peasants, and workers in the cities. Tapping a vein of social discontent that had troubled much of Europe since at least the middle of the previous century, they were determined to achieve both a complete break with Rome and the overthrow of the feudal order.

The revolutionary upsurge was strongest in the countryside and was reflected in the rapid growth of a radical group that, having seized the fortress of Hradiste in southern Bohemia, built its headquarters on a nearby hill, to which the biblical name of Tabor was given. Unlike the Utraquists, the Taborites believed that the word of God should be applied in every sphere; their aim was the creation of a new Zion in which there would be neither barons nor prelates, and Christ alone would be king.

An estimated 40,000 people attended the first Taborite gathering, in July 1419. The meeting began at daybreak, and from then until noon, teams of Taborite priests were busy preaching, hearing confessions, and giving Communion in both kinds. Lawrence of Brezova noted how at noon, when there was a break for refreshment, the congregants were "convivial together in brotherly love, not to the extent of indulging desire or drunkenness, not levity nor dissoluteness, but to the greater and stronger service of God. There all called each other brother and sister, and the rich divided the food that they had prepared for themselves with the poor."

The community that was subsequently established at Tabor was run on strictly egalitarian lines. Its leaders were elected by popular vote and all goods were held in common. As the Taborite code described it, there was "nothing mine and nothing

This illustration from the margin of a Czech manuscript Bible commissioned by a Hussite supporter, Peter of Mladonovice, shows the preacher Jan Hus being burned at the stake. The figure in black probably represents Peter himself, who witnessed Hus's trial for heresy at the Council of Constance in 1415 as well as his death. According to the account written by Peter, Hus continued to pray and to swear his innocence as he died amid the flames of two cartloads of wood. His charred body was then taken down and consumed on a second pyre.

A late-fifteenth-century manuscript illustration shows a blindfolded Jan Žižka, who lost his sight in battle, leading a peasant army bearing farm implements as weapons. The banner held aloft behind him is decorated with the Hussite chalice.

The Taborites forged lethal flails from farm tools normally used to thresh grain. Maces were also often improvised from wooden cudgels or clubs, although the metal-tipped example shown here *(far left)* would have required more sophisticated manufacture.

Facing armies well provided with heavily armed knights and backed by the emperor and the pope, a makeshift force of Bohemian peasants held out for nearly two decades. Much of the credit for this achievement belonged to Jan Žižka, a professional soldier and landowner who led a radical Hussite faction, the Taborites. From previous experience, Žižka well understood the agonies his horseless and impoverished farmers could expect from a cavalry charge. He was therefore especially careful to develop their defensive capability.

Utilizing any available equipment, Žižka had his men convert their farm implements into tools of carnage, such as the flail shown on this page. He showed similar ingenuity in making the best possible use of artillery, bought with money provided by his supporters or made by Hussite artisans. To increase their mobility, many of these pieces were mounted on wagons.

Žižka's most effective innovation, however, was not a weapon but a tactic: use of the wagon-fortress, a rectangular or circular grouping of converted farm carts that could hold a well-chosen position, preferably on high ground, against a cavalry attack. Gaps between the wagons were bridged with shields known as pavises.

From within the stockade, Taborite soldiers directed a barrage of fire at the advancing enemy. Any cavalry who managed to advance as far as the wagons were toppled from their horses by Taborites wielding flails or long poles fitted with hooks. After the enemy had spent its energy in futile charges, mounted soldiers emerged from within or behind the defenses to pursue the retreating forces.

The combined effect of Žižka's tactics was terrifying. The flashes of gunfire and the thick smoke erupting from the Hussite artillery were often by themselves sufficient to disorient attackers.

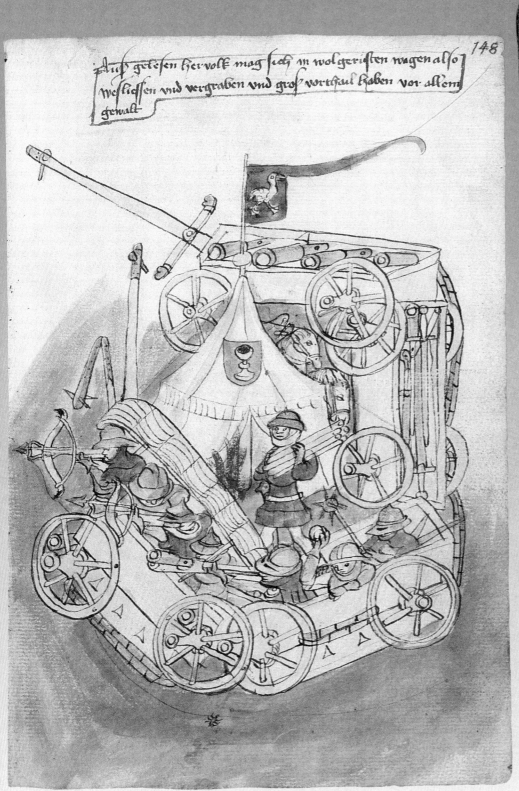

Aus gelesen hervolck mag sich in wolgerusten wagen also
wesliessen und vergraben und groß vortheil haben vor allem
gewalt

Propped up from behind with staves, pavises—wooden shields covered with canvas or leather—such as the one above spanned gaps in a wagon-fortress's tight formation. This pavis bears the town symbol of Prague.

This simplified image of a wagon-fortress shows a chilling array of fifteenth-century weapons: artillery, swords, stones, spiked maces and flails, and crossbows. The soldiers wear "kettle-hat" helmets, some of which have eye-slits. The bird on the banner is a punning reference to the name of Hus, which means "goose" in Czech. An actual fortress might comprise several hundred war wagons, which had canvas hoods and hinged boards that could be lowered to provide protection down to ground level.

yours, but everything in the community is possessed equally, so everything should always be in common for all.''

As the Taborites became stronger, the apprehensions of the Utraquists increased. It was not in the countryside, however, but in the city of Prague that the tensions between the rival Hussite factions first exploded into open conflict. The flash point came in November 1419, when a leading Hussite nobleman, Cenek of Wartemberk, in alliance with the Catholic supporters of Sigismund, decided to suppress the city's radical contingent. After several days of bitter fighting, the radicals were defeated, and some of their leaders left Prague to pursue the struggle in the provinces.

Most prominent among these was Jan Žižka. Born around 1360 in southern Bohemia, Žižka was a minor landowner and professional soldier who had lost one eye in an early skirmish. In 1411, he had entered service as an officer in the royal bodyguard, and it may have been as an escort of Queen Sophia that he first visited the Bethlehem Chapel and heard the preaching of Jan Hus. In any event, he became a fervent reformer, joining the popular protest that swept Prague in the summer of 1419 and leading the New Town militia in the unsuccessful November confrontation with Wartemberk and the Catholic royalists.

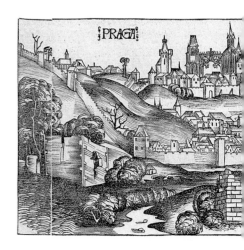

He was to find his spiritual home among the puritan radicals of Tabor. After arriving there in March 1420, Žižka was elected one of the community's four captains, or military commanders, and quickly assumed responsibility for the training and leadership of the Taborite army. His guiding principle was improvisation. Most of his troops were peasants, who possessed few conventional arms. Žižka pragmatically sought to convert what they did have at hand—scythes, clubs, and grain flails—into weapons of war. The most formidable of the resulting makeshift devices was the flail, especially when studded with an iron spike; wielded in close combat, it rarely failed to break through the enemy's ranks.

The greatest problem confronting Žižka was matching his army, mainly made up of foot soldiers, against the mounted and mail-clad knights of the royalist forces. According to the conventional wisdom of the time, even a large infantry formation could not normally expect to withstand, let alone defeat, a concentration of armored cavalry. Žižka's solution was the war wagon—a reinforced farm cart, armed with cannon and defended by crossbowmen. Separately, the carts had the advantage of mobility; bound together into circles, they provided the Taborites with strong defensive positions that were almost impossible for horsemen to penetrate. Žižka's deployment of these movable fortresses in the next few years was to do much to end the ascendancy of the mounted knight.

The launching of the Taborite army coincided with Sigismund's long-delayed invasion of Bohemia. Following the November fighting with the radicals, the conservative Hussites, centered in Prague, had striven for an agreement under which they would have enjoyed Communion in both kinds as well as the benevolent toleration of the emperor. But the emperor was not in a benign mood, and on April 23, 1420, after Pope Martin V had proclaimed a crusade against the Czech heretics at his behest, he crossed the border from Silesia with an army made up largely of Germans and Hungarians. It was clear that his main objective would be Prague, and the two Hussite factions within the city, radical and conservative, issued an urgent and united appeal for assistance from other parts of the kingdom.

Their plea was answered by a number of Hussite centers in the provinces, but the strongest and most effective help came from Tabor—some 9,000 men led by Jan Žižka. The Taborite soldiers, many of them accompanied by their wives and children, received a tumultuous welcome from the overjoyed people of Prague. To the militants from the south, however, Prague appeared to be much like a latter-day Sodom, sinking in sinful pride and luxury. The strait-laced newcomers were particularly outraged by the long mustachios of the well-to-do townsmen, and their attempts to cut off the offending objects naturally caused much angry resentment. Complaints were made to the Taborite commanders, who threatened severe punishment for anyone continuing to interfere with Prague citizens.

It was not long before the Taborites were able to vent their wrath on the real enemy. Sigismund reached the city around the middle of June. Although his huge army by now included contingents from virtually every part of Christian Europe, it was quickly demoralized by the defeat at Vitkov Hill—where the Taborite counterattack was led by Žižka himself—and by the end of July, the first great anti-Hussite crusade had collapsed. The Vitkov was to be known from that time on as Žižka's Hill.

In the aftermath of their victory, the conservative and radical Hussites produced a joint manifesto enshrining the minimum beliefs on which they agreed. Known as the Four Articles of Prague, the declaration demanded freedom of speech in the pulpit; Communion in two kinds for all Christians, laity as well as priests; the abolition of excessive clerical wealth; and the punishment of those who committed mortal sins, even if they were priests. Deep differences still existed between the two wings of the movement, however, and in September 1420, the Taborites elected their own bishop—an act of theological defiance that widened the gulf not only between Tabor and Rome but also between Tabor and Prague.

During the next few months, Sigismund made two additional attempts to win his kingdom by force, both of which were decisively defeated. A convocation of the Bohemian estates subsequently declared him deposed, calling him "the deadly enemy of the honor and the people of the Czech nation." A regency council, which included Žižka, was appointed to rule in his place.

The hatred of the rebellious Czechs for the emperor was fanned to white heat by the depredations of his crusader allies. The Czechs themselves, including even the more fanatical Taborites, were, with very rare exceptions, careful to spare the lives of women and children throughout the Hussite wars. The crusaders, on the other hand, were usually indiscriminate in their slaughter. Prisoners who were not immediately burned to death or dismembered were marched off to the predominantly German silver-mining city of Kutná Hora, about sixty miles east of Prague, to be thrown alive into the abandoned mine shafts.

Despite Sigismund's withdrawal to Hungary, the Czechs had no doubt that they would soon be facing a second crusade. This came in the autumn of 1421 and was spearheaded by a German army under Frederick of Wettin, the margrave of Meissen. On August 5, Frederick's forces clashed with an army of Praguers at Most, in the

Dominating the skyline of this 1493 view of Prague are the city's castle and Saint Vitus Cathedral, on Hradcany Hill. The cathedral was built by Charles IV, who became Holy Roman emperor in 1355 and made Prague, his native city, the imperial capital. There Charles founded the first university in central Europe and constructed the Charles Bridge across the Vltava River. During the early fifteenth century, the city was a stronghold of followers of Jan Hus, who was appointed preacher at Prague's Bethlehem Chapel in 1402. In the wars, Hussites from the provinces flocked to Prague to defend the city against the armies of Sigismund.

northwest of Bohemia, and won a resounding victory—the first for Sigismund's supporters since the start of hostilities. However, when the news arrived that reinforcements were on the way from Prague with Jan Žižka at their head, Frederick and his men promptly returned to Meissen. In October, a second and much more formidable German army—estimates of its size range from 125,000 to 230,000—which had invaded Bohemia from Bavaria and was now laying siege to the Hussite town of Žatec, also took flight at the news of Žižka's approach. The garrison of Žatec gave chase and inflicted heavy losses on the frantically retreating crusaders.

The invaders might have shown more nerve had they realized that the leader they feared above all others was now totally blind. While directing an assault on the royalist stronghold of Rabi, near Pilsen, in June, Žižka had been struck in his one good eye by an arrow. The injury had caused an infection that brought him close to death, as well as leaving him without sight. He showed remarkable powers of recovery, and within a few weeks, he was once more in full command, although his horse now had to be led by the bridle.

In October 1421, Sigismund again crossed the border from Hungary into Moravia. His plan had been to attack the Hussites from the east while they were still tied down by the Germans in the west. But as a result of the rout of the Germans at Žatec, Sigismund was left in the position of having to carry on the crusade with his own, mainly Hungarian army, comprising some 60,000.

While the emperor was moving slowly across Moravia, Žižka decided to deal with an enemy closer to home. The atmosphere of pious fervor generated at Tabor had given rise to a number of outlandish groups, but none more fanatical, or more offensive to Žižka and his puritan colleagues, than the sect known as the Adamites. Denying the existence of the devil and of original sin, they asserted that all human impulses, including sexual desire, were manifestations of the divine will and should therefore be given free rein.

Žižka had condemned seventy-five members of the sect to be burned as heretics in April 1421, but the survivors, numbering around 300, then escaped southward to establish what they called a new Garden of Eden on an island in the Nezarka River. According to Lawrence of Brezova, "some of them fell into such insanity that men and women threw off their clothes and went nude, saying that clothes had been adopted because of the sin of the first parents, but that they were in a state of innocence. From the same madness they supposed that they were not sinning if one of the brethren had intercourse with one of the sisters, and if the woman conceived, she said she had conceived of the Holy Spirit."

To those outside their sect, the Adamites were less tender, and their nighttime raids on neighboring villages caused much terror and destruction. In response to the appeals of these villagers, Žižka, on October 21, 1421, ordered 400 of his troops to attack the sect's island stronghold. Believing themselves to be immortal, the Adamites, both men and women, fought back with reckless bravery, and not until Žižka had sent in reinforcements was the colony destroyed. Only forty Adamites were taken prisoner; all of them were burned to death except one man, who was spared for the purpose of questioning by Žižka.

In December, the blind general turned his attention back to Sigismund and the crusaders. The emperor's forces, having finally crossed the Bohemian border, were now heading toward Kutná Hora. It was in this direction, therefore, that Žižka and his combined army of Taborites and Praguers also went. The city had been threatened by a Hussite army in the previous year and had saved itself then by declaring its support for the Hussite cause. It did the same again now, sending out a delegation to welcome Žižka. In fact, the people of Kutná Hora had already been in touch with Sigismund, and the goodwill they showed to Žižka was feigned.

The trap was sprung on December 21, when Sigismund's army reached Kutná Hora and joined battle with Žižka's forces outside the city gates. On a prearranged signal from the crusaders, the civilians started massacring the Hussites in the city, and the Czech army found itself suddenly fighting on two fronts. To Žižka, with only 10,000 men and already outnumbered by four or five to one, the situation must have seemed desperate. By using the guns on his war wagons for attack rather than defense, he managed to blast a way through the enemy lines, regrouping his forces at the village of Kolín, about ten miles to the northwest.

From here, on January 6, Žižka, joined by fresh troops, launched his own offensive. The crusaders, dispersed among villages in the area—Kutná Hora was large enough to accommodate only the royal entourage and one army contingent—and not expecting further campaigning until spring, were soon in headlong retreat. Sigismund, fearing that he might be surrounded, joined the flight, which continued, despite unsuccessful rearguard actions, to the Hungarian border.

A third crusade followed in September, but this one was a relatively small-scale affair, involving only minor skirmishing, and before the end of 1422, the invaders had withdrawn. Five more years would pass before the soldiers of a crusading army would again set foot in Bohemia.

Once the external threat had receded, the Hussites began another period of factional strife that in August 1423 exploded into open war. The most serious clash occurred in June 1424, when the conservative Utraquists united with the Catholic royalists to deal what they hoped would be a deathblow to Jan Žižka. By now, Žižka was no longer associated with the Taborites. Exasperated by the interference of Taborite clergy in military matters, the old general had accepted in 1422 the leadership of a somewhat less radical group, the Orebites. In the eyes of the Utraquists and their allies, however, he remained as dangerous as ever.

The decisive battle came on June 7, near Malešov on the Malesovka River. Though commanding a new army, Žižka had forgotten none of his old tricks. His opponents, vastly superior in number, were crossing the river into a narrow valley when the general attacked them from his wagon-fortresses, drawn up on one of the nearby slopes. This time, Žižka used not only guns and crossbows to break up the enemy advance but also supply wagons loaded with rocks, which he sent lumbering down the hill. Once these had disrupted the enemy formations, he ordered his troops to charge. Unable to employ their battle order, the Utraquist forces took to their heels.

But Malešov was to be the old general's last victory. On October 11, 1424, while besieging the castle of Pribyslav on the Moravian border, he died of the plague. To signify their loss, the Orebites changed their name to the Orphans. The true successor to Žižka came from among the Taborites—and, ironically, he was a priest, John Prokop, known as Prokop the Bald.

Born around 1380 into a wealthy Prague family, Prokop had joined the Taborite movement at an early stage, mastering the military arts under Žižka's harsh guidance. Prokop displayed his own brilliance as a commander in June 1426, when he led the united Hussite armies on an expedition to relieve Ústí, in northern Bohemia. The city

FANCIFUL VISIONS OF THE FUTURE OF WAR

The innovative tactics of Jan Žižka and other Hussite commanders stimulated a renewed interest in the theory and practice of warfare. The colored pen-and-ink drawings on these pages are from an encyclopedic survey of contemporary military technology compiled by Johann Hartlieb, who was a scholar and the personal physician and counselor to two Bavarian rulers.

Hartlieb's *Kriegsbuch (Book of War)* included accurate depictions of armor, artillery, and fortifications, as well as of episodes from the Hussite wars. But many illustrations take flight into the realm of fantasy, showing inventions conspicuous more for ingenuity than practicality.

Held aloft by a mounted knight, this fire-breathing demon was designed to terrify enemy soldiers; the whole apparatus was intended to be filled with combustible materials and then set on fire.

This elaborate prototype tank consists of a wheeled wooden frame with cutouts for guns and for the horses that propelled it. A canvas awning protects the lead horses; the palisaded platform shelters soldiers. Although siege towers and other mobile structures were used in fifteenth-century warfare, this model was probably never constructed.

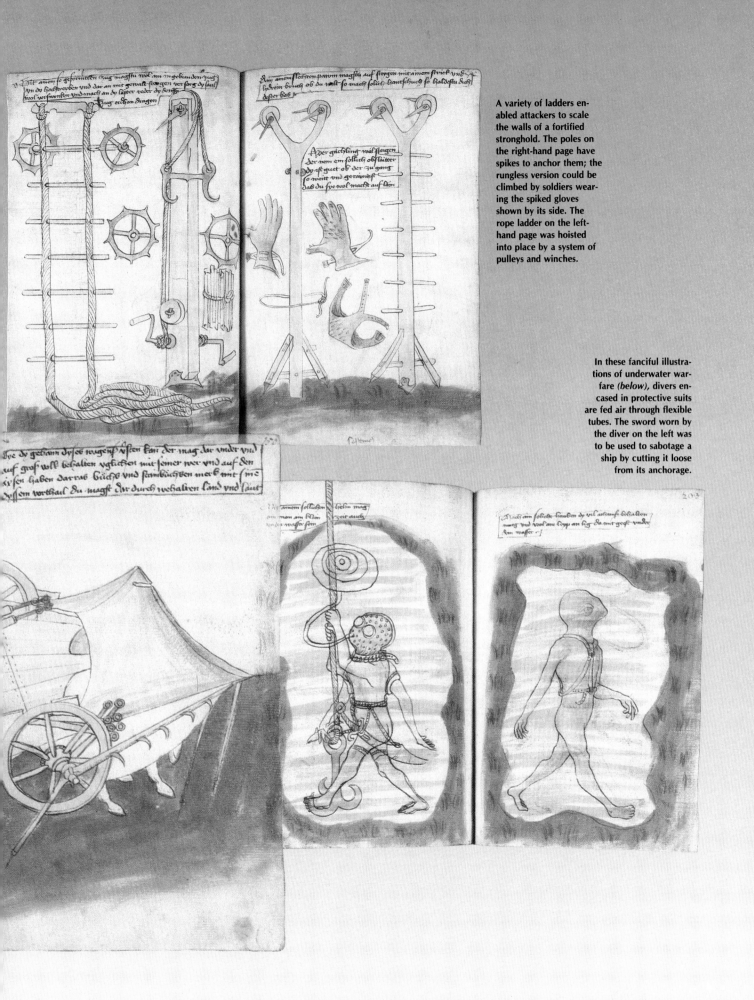

A variety of ladders enabled attackers to scale the walls of a fortified stronghold. The poles on the right-hand page have spikes to anchor them; the rungless version could be climbed by soldiers wearing the spiked gloves shown by its side. The rope ladder on the left-hand page was hoisted into place by a system of pulleys and winches.

In these fanciful illustrations of underwater warfare (below), divers encased in protective suits are fed air through flexible tubes. The sword worn by the diver on the left was to be used to sabotage a ship by cutting it loose from its anchorage.

had been awarded by Sigismund to the elector of Saxony in return for financial favors, and the elector dispatched an army of 70,000 to aid its garrison against the Czechs, who had only 24,000 troops. In spite of their overwhelming numerical superiority, the elector's forces suffered a catastrophic defeat, with 15,000 dead, according to the German chroniclers of the event.

The enormous crusader army that invaded western Bohemia in the summer of 1427 fared little better. Operating under the command of Cardinal Henry Beaufort, a half brother of King Henry IV of England, it began laying siege to the town of Stříbro. However, the crusaders turned tail at the mere sight of a Hussite relief army led by

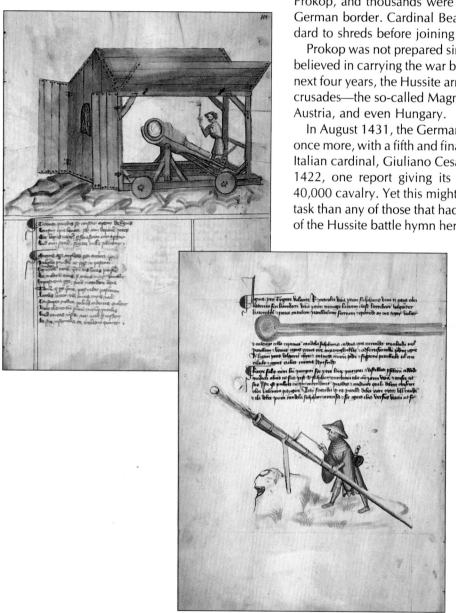

Prokop, and thousands were cut down in the headlong flight toward the German border. Cardinal Beaufort, in his anguish, tore the imperial standard to shreds before joining the crusaders' inglorious retreat.

Prokop was not prepared simply to wait for another invasion. Instead, he believed in carrying the war back into the enemy's territory, and during the next four years, the Hussite armies under his leadership mounted their own crusades—the so-called Magnificent Rides—thrusting deep into Germany, Austria, and even Hungary.

In August 1431, the German princes and the pope went on the offensive once more, with a fifth and final crusade against the Czechs. Led by a young Italian cardinal, Giuliano Cesarini, it was the largest to be mobilized since 1422, one report giving its strength as 130,000—90,000 infantry and 40,000 cavalry. Yet this mighty host proved to be no more adequate to the task than any of those that had preceded it. On August 14, when the sound of the Hussite battle hymn heralded the approach of Prokop's army toward Domažlice, near the Bavarian border, the crusaders immediately began fleeing in panic. Cardinal Cesarini, gold crucifix in hand, tried to halt the stampede; finally, he, too, was forced to flee for his life, disguising himself as a common soldier and riding bareback. His gold crucifix and cardinal's hat were among the booty taken by Prokop's triumphant troops.

The fiasco of the fifth crusade at last convinced even the Hussites' most determined enemies that only a diplomatic initiative could succeed in bringing Bohemia back into the Catholic fold. Moves for a peace settlement had been made as far back as 1429, but it was not until after Domažlice that both sides showed a willingness to begin serious negotiations. The Hussites, in spite of their spectacular military victories, had compelling reasons of their own for wishing to end the conflict. More than ten years of fighting had had a disastrous effect on the Bohemian economy, reducing trade and production, forcing up prices, and making life progressively harder for everyone, especially the poor.

Thus, in May 1432, at the western Bohemian town of Cheb, the Hussite leaders met with representatives of the church council that had been convened in Basel, Switzerland, the previous year. Eight months later, the Czechs traveled to Basel, where they were warmly greeted by their old enemy Cardinal Cesarini, the council's president. (As a concession to Hussite sensibilities, the city's brothels were closed down for the duration of the talks.)

Negotiations, always strained, often acrimonious, centered on the Czechs' demand for an unconditional acceptance of the Four Articles. After three months had passed with no agreement in sight, Prokop and his companions went home. However, it was thought worthwhile to hold further discussions in Prague, and representatives from Basel arrived there in June 1433. Their basic plan of action was defined by the Spanish prelate Juan Palomar, who was to play a prominent part in the negotiations: "The Czechs are like a prancing, untamed stallion. He must be approached with soft words and promises and be given a halter. As soon as the stallion is haltered, he can be tamed, he may even be thrashed."

The soft words were directed at the Utraquist nobles, whose resentment of Prokop and the radicals the Spaniard assiduously exploited. In return for their agreement to rejoin the Church, he guaranteed the Utraquists the right to go on receiving Communion in two kinds and promised to provide them with money for a military campaign against the radicals.

On May 30, 1434, the culmination of the conspiracy came when a league of Bohemian nobles, comprising both Utraquists and royalists, faced the Orphans and Taborites near the village of Lipany, about thirty miles east of Prague. Žižka had been confronted by a similar coalition ten years before, at Malešov, and had achieved one of his most spectacular triumphs. Prokop, though outnumbered—he had only 18,000 compared with the enemy's 25,000—was served by battle-hardened veterans of the Magnificent Rides. Indeed, when the troops of the Barons' League began what seemed to be a headlong retreat, Prokop's forces saw victory within their grasp. But the retreat was a ruse, and when the Orphanite and Taborite troops rushed from their wagon-fortress to give chase, they found themselves cut off by enemy cavalry that had been lying in wait in a nearby valley. After that, the Hussite troops stood no chance. Their losses were enormous—one report gives a figure of 13,000 dead—and included Prokop the Bald himself. Many prisoners were taken; about 1,000 of them were locked in barns, which were then set on fire.

The final agreement between Utraquist Bohemia and the Council of Basel was signed at the Moravian city of Jihlava on July 5, 1436. Known as the Compacts, it was based on the Four Articles of Prague, and though a watered-down version of the

The Hussites' ingenious deployment of a limited number of artillery weapons made up for their lack of conventional arms and enabled them to beat the odds in the struggle against the might of the Holy Roman Empire. Their strongholds were protected by artillery sheds on wheels that resembled the one depicted in an early-fifteenth-century manuscript on the art of war (opposite). The roof protected the gun and its powder from the elements, while the walls, which were hinged to allow smoke to escape, shielded the gunner from enemy attack. Also illustrated in this German manuscript is a large handgun set in a wooden stick, of a type probably familiar to the Hussites. Wheeled guns (below) were a subsequent development, rarely used on the battlefield until the late fifteenth century. In this Viennese example, an iron pin could be inserted in a pierced bar to alter the elevation of the gun barrel.

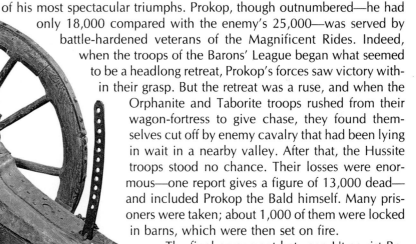

original, the Compacts still went a great deal further than most ecclesiastics, including Pope Eugenius IV, would have wished. The acceptance of the Compacts was due largely to pressure from Emperor Sigismund, who perceived the agreement as the only means by which he could finally take possession of his Bohemian heritage. On August 16, he solemnly pronounced the restoration of peace between Bohemia and the Catholic world; a week later, after seventeen years of struggle, he at last entered Prague as the king of Bohemia.

One of his first acts was to deal with the hard-line Taborites who refused to acknowledge his sovereignty. In the autumn of 1437, following a six-month siege, imperial troops forced their way into the castle of Zion, north of Prague, where the Taborite commander, John Rohac of Duba, and his men had found a last refuge. Many defenders were killed on the spot, but sixty of them, including Rohac, were taken to Prague to be tortured and hanged. Sigismund had little time to savor his triumph, for on December 9, 1437, he died en route to Hungary, fleeing from the revolt that his immoderate policies had already stirred up among the Czechs.

Sigismund's death without an heir extinguished the line of Charles IV, leaving a power vacuum that was to be filled by a long succession of mainly foreign monarchs. Indeed, the only native-born Czech to rule Bohemia after Sigismund was George of Podebrady, an Utraquist nobleman who, during his reign from 1458 to 1471, did his best to promote religious tolerance and domestic stability. Unfortunately, he was unsuccessful in his attempts to win papal approval of the Compacts, and in 1462, Pius II repudiated any obligation of the Church to abide by the agreement. In 1466, Pius's successor, Paul II, went even further, declaring George a heretic and inciting George's ambitious son-in-law, King Matthias of Hungary, to attack Bohemia. However, as so often before, Czechs of all classes rallied to the defense of their country, and the invasion was crushed.

It was an illusory victory, at least for the poorer section of the community. After a protracted period during which Bohemia functioned more or less as an oligarchic republic, by the end of the century, the nobility had consolidated its political, social, and economic power. This aristocratic backlash eventually reduced the peasants to a worse state than they had known before their moment at center stage in the days of the Taborite victories.

Nonetheless, the Hussite revolution in Bohemia was the most dramatic and sustained of all the popular insurrections that disturbed Europe in the troubled centuries of the waning Middle Ages. It was also a forerunner of events to come. Just 102 years after the burning of Jan Hus, another dissident cleric would take offense at the moral standards of the Church and in particular at the sale of indulgences, stating his position in a list of ninety-five theses nailed to the door of a German church. His name was Martin Luther, and the Protestant Reformation that he set in motion would destroy the unity of the Roman Catholic Church.

MACHINES TO MASS-PRODUCE KNOWLEDGE

Of all the technological developments that marked Europe's transition from the Middle Ages to the modern world, the most significant was the invention of printing. Known to the Chinese in the eleventh century, the principle of movable-type book production was to have a much greater impact in the West than in the Orient, largely because the technique was much better suited to a Western letter alphabet than to the Chinese language with its many thousands of ideograms.

The main developer of the process in the West was a German goldsmith called Johannes Gutenberg, who drew on the technique, familiar to all his colleagues, of producing coins by stamping metal in a die. His innovation was to use the stamps to make individual letters of the alphabet, which could then be laid out in limitless combinations and assembled on presses adapted from other industries. Exploiting advances in the production of oil-based, metal-adhesive ink and using paper from water-powered pulping mills, Gutenberg was able to transform the reproduction of the written word from the painstaking copying-by-hand of manuscript scribes to a mass-production process. By 1455, his first

major project, a printed edition of the Bible, had been completed.

Other entrepreneurs, perceiving the financial potential of the invention, abandoned jobs as scribes and booksellers in a rush to set up as printers. By the end of the century, about 1,000 printing offices in more than 250 locations had brought out some 30,000 editions and at least 10 million individual books. In contrast, only an estimated 50,000 manuscripts were produced in the course of the whole century.

The availability of books vastly increased the market for reading matter. The demand for Bibles never waned, and devotional works such as the German monk Thomas à Kempis's *Imitation of Christ* also enjoyed a surge of popularity as religion acquired an individual dimension. At the same time, a counterbalancing interest arose in the authors of classical antiquity, and Cicero, Ovid, Virgil, and other secular writers were disseminated in abundance. Everywhere, demand for the newly accessible information manifested itself: People who had never owned manuscripts now clamored for books; universities imported them by the shipload. With the advent of printing, the floodgates of knowledge burst open.

This reconstruction of an early press shows the mechanisms used for printing. In preparation, the form was placed on the stone, the type well inked, and a sheet of paper pinned securely to the tympan. The frisket was folded down over the tympan, exposing only that area of paper intended to receive the print. Both parts were folded down together onto the form, and the whole assemblage was then slid under the platen. The bar—a lever inserted into the spindle—lowered the platen.

Bar

Spindle

Platen

Type

Chase

Frisket

Tympan

The screw presses used in wine and oil production provided Gutenberg with a prototype mechanism for his movable type. The construction of an early printing press posed few technical problems for experienced carpenters and metalworkers.

The first stage of the printing process was to compose the text for the press. The compositor selected type from trays bearing an array of pigeonholes, each containing a specific letter. He inserted the characters into a slotted receptacle, known as a stick, to form words and eventually whole lines. The line was then removed from the stick and placed in a small tray, or galley. Once a full page had been composed, the type was secured by wedges in a low metal frame called a chase. The assemblage of type and chase, known as the form, was placed on the stone—the press's smooth marble bed—and inked with leather pads. Paper was placed over the type, and the screw mechanism was turned to lower a flat plate, or platen, that pressed the paper hard against the type. Considerable power was needed to make the impression, and to counteract the downward pressure of the screw, the press was equipped with a sturdy upper section and braced against the ceiling of the printing shop.

Early printers had several practical problems linked with this basic procedure. First, it was impossible to raise the platen high enough to reink the type for the next imprint. This obstacle was overcome by setting the stone in a wood frame mounted on rails, which allowed the form to be slid from beneath the platen.

The other difficulties involved the printing itself. Ink tended to splash and smudge the margins of the paper, and slight differences in the height of the type produced an uneven impression. These problems led to the development of the cushioning system known as tympan and frisket *(opposite)*. Hinged onto the frame holding the stone, the tympan consisted of two parchment-covered frames sandwiching a sheet of thick flannel. This flannel absorbed pressure from the platen, reducing the problem of uneven print.

The frisket, another parchment-covered frame hinged to the upper side of the tympan, was designed to do away with inky margins. Its parchment shielded the paper from the ink except in those places where it had been intentionally cut away to let the type meet the paper.

The initial step in casting movable type—a process shown from left to right in this illustration—was to engrave a relief letter in reverse on a steel punch, or patrix. This was then used to strike a matrix made of softer metal. Any irregularities in the matrix were filed down, and it was placed face up in a deep mold, into which molten lead alloy was poured. When cooled, the resulting reverse image would print a correctly oriented letter. Nicks cut into the letters' shanks helped the compositor align them rapidly in his stick the right way up.

PIONEERS OF PUBLISHING

Illuminated margins, rubricated text, and a typeface based on formal German script give a traditional manuscript appearance to this page of the Gutenberg Bible. Also known as the *42-Line Bible*, from the length of its columns, the Bible was issued both on vellum and on paper, a total of almost 200 copies.

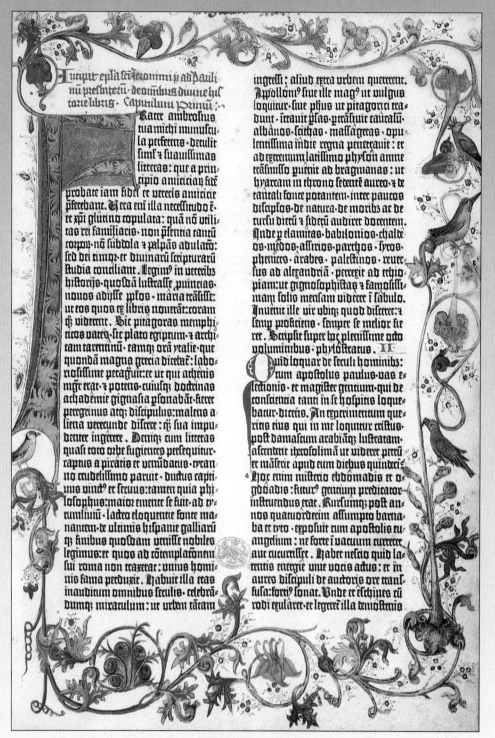

In 1455, the first book in Europe to be printed with movable type was published. It was a copy of the Vulgate—the Latin translation of the Bible—which had taken more than two years to complete, and it became known, after its printer, as the Gutenberg Bible.

Yet by the time the book came out, Gutenberg no longer owned the printing house that produced it. Johann Fust, a wealthy goldsmith, had funded Gutenberg's experiments since 1450 and later became a partner in the enterprise. In 1455, with production of the Bible almost finished, Fust claimed breach of contract and sued to recover his investment. Gutenberg was forced to retire, and Fust, in partnership with his son-in-law, Peter Schöffer, assumed complete control.

Ruthless tactics they may have been, but in the hands of Fust and Schöffer the continuation of the printing business was ensured. They intended their books to replicate the lavish appearance of manuscripts, which commanded very high prices. To this end, experienced calligraphers were used to rubricate, or pick out in red, the text, just as a manuscript would have been rubricated.

Subsequent printers followed suit, with the result that the earliest printed books look much like manuscripts. Soon, though, typefaces that had been based on the handwriting of scribes were simplified in the interests of standardization. Initial resistance from some copyists and stationers to the newfangled competition gave way to grudging acceptance, and manuscripts and printed books were sold side by side.

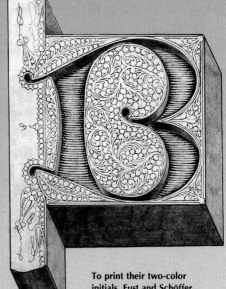

To print their two-color initials, Fust and Schöffer used a device similar to that above, consisting of two interlocking metal sections: one carved to print the letter only, fitting inside a separate block for the surrounding ornament. The constituent parts were inked separately, then assembled and inserted in the form with the rest of the text type.

ENHANCING THE TEXT

Emboldened by their initial successes, the pioneer publishers soon strove to expand their craft by tackling a series of technical problems. Renewed interest in mathematics and classical geometry spurred them on to address the difficulties of producing mathematical diagrams typographically. Erhard Ratdolt, in his 1482 edition of Greek mathematician Euclid's *Elements of Geometry*, met the challenge with remarkable success, producing the superbly defined lines of his diagrams by shaping thin metal and securing these shapes with molten lead.

Printing music was an even greater challenge, since it required superimposing the musical notation accurately upon the staff lines. Few printers were successful: Some reproduced the staff lines only, others the notes only; in both cases, the rest had to be filled in by hand.

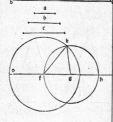

Ratdolt's version of *Elements of Geometry* broke new ground in three ways: as the first printed edition of Euclid, the first printed book with mathematical figures, and (in some copies) the first one to use gold printing.

This page from Michel de Toulouze's dancing manual *L'Art et Instruction de Bien Dancer* of 1496, is the first known attempt at reproducing measured musical notation with movable type. Using two impressions, he first printed the red staffs, followed by the notes in black type.

In 1500, having taken five years to prepare the elegant Greek type used for this philosophical treatise, the Venetian printer Zacharias Callierges decorated the first page of certain copies with a celebratory touch of gold. He applied gold leaf to heated type, which was subsequently pressed to the paper. The heat melted the powdered adhesive with which the paper had previously been dusted and—provided enough pressure was applied—the metal was transferred to the paper.

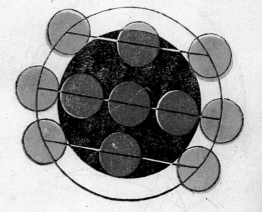

In Johannes de Sacrobosco's astronomical treatise *De Spheara* of 1485, Ratdolt extended the techniques of color printing by using several colored inks on one page. In this illustration, probably one color was printed with the outline and the other two were stenciled in later.

MECHANIZING THE ILLUSTRATOR'S ART

In the early decades of the new technology, printers drew on the services of traditional manuscript artists to illustrate their books—a time-consuming and expensive partnership that negated the advantages of printing. The first occasion on which the speeds of text and picture production were brought into line was in 1460, when Albrecht Pfister of Bamberg introduced the woodcut—an art well established in picture printing but never before combined with movable type.

Made of hard, fine-grained wood, onto which was drawn or traced the design to be carved out by the block cutter, the woodcuts fitted in the form beside the type and were sturdy enough to be reused many times.

Normally, both illustration and text were printed in the same impression with the same ink. Colored illustrations could also be printed, but most woodcuts were hand-colored, as shown here—a job often performed by the printer himself.

Birds identified fancifully as a sea eagle and an auk are just two of more than 1,000 creatures, plants, and precious stones in a late-fifteenth-century natural-history text.

Scenes from the laboratory and marketplace mingle to open a 1486 encyclopedia entry on such bafflingly diverse subjects as colors, odors, eggs, measurements, and music. The book was printed not in Latin but in French—a hallmark of printers from Lyons, whose titles gained widespread appeal.

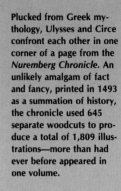

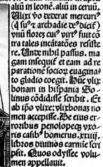

Plucked from Greek mythology, Ulysses and Circe confront each other in one corner of a page from the *Nuremberg Chronicle*. An unlikely amalgam of fact and fancy, printed in 1493 as a summation of history, the chronicle used 645 separate woodcuts to produce a total of 1,809 illustrations—more than had ever before appeared in one volume.

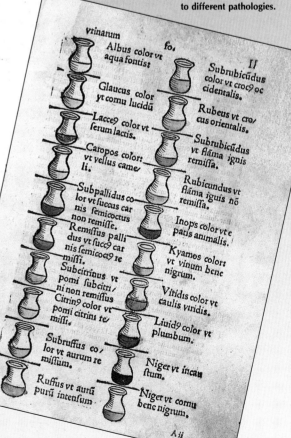

Urine charts, such as this example from an early-sixteenth-century medical textbook, were useful diagnostic aids for the medieval physician. Such guides differentiated between twenty shades of urine, each of which was considered to correspond to different pathologies.

THE LAST GREAT HINDU EMPIRE

In May 1498, the Portuguese explorer Vasco da Gama and his little fleet made the first European landfall in India, arriving at the port of Calicut. He and his men set off from their boats to pay homage to the local ruler, the *zamorin,* bearing their customary gifts of caps and trinkets. But when they reached the residence of the potentate, their offering was not well received by the palace officials. "When they saw the present, they laughed at it," the expedition's diarist noted ruefully, "saying that it was not a thing to offer a king, that the poorest merchant from Mecca or any other part of India gave more, and that if he wanted to make a present it should be in gold." Da Gama and his men found themselves to be unwanted guests of a civilization in many ways richer and more sophisticated than their own, and they were treated with barely disguised contempt for the rest of the visit.

For all his wealth and pretensions, the zamorin of Calicut was only a tributary ruler on the fringes of a great empire, founded a century and a half before and now in the ascendant. Its authority was recognized, at least in theory, from the Krishna River in south-central India's Deccan plateau to Cape Comorin in the south, where the Indian Ocean meets the Bay of Bengal. Like the empire of Rome, it was to take its name from its capital, Vijayanagar, the "City of Victory," a glittering metropolis located far inland in the Deccan foothills at the center of a network of roads that drew the wealth of southern India to its rulers.

Da Gama, baffled by language problems and treated with disdain by everyone he met, probably never even heard of the empire's existence. Fifty years earlier, though, a better-informed traveler had passed through Calicut: Abdur Razzak, roving ambassador-at-large of the king of Persia. He was told—although he sensibly doubted the fact—that there were 300 such ports in the ruler of Vijayanagar's dominions, which were said to stretch the distance of a three months' journey.

Shortly afterward, Vijayanagar's raja invited the Persian to visit the city himself, and the diplomat was able to send home an eyewitness report of the capital. Vijayanagar, Abdur Razzak wrote, "is such that the pupil of the eye has never seen a place like it, and the ear of intelligence has never been informed that there existed anything to equal it in the world." He told of impregnable fortifications constructed in concentric rings, glorious palaces, arcaded bazaars thronged with free-spending multitudes, colonnaded avenues lined with sculptures (and courtesans), "numerous running streams and canals formed of chiseled stone," and lavish festivals whose participants (including a thousand caparisoned elephants) "presented the appearance of the waves of the sea, or of the compact mass that will be assembled together at the day of resurrection."

As a diplomat, Abdur Razzak was trained to observe people and their works, not nature, and he scarcely mentioned the city's most extraordinary feature—its location.

Adorning the entrance to the ceremonial hall of the Jalakanthesvara Temple in the southern Indian city of Vellore, sculptured pillars depict a prancing horse and two mythical beings known as *yalis,* half-lions and half-elephants. Lavishly ornamented stonework was typical of the architecture of the Vijayanagar empire, which dominated the southern part of the subcontinent in the fifteenth and early sixteenth centuries.

It lay on the south bank of the Tungabhadra River, a major tributary of the Krishna cutting eastward through the lower Deccan, amid a lunar landscape of boulder-strewn hills. The boulders, indeed, were often more apparent than the hills: great weathered blocks of granite and gneiss, black, gray, and gold, larger than houses and scattered everywhere. Sometimes they formed labyrinthine passageways, often choked with smaller, merely human-size rocks; elsewhere the workings of time and erosion, the hot days and chilly nights of the plateau climate left them heaped in precarious, though ancient, equilibrium.

These boulders were the raw material on which the city's stoneworkers labored. Some the masons hewed neatly into blocks, dragging the stones to the chosen sites of palaces and temples. Other stones they left in place, carving sculptured shrines from the living rock or hacking out a stairway up the wild jumble of a hillside. Sometimes the masons blended artifice with nature: The massive square stones of the city walls merged imperceptibly with adjoining ramparts that had been shaped by the chance workings of nature, and from a distance, it was difficult for an observer to differentiate a pillared watchtower laboriously built upon a hilltop from the natural castle keeps that studded the horizon of the city. It was as if Vijayanagar had simply grown up out of the landscape, raised less by the hands of humankind than by the slow, inexorable forces of the earth itself.

Vijayanagar had developed with astonishing speed. Less than a century before Abdur Razzak's visit, there was only a scattering of unpretentious villages to be found around a fort on the site of the future city. It would have been hard to see the area as the birthplace of a great city, let alone the imperial capital that Vijayanagar was to become. Yet for 200 years, the rulers of this arid upland realm were to hold sway over most of central and southern India, building a great Hindu empire in a subcontinent increasingly dominated by Muslims.

At the time of the city's foundation, history as well as geography seemed set against such an enterprise. By the early fourteenth century, most of India's Hindu rulers had been reduced to the status of underlings of great Muslim dynasties. Beginning in the eighth century, Arab rulers had held power over the Indus Valley, cradle of the subcontinent's most ancient civilization, and Muslim traders had es-

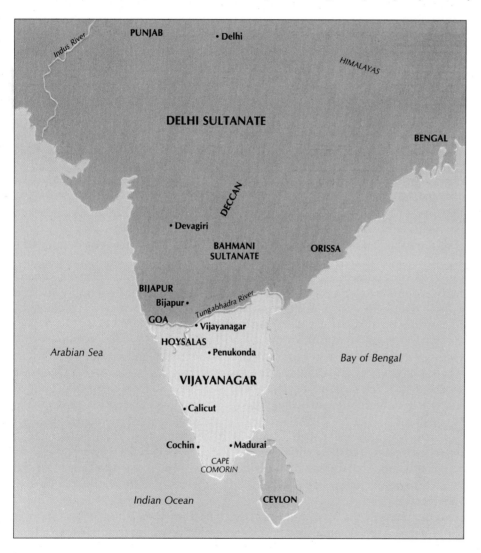

Vijayanagar was the last great Hindu empire. From its capital of the same name on the Tungabhadra River, its realm embraced all of southern India, from the extensively irrigated Deccan uplands to the green river valleys of the south. Rich in labor resources and in revenues from agriculture and foreign trade, Vijayanagar stood as a bulwark against the Muslim sultanates to the north. But its armed rivalry with Hindu Orissa eventually weakened both states and left them unable to withstand the impact of a Muslim alliance.

tablished enclaves in almost every significant Indian port. But the most devastating Islamic incursions had come not from the Arabs but from the Turkic peoples of central Asia and Afghanistan. From the eleventh century onward, massive Turkish raids had ravaged the whole northern Indian plain, and in the way of raiders, they eventually found the exercise of power more profitable than plunder. The congeries of quarreling Hindu kingdoms that were in nominal control of the region were no more capable of halting the northern conquest than they had been able to stop the looting expeditions that had preceded it, and in 1206, the newcomers established a separate Turko-Afghan dynasty in the old city of Delhi. The long rule of what was to be called the Delhi sultanate had begun.

It was one thing to conquer the north and quite another to win the Deccan and the south, particularly since the heirs to the new dynasty spent most of their time in the thirteenth century murdering one another in vicious palace intrigues. Southern India remained untouched, and even in the north the dynasty's control was challenged: Bengal, supposedly a part of the sultanate, was virtually independent, and Genghis Khan's world-conquering Mongols seized the Punjab. But when Alauddin Khalji became sultan in 1296—which he accomplished by assassinating his predecessor, who was both his father-in-law and his uncle—he set about consolidating and expanding the authority his ancestors had won.

Clearly, Alauddin had a high opinion of himself: He called himself the "second Alexander," after the great Macedonian conqueror of the fourth century BC, and even went so far as to have the title stamped on his coinage. Remarkably, though, he had the ability to match his ambition. His armies advanced as far as Madurai, deep in the Hindu south, returning with vast quantities of loot and leaving behind them a chain of burned cities whose surviving rulers pledged a fearful allegiance to the triumphant sultanate. In the north, he beat back a whole succession of Mongol attacks with a ferocity that matched the Mongols' own.

Alauddin's success, like that of most of his fellow Muslim rulers, depended on using the new military methods the Turko-Afghans had brought to India. The Hindu way of fighting had not changed much in the centuries since Alexander the Great's wars against them. Hindu armies were usually as large as possible: Great numbers marked a ruler's might and could generally be relied on to terrify an enemy. But only a small part consisted of trained, well-armed troops, and the sheer size of such forces made them snail-like in maneuver and virtually unmanageable on the battlefield. The Muslims placed less emphasis on quantity and more on quality. Their cavalry and their archers, many of whom also went into battle mounted on horseback, were especially formidable: Horsebreeding had been a highly developed art for centuries in both Arabia and central Asia, so the Muslims' mounts were consistently far superior to anything the Hindus had.

Alauddin was also a skilled administrator, the first ruler of the Turko-Afghan line to raise more revenue by the levying of taxes than from the seizing of plunder. And his coinage was by no means simply a form of self-advertisement: Increased cash circulation meant a thriving economy. It also meant that at least some taxes were paid in real money instead of in kind, which made it much easier for Alauddin in turn to pay the wages of, and hence to control, the standing army on which his authority ultimately rested. As Alauddin himself frequently complained, his word was law only within the immediate vicinity of Delhi. Farther afield, troops alone could ensure that the sultan received his due respect.

The exercise of power at a distance, in a world of poor communications and strong local loyalties, was a problem that bedeviled almost every ruler, not just in India. Even Alauddin, with his fearsome reputation and efficient administration, was never able to subjugate the south. When his mid-fourteenth-century successor, Muhammad Tughluq, tried to consolidate the sultanate's hold, he met with disaster. He moved his capital southward from Delhi to the ancient city of Devagiri (present-day Daulatabad), more than 600 miles away, at the cost of countless lives, since a large part of the population of the old capital—some chroniclers said all of it—was forced to make the journey. The move brought the southern provinces more firmly under the sultan's control, but at the same time the northern provinces became extremely difficult to govern. Muhammad also made an attempt to bring his whole domain under the direct administration of his single central authority, an idea that might have been admirable in theory but that turned out to be almost impossible in practice. There was never enough money to pay for an effective administration, and without such an administration, there was no reliable method of collecting the money. The only practical way for the sultanate to extend its rule was through a kind of military feudalism, and that brought a vicious circle of another set of problems. Weak governors were useless and encouraged rebellion among their subjects; strong governors were always ready to rebel themselves.

In the end, Muhammad abandoned Devagiri and returned to Delhi, the chastened ruler of a much smaller sultanate. He had scarcely left his short-lived southern capital when it fell to one of his former officers, a mutineer who went on to found a dynasty and a kingdom, the so-called Bahmani sultanate. Other Delhi provinces went the same way, and Muhammad's shrinking empire left behind it a tangle of successor-states, most in the hands of warlike adventurers.

For the great mass of the Hindu population, still ruled by a tiny alien elite, the change made little difference. The new Muslim principalities were built everywhere on the wreckage of earlier Hindu states. By mid-century, only two major Hindu kingdoms remained: Orissa, on the eastern seaboard, and the kingdom of the Hoysalas, bordering the newborn and aggressive Bahmani sultanate. The Hoysala territory looked to be the next to fall.

But in 1346, when the last of the Hoysala kings died (surprisingly enough, for those times, of natural causes) without having produced an heir, the two brothers who took over the modest realm chose just that inauspicious moment to found a new city and a greater kingdom. At a time of disastrous defeat for Hindu arms and culture, the name that they chose—the "City of Victory"—must have seemed outrageously optimistic. Nonetheless, for more than two centuries, they and their descendants were to succeed in providing the promised victories.

The exact details of the city's creation have been lost, along with most other knowledge of the brothers' background and early history, obscured less by the passage of time than by the glowing cloud of legend with which Hindu chroniclers endowed them. According to one traditional account, the brothers found themselves at one point taken prisoner by the sultan of Delhi and forcibly converted to the faith of Islam. Ordered to go south in the service of their new master, they returned to their ancestral religion because of the influence of a great sage and became leaders of a Hindu rebellion on the fringes of the Muslim sphere of interest. Their success was predetermined, the story had it, for the brothers were none other than the representatives on earth of the god Virupaksha, a manifestation of mighty Shiva himself, the destroyer and the renewer.

Recently deciphered inscriptions point to a more prosaic, but more probable, beginning. The brothers—at least their names, Harihara and Bukka, are common to all accounts—were Hoysala warriors, sent to hold the northern marches of the kingdom against Muslim invaders. When they learned that their king had died, they simply seized the opportunity that presented itself. They would doubtless have encouraged the making of myths and legends, knowing that no true believer would challenge the legitimacy of god-sent protectors of the faith. A temple to Virupaksha featured prominently in the new city's groundplan, and later rulers unabashedly used the god's name to sign state documents. The brothers' successors were also to make much of their status as protectors of Hindu temples and Brahman priests. To the religious establishment, Harihara and Bukka must have seemed a bulwark against the onward march of image-smashing Muslims.

Yet Vijayanagar was far from being a die-hard's holdout, the last stronghold of Hindu tradition on a subcontinent in the throes of conquest and change. In fact, the new kingdom immediately made a point of adopting many of the Muslims' ways, especially in warfare. Vijayanagar learned to use cavalry and mounted archers almost as well as its enemies. War-horses became a major import. The cash to pay for them came from Vijayanagar's generally thriving economy, for here, too, the empire's rulers followed the Muslim administrative example, raising revenues in money whenever it was possible and taking a profitable part in the flourishing international trade that had developed along India's southern coasts, mostly under Muslim guidance, from the thirteenth century onward.

But the greatest difference between Vijayanagar and the Hindu states that had preceded it was a matter of climate and geography rather than style or administrative methods. Every southern Indian empire of the past—that of the Cholas, for example, who three centuries before had dominated all of southern India and Ceylon—was based on rice-rich river valleys and the agricultural surpluses they were almost sure to yield. In the dry Deccan upland around Vijayanagar, however, extensive irrigation works were essential if rice and other crops were to grow: Wells and storage tanks had to be constructed and maintained to preserve the life-giving waters of the seasonal monsoons.

As the population of the region swelled during the Vijayanagar peace, so the works necessary for survival grew in size and complexity. Because they controlled many of the water tanks, the temples gained importance. At the same time, the armies also grew in importance as they maintained order in areas unfamiliar with large-scale administration. Such order was essential if the empire was to survive, much less expand.

And expand it did, almost from the beginning. War with the Bahmanis pushed the northern frontier of Vijayanagar as far as the Krishna River, and a campaign in the early 1370s swallowed up the sultanate of Madurai, the only remaining Muslim power in the south. Within thirty years of the city's foundation, the dominions of Vijayanagar approached the dimensions that earlier Chola rulers had struggled for centuries to attain. But the borders were far from peaceful. There was almost constant war-

Vasco da Gama, leader of the first European fleet to reach India, sailed into Calicut, a tributary port of Vijayanagar, in 1498. The Portuguese explorer, shown here in a Spanish engraving, failed to conclude a treaty with the local ruler and most likely departed unaware of the empire's existence. He returned four years later with a second fleet, however, intent on making his presence felt by force. He demanded the immediate banishment of the local Muslim trading community, who had shown themselves bitterly hostile to Christian competition. When the local ruler failed to respond, da Gama retaliated by bombarding the port and slaughtering thirty-eight Hindu fishermen who sailed out innocently to trade with his crew.

Some of the most vivid and charming depictions of life in southern India at the time of the Vijayanagar empire are found among a series of 141 watercolors painted by an unknown artist in the first half of the sixteenth century. Together they formed a pictorial record of life in lands around the Indian Ocean, from East Africa to Indonesia, and were probably intended to illustrate a Portuguese traveler's account of the recently discovered territories. There was at the time something of a vogue for such books, which not only introduced readers at home to the wonders of the Indies but also prepared potential voyagers for the unfamiliar sights and customs they could expect to meet.

The artist—possibly an Indian—may have seen for himself only some of the scenes that he illustrated. The inspiration for other incidents is thought to have come from two of the better-known contemporary guidebooks: Duarte Barbosa's *Book on What Can Be Seen and What Can Not Be Seen in the East* and Tome Pires's *All the Orient from the Red Sea to China*.

Pirates were a constant hazard to merchant ships in the Arabian Sea. This picture of a galley that operated along Vijayanagar's Malabar Coast shows that the buccaneers were no strangers to firearms.

fare with the Bahmani sultans: Neither side was strong enough to eliminate the other, and the wretched peasants in the disputed area were hard-pressed by constant looting raids. By the early fifteenth century, Vijayanagar's enemies were Hindu as well as Muslim: Its northeastward expansion brought it into conflict with Orissa, and there ensued a century of sometimes bloody frontier bickering that sapped the strength of both Hindu powers.

By the time of Abdur Razzak's mid-century visit, though, the empire was more or less stable and exercised at least some sort of authority as suzerain over all of the south of India. Of course, the empire did not rule in the tightly organized manner of a modern state. Instead, it governed through intermediaries of two sorts. In the dry, upland areas, where trading was still in kind, the Vijayanagar emperors would normally recognize a *palaiyakkarar*, or fortress holder, as local king. In return, he would supply arms, men, and livestock from the levies he imposed on the villages under his control. In the well-irrigated river valleys where state control was stronger, administration was in the hands of officials called *nayaks*, literally "military officers," who were directly appointed by the state to raise revenue in cash or kind. Some areas existed in which neither palaiyakkarar nor nayak could function. Throughout the

Moneychangers—such as this one in a western Indian port—would have been familiar to travelers journeying overland to southern India through the Middle East or sailing around the Arabian Sea.

xarafo quieros chamamos canbador de keyno deanbaya

empire, even in its heartland, there were pockets of mountainous or jungle territory whose tribal peoples remained a law unto themselves, with their own languages and their own pre-Hindu animist religions.

For most of the fifteenth century, Vijayanagar's biggest problem, however, was protecting itself from its aggressive Bahmani neighbor, whose armies more than once approached the city walls and had to be bought off with tribute. According to the principal Muslim chronicle of the period, Vijayanagar's Raja Deva Raya II sought a new solution sometime in the 1440s. His lands and revenues were greater than those of the Bahmani sultans, the angry ruler told his nobles, and his army more numerous; why then should he suffer such humiliations? The raja's council cited the Muslims' horses by way of reply but also pointed out that the sultans kept "a great body of excellent archers."

The raja forthwith ordered Muslim soldiers to be taken into his service, honored, and granted estates; he even built them a mosque and, according to the chronicler, "commanded that no one should molest them in the exercise of their religion. He also ordered a Koran to be placed before his throne, on a rich desk, that the Muslims might perform the ceremony of obeisance in his presence, without sinning against their laws." A Muslim quarter grew up within the city, and Muslim styles of architecture became a powerful influence on traditional Hindu forms; soon domes and pointed arches were decorating halls and monumental gateways.

The military situation, however, remained more or less unchanged. War with the

This wedding scene illustrates the brightly dyed Indian fabrics that were unequaled for their brilliance and fastness of color. Indian dyers were the only medieval artisans to use fixing agents.

Bahmani sultanate was endemic but indecisive, with each side enjoying its share of victory and defeat. The most obvious effect was to increase the power of a number of Vijayanagar's provincial commanders at the expense of the imperial center. After the death of Deva Raya in 1446, a succession of weak rulers made matters worse, and for the forty years that followed, the empire seemed likely to tear itself apart at any moment in factional fighting.

The crisis came to a head in 1485, when the ruling dynasty extinguished itself in a welter of assassinations, and the throne passed to a victorious frontier general, whose attempt to establish a ruling line foundered amid yet more murders and

The widow of a mule driver of the Lingayat sect is buried alive in the grave of her husband—a variation on the Hindu rite of sati, which usually involved self-immolation on a funeral pyre.

usurpations. Not until 1509, the year of the accession of Krishna Deva Raya, did Vijayanagar again acquire a strong, unchallenged ruler.

The empire had survived the civil wars only because its enemies were in no better shape. The Bahmani sultanate had suffered the fate so narrowly avoided by Vijayanagar and split into a handful of rival subkingdoms. They managed to unite for long enough to greet Krishna Deva Raya's accession with an invasion, but the new raja defeated the alliance. He even succeeded in capturing the last of the old Bahmani sultans, and with a masterstroke of diplomacy, he released and reinstated his enemy as a vassal of Vijayanagar. In this way, Krishna Deva Raya acquired the remarkable title of "Master of the Foundation of the Sultanate," at the same time encouraging the deadly rivalry among his northern neighbors. From then on, Vijayanagar employed a policy of shifting alliances with one or another of the Deccan sultans, finding strength in keeping them divided.

Vijayanagar enjoyed a golden age under Krishna Deva Raya. He reasserted the empire's weakened authority over the far south, brought the kingdom of Orissa to its knees, and spent much of his increased revenues on a flurry of temple building. The great city thrived as never before, rich from tribute and from trade with Asia, Arabia, and now Europe.

The Portuguese recovered quickly from Vasco da Gama's rebuff. Their goods at first were inferior to those of their Arab and Indian competitors, but their ships and cannon were much better. The Portuguese used both ruthlessly in a series of annual expeditions that were as much pirate raids as merchant ventures. In 1510, they seized the small port of Goa, which they built up as a base for commerce and for future plundering. Although Goa had once formed part of the Vijayanagar empire, it had been under Muslim control for generations, and Krishna Deva Raya had no objection to the interlopers, particularly since they promised him a non-Muslim source of much-needed war-horses.

Trade with the empire in weapons, including firearms, as well as horses served as Goa's mainstay for fifty years; on occasion, Portuguese troops even fought to defend Vijayanagar. The different culture of India naturally aroused great interest in Europe, and several Portuguese merchants wrote long, lucid accounts of the imperial capital in its heyday for the benefit of their compatriots at home.

To one frequent visitor, the merchant Domingo Paes, the city seemed "as large as Rome, and very beautiful to the sight; there are many groves of trees within it, in the gardens of the houses, and many conduits of water that flow in the midst of it. . . . The people in this city are countless in number, so much so that I do not wish to write it down for fear it should be thought fabulous; but I declare that no troops, horse or foot, could break their way through any street or lane, so great are the numbers of the people and elephants."

Paes recounted tales of lavish festivals, including parades of women heavily bedecked in jewelry: "So great is the weight of the bracelets and gold and jewels carried by them that many of them cannot support them, and women accompany them, assisting them by supporting their arms." As for the military resources of the empire: "When the king wishes to show the strength of his power to any of his adversaries amongst the three kings bordering on his kingdom, they say that he puts into the field two million soldiers; in consequence of which he is the most feared king of any of these parts." The troops were raised by captains, "the nobles of his kingdom," who

A fifteenth-century bronze casting of the gentle Mother Goddess, Parvati, includes the conical headgear that was a typical feature of Vijayanagar statues. In Hindu mythology, Parvati is the beautiful wife of the god Shiva, whose meditations are believed to generate the spiritual force that maintains the cosmos. Like all Hindu deities, however, she can take on other forms; as the fierce Kali, often represented as a black giant with a huge red tongue and tusks, she embodies the cruel and destructive face of nature.

also had to make annual payments to the king, who "has his own salaried troops to whom he gives pay."

A contemporary of Paes's named Duarte Barbosa, who worked for the Portuguese government in India during the first decades of the sixteenth century, wrote illuminatingly of the social customs of the kingdom. He noted with surprise the parasols—"hats with handles," he called them—with which the wealthy were shaded by their attendants. What most aroused Barbosa's curiosity were certain of the customs governing the behavior of women and girls. He described ceremonies in which maidens, some as young as twelve years of age, would offer up their virginity to the god Shiva on phallic altars, and he told of thanksgiving rituals that called for young women to demonstrate their gratitude for winning the husbands of their choice by impaling themselves on iron hooks.

Barbosa also recounted in great detail the practice of *sati*, the ceremonial suicide practiced by Indian widows. According to his account, the wife of a man of high rank would, on his death, hold a great funeral banquet, in the course of which she would give away all of her possessions to her friends and relatives. Then, shortly before dawn, she would ride through the city to the burial pit where the body of her husband had been cremated. Mounting a small scaffold, she would divest herself of all her clothing, except for a loincloth, before anointing her head with oil. Turning toward the rising sun, she would intone prayers of greeting; then she would hurl herself down into the rekindled fire. Her kinfolk, assembled at the spot, would throw oil and butter into the flames to hasten her end. Barbosa reported with some astonishment that when a king died, as many as 500 of his concubines might immolate themselves in this manner.

Barbosa and Paes were writing of Vijayanagar at the height of its affluence and power under Krishna Deva Raya. His heirs were not of the same caliber, and after his death, real authority soon passed to a born conspirator named Rama Raya, the great king's son-in-law. In 1542, Rama Raya was officially appointed regent for the new king, Sadashiva; to ensure that his regency was untroubled, Rama Raya immediately had the monarch imprisoned.

The power struggle was not confined to Vijayanagar. The Deccan sultans—four of them by now controlled the old Bahmani domain—took sides and were even courted by disgruntled Vijayanagar factions. The Portuguese were also involved in what became a murderously confused, six-sided game, ruthlessly improving their position in India at the expense of whoever happened to be temporarily the weakest. They even added aggressive Catholicism to an already-explosive religious mixture—the Holy Inquisition had been established in Goa—and their destruction of Hindu temples goaded Rama Raya into a brief war with the Europeans. He did not dare alienate his main source of supply of horses and munitions, however, so an uneasy peace was hastily patched together.

But events were moving toward a crisis. In 1564, the Muslim sultans at last buried their differences and formed a fighting alliance expressly directed against Vijayanagar. They claimed religious provocation: During a recent campaign, in which Rama Raya had adroitly aided one sultan against the others, the Vijayanagar infidels had, according to one Muslim source, "insulted the honor of the Muslim women, destroyed the mosques, and failed to respect even the sacred Koran."

In December of 1564, when the weather turned cool and dry, the Muslim allies

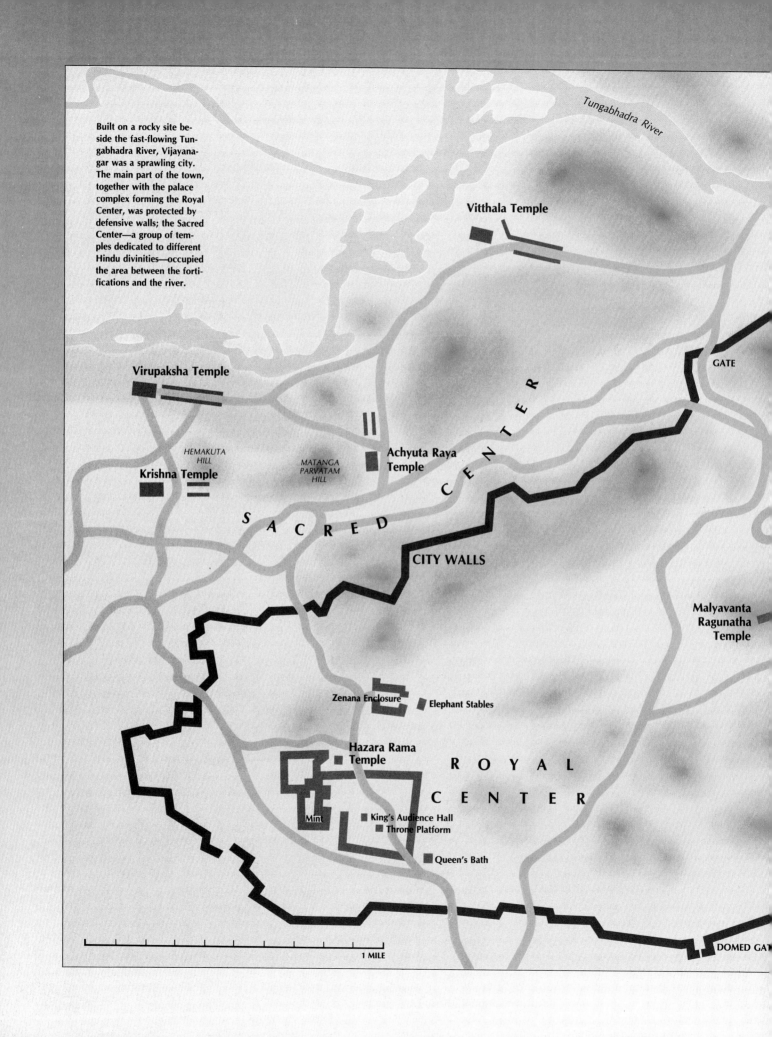

Built on a rocky site beside the fast-flowing Tungabhadra River, Vijayanagar was a sprawling city. The main part of the town, together with the palace complex forming the Royal Center, was protected by defensive walls; the Sacred Center—a group of temples dedicated to different Hindu divinities—occupied the area between the fortifications and the river.

Tungabhadra River

Vitthala Temple

GATE

Virupaksha Temple

HEMAKUTA HILL

Krishna Temple

MATANGA PARVATAM HILL

Achyuta Raya Temple

S A C R E D   C E N T E R

CITY WALLS

Malyavanta Ragunatha Temple

Zenana Enclosure ■ **Elephant Stables**

Hazara Rama Temple

R O Y A L

C E N T E R

Mint

■ King's Audience Hall
■ Throne Platform

■ Queen's Bath

1 MILE

DOMED GATE

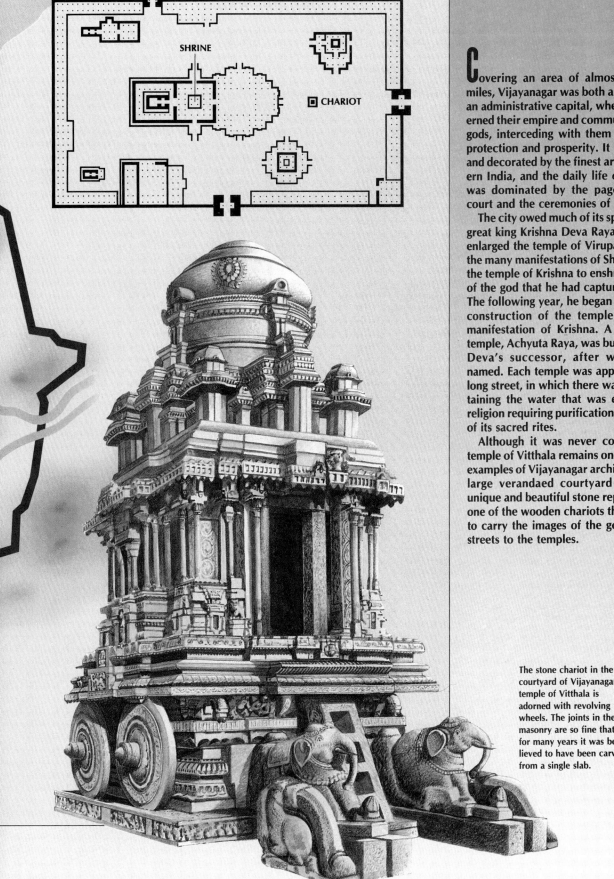

SHRINE

☐ CHARIOT

Covering an area of almost ten square miles, Vijayanagar was both a religious and an administrative capital, where kings governed their empire and communed with the gods, interceding with them to ensure its protection and prosperity. It was designed and decorated by the finest artists of southern India, and the daily life of its citizens was dominated by the pageantry of its court and the ceremonies of its temples.

The city owed much of its splendor to the great king Krishna Deva Raya. In 1512, he enlarged the temple of Virupaksha (one of the many manifestations of Shiva) and built the temple of Krishna to enshrine an image of the god that he had captured in Orissa. The following year, he began a massive reconstruction of the temple of Vitthala, manifestation of Krishna. A fourth great temple, Achyuta Raya, was built by Krishna Deva's successor, after whom it was named. Each temple was approached by a long street, in which there was a tank containing the water that was essential to a religion requiring purification for almost all of its sacred rites.

Although it was never completed, the temple of Vitthala remains one of the finest examples of Vijayanagar architecture. In its large verandaed courtyard was built a unique and beautiful stone reproduction of one of the wooden chariots that were used to carry the images of the gods along the streets to the temples.

The stone chariot in the courtyard of Vijayanagar's temple of Vitthala is adorned with revolving wheels. The joints in the masonry are so fine that for many years it was believed to have been carved from a single slab.

assembled at Bijapur the largest force that Vijayanagar had ever had to face. They were in no great hurry; they planned a decisive confrontation, not a sneak attack, and although on the march south there were both plenty of fresh forage for their cavalry and roads that were firm enough for the teams of oxen drawing their cannon, it was mid-January before the sultans reached the small town of Talikota, just north of the Krishna River.

More than ninety miles away in Vijayanagar itself, Rama Raya was not impressed. He believed the city to be impregnable behind its massive walls; after all, its empire had withstood assault for centuries. The new Muslim alliance meant that his diplomacy had failed at last, but the old arch-intriguer had beaten each of the sultans on the battlefield before separately and he was ready to take them on again together. Despite his ninety-odd years, he acted with energy and dispatch. To deny the Muslims a river crossing, he ordered his brother Tirumala north with all the troops immediately at hand. As reinforcements flooded in from the empire's provinces, he sent a second brother with a supporting army. When the empire's remaining forces had assembled, Rama Raya led them to the Krishna—the old man was carried in a litter—and assumed overall command.

One chronicler numbered the combined army at 600,000 infantry and 100,000 cavalry; another claimed there were almost a million soldiers, all told, and 2,000 war elephants. Even allowing for exaggeration, it was a stupendous force. But very few in Vijayanagar's army were disciplined regulars. There were several divisions of Muslim cavalry, mercenaries who had long fought for Vijayanagar gold against their coreligionists, and there were many contingents led by subsidiary princelings, varying widely in equipment and training. The great mass of the army consisted of poorly armed, ill-organized militia, impressive in their sheer numbers but utterly ineffective in real combat.

The sultans' army seems to have been about half the size of Rama Raya's—not necessarily a disadvantage, since the number of skilled soldiers on each side was probably about equal. For days, the two hordes marched and countermarched against each other on opposite sides of the Krishna. At length, the less cumbersome Muslims managed to trick the Hindus into leaving a ford unguarded, and their whole army crossed safely.

Their enemies were undismayed. The following morning, January 23, 1565, the two unwieldy armies deployed themselves into line and clashed head-on. Since only

Elephants, camels, hunters, and soldiers decorate the throne platform in the royal palace at Vijayanagar. Rising in tiers from a 430-square-foot base, the pyramidal dais—built by Raja Krishna Deva Raya to celebrate a victory over Orissa—elevated the ruler forty feet above those to whom he gave audience. The platform was the centerpiece of a great hall adorned with carved wooden pillars and a copper-plated roof. The room was used principally during an annual rite known as the Nine Days' Festival, when the king sat in splendor on a jeweled throne to receive his rents and review his horses and the women of the royal harem.

the first few ranks could come to blows, most of the soldiers were mere bystanders; and with the center of the battlefield soon shrouded in smoke from the era's crude gunpowder, they could see little of the actual fighting.

According to Muslim accounts, the Hindus at first had the better of it. But the Muslim artillery had loaded their guns with small copper coins instead of cannon-balls, and when the Hindus closed in for the kill, they were cut down by a hail of primitive grapeshot. The Muslim cavalry surged forward into the confusion, and disaster struck Vijayanagar. Rama Raya was commanding from his litter, not a war-horse. Thus, when an advancing war elephant put his bearers to flight, the old general was captured easily. A quick-thinking Muslim officer lopped off his head and raised it on the point of a lance.

Few of Rama Raya's troops could have seen the grisly trophy, much less recognized it. Nonetheless, panic spread like wildfire through the close-packed, blinded ranks of ill-trained soldiery. There may also have been treachery: Hindu sources claim that Vijayanagar's Muslim mercenaries changed sides at the critical moment. Whatever the cause, there was no doubting the effect. One moment there was an army; the next, only a rabble of terrified men fleeing for their lives.

Once the army had begun to run, there was no stopping it. The Muslims slaugh-tered everyone they could catch—more than 100,000 people, according to one chronicler—while the rest of the Hindus simply scattered. There was no lack of good defensive positions in the country between the Krishna River and Vijayanagar, but no one made any attempt to stand and fight. And when Tirumala, the sole surviving senior general, reached the city with some of the royal princes and the remnants of his household troops, he gave no thought to its defense. Instead, he seized all the remaining modes of transportation, from elephants to oxcarts, loaded what treasure he and his men could carry, and pausing just long enough to collect the wretched King Sadashiva from his prison, he hurried off to the south.

Only then did the inhabitants of Vijayanagar realize the extent of the catastrophe that had befallen them. The great walls of the city were intact, but there were no soldiers to defend them, and since there was scarcely a horse or a cart left in the city, flight was impossible. Looting started even before the Muslims arrived. The region's tribal peoples, who had been only loosely incorporated into the realm by the offer of gifts or by the threat of punitive military raids, had always detested its power and arrogance. Now they revenged themselves on the helpless citizenry.

But the real horror began three days after the battle, when the first of the Muslim invaders swept over the abandoned defenses. Most of the city's inhabitants were murdered or enslaved in the first few days. But week after week, for nearly six months in all, the slower work of destroying buildings went on. To the Muslims it must have been doubly satisfying: By smashing the temples and palaces of the idolatrous infi-dels, they gained in religious merit while they enriched themselves beyond their dreams by plundering one of the wealthiest cities in the world. Gunpowder was too precious to be wasted on demolition, so anything that would not burn had to be wrecked with hammers and crowbars. Vijayanagar was finished forever as an im-perial capital. Two years later, an Italian traveler who visited the site found some buildings still standing but living there was "nothing, as is reported, but tigers and other wild beasts."

The alliance of the city's Muslim conquerors barely outlasted their victorious campaign. They mopped up what fragments of the empire they could but spent most

of their energy warring among themselves. All of them were swallowed up by the Moguls, India's next great rulers, who had annihilated the old Delhi sultanate in 1526 and would spend the following 150 years expanding southward.

The fate of Vijayanagar's empire was simply to waste away. Tirumala ruled what was left of it from the southern fortress of Penukonda, but without the majesty of the great city to act as an imperial center of gravity, the regions that remained outside Muslim control were increasingly reluctant to continue their payments of tribute. When the luckless Sadashiva died in 1567, Tirumala founded the so-called Fourth Dynasty of the empire. Tirumala, however, lacked the military force as well as the prestige to impose his will. In the manner of Indian empires, the Vijayanagar state did not so much disappear as slowly disintegrate, its authority fragmented among dozens of petty local kings.

In the far south, though, some remnants of the old empire persisted: the nayaks, successors of Vijayanagar's imperial officials. They had won independence in the wake of the empire's collapse. In Madurai, Tanjore, and elsewhere, they maintained flourishing local dynasties; and in 1639, when the first English traders in India were granted title to Fort Saint George, Madras, it was on the authority of one Shri Ranga Raya IV, nayak of Kalahasti, who styled himself king of Vijayanagar much as some European ruler of the Dark Ages might have invoked the name of the Roman Empire to embellish his title. The fame of the vanished empire still commanded respect—so much so that its name appeared on land grants as late as the eighteenth century, by which time English traders were hacking out a vigorous empire of their own.

As for the imperial city itself, it was never repopulated as a major urban center. Its empty, mutilated temples and palaces became the domain of monkeys and lizards. But the stone-cut water channels remained, their solid construction proof against devastation. Amid the shattered monuments was good, green, fertile land, once a few seasons' rain had completed the ruin of the streets. The imperial capital's gardens and bazaars fell to the region's stolid farmers, and the marvels of its stonework became mere obstacles to the plow.

The first western Europeans to gaze upon the city of Tenochtitlán, less than a century after it had become the center of the most powerful state in Middle America, were entranced by its beauty. One of the Europeans, the conquistador Bernal Díaz del Castillo, later wrote that "these great towns and pyramids and buildings rising from the water, all made of stone, seemed like an enchanted vision. . . . It was all so wonderful that I do not know how to describe this first glimpse of things never heard of, seen, or dreamed of before."

Díaz was writing about the capital of one of two great New World empires that, without any contact with or knowledge of each other, rose to dominance in the course of the fifteenth century. Both empires—one in what is now Mexico, the other stretching along the western rim of South America—had complex social structures and constructed sizable cities: Tenochtitlán itself was probably larger than any European capital of its day. Their arts and crafts achieved high levels of sophistication, yet they had neither wheeled vehicles nor ironwork, and the only script used was pictographic, which was beautiful to look at but very cumbersome as a method of conveying information. Both societies showed care and ingenuity in providing for their people, while also practicing ritual human sacrifice—in one case, on a scale never equaled. These alternative worlds, sometimes eerily echoing features of Eurasian cultures, sometimes startlingly original, were the empires of the Aztecs and the Incas, which within a few decades of the year 1500 were, with the arrival of the Spanish conquerors, destroyed.

The story of the Aztecs—the builders of the city of Tenochtitlán—had begun a little more than two centuries before, when they had arrived in the fertile Valley of Mexico as an impoverished band of barbarians, dressed in rough sisal clothing and devoutly bearing the image of their tribal god, Huitzilopochtli. The Aztecs had been forced to leave their homeland to the northwest by climatic changes that had turned their productive fields into inhospitable desert. Other tribes from the same area beat out the Aztecs in the scramble for the choice farmland in the Valley of Mexico, and during the decades between 1220 and 1260 founded city-states on the fringes of Lake Texcoco. These rival tribes filled the vacuum left by the collapse of the Toltec empire and soon dominated the refugee remnants of that civilization through military might. A handful of surviving Toltec city-states, such as Xicochimalco and Colhuacán, managed to hold their own into the new age, impressing the conquering immigrants with their culture and traditions. Their proud rulers adapted to the changed circumstances by graciously allowing their daughters to marry incoming chiefs. Gradually, a way of living was established.

When the Aztecs first made their appearance, they were regarded by the other

Portrayed life-size in ceramic, an Aztec warrior wears the parade uniform of the Eagle Knights, an exclusive military order dedicated to the sun god Huitzilopochtli. The feathered costumes, complete with eagle-head helmets and wings, were donned for ceremonies at which the knights performed ritual dances; on the battlefield, more practical—if less elaborate—suits of quilted cotton armor about an inch thick protected the soldiers, who in the course of the fifteenth century carved out an extensive Middle American empire.

The two great civilizations of fifteenth-century America developed in total ignorance of each other's existence, separated by more than 1,550 miles of mountain and jungle *(above)*. The Inca empire, centered in Cuzco in present-day Peru, stretched over 2,175 miles of the Andean region of western South America. The Aztecs dominated most of present-day Mexico from their capital of Tenochtitlán. Within their domains, however, they tolerated the existence of independent enclaves such as Tlaxcala and Huexotzinco *(below)*, because these were a convenient source of an indispensable commodity: prisoners of war to sacrifice to the gods.

occupants of the valley as little more than squatters, who maintained such primitive customs as stealing women from their neighbors and cutting off their enemies' ears. Moved on from one patch to another, they eventually took service under King Coxcox of Colhuacán, first as serfs and then as mercenary soldiers. In 1323, the monarch agreed to the marriage of his daughter to the Aztec chief.

The Aztecs had assimilated the local belief in Toltec cultural superiority, but their desire to imitate their overlords did not prevent them from continuing with their own tribal rituals. Hoping to ingratiate themselves with Xipe Totec, the "Flayed One," they welcomed the Colhuacán princess and then ritually sacrificed her and flayed her. King Coxcox, arriving to witness her wedding, was aghast to find an Aztec priest wearing her skin as a dance costume.

Having outraged their benefactor, the Aztecs—still probably numbering in the hundreds, rather than thousands—fled, finally taking refuge on a small, remote, and desolate island surrounded by marshes in western Lake Texcoco. According to legend, they found there an eagle seated on a prickly pear cactus holding a serpent in its beak—a long-awaited sign predicted by their priests as indicating the site of their future capital. One legend has it that they named the settlement Tenochtitlán after Tenoch, the leader who had first brought them to the Valley of Mexico. There they built a small temple in honor of Huitzilopochtli.

In time, the site's many disadvantages were overcome and even turned to the Aztecs' favor. The small island, well defended by the waters of the lake, was extended by reclaiming mud banks and marshes. Rectangular artificial islands, called *chinampas,* were made by anchoring piled-up mats of cut water reed with stakes and planting willow saplings to secure the mats. Rich sediment, dredged from the lake, was dumped on top to form fertile garden plots producing at least two crops of corn, beans, tomatoes, chili peppers, and other staples each year. Food supplies were thus

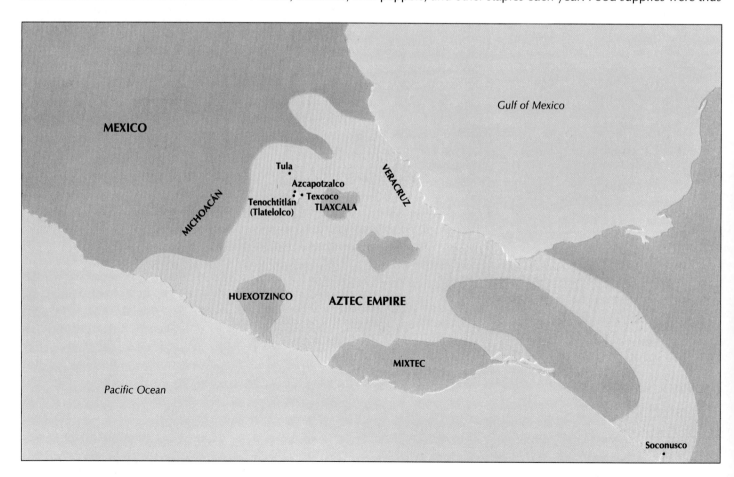

ensured, and the settlement could expand: By the year 1500, Tenochtitlán had grown to an area of about six square miles.

The Aztecs' reputation as fierce fighters—they would eventually style themselves Warriors of the Sun—also helped to secure their island stronghold. In the mid-fourteenth century, the Aztecs were only one of about twenty groups vying for supremacy in the Valley of Mexico; each group was organized as a city-state, with populations that may have averaged as many as 10,000 people. Rulers of one of the most powerful, Azcapotzalco on the western shore of the lake, employed the Aztecs as mercenaries, paying them with a share of the spoils of war. Later, as allies, the Warriors of the Sun were rewarded with territory on the mainland.

In the service of Azcapotzalco, the Aztecs acquired both a formidable knowledge of military matters and many of the trappings of a civilized state. With the encouragement of their allies, their society metamorphosed from a tribal chieftaincy into a hierarchical monarchy whose ruler was elected from the hereditary nobility. But as the Aztecs grew in power and ambition, they became increasingly unhappy with their inferior status. Led by their fourth king, Itzcoatl (Obsidian Snake), they decided to annihilate their erstwhile masters. With pent-up fury, they sacked the city of Azcapotzalco in 1428, committing brutal massacres in retaliation for what they saw as eighty years of subjugation. They took over the tributes from all the city-states formerly dominated by Azcapotzalco, thereby gaining vast riches and enormous influence. At a stroke, the Aztecs had become the greatest power in Mexico, and from that point on, their history was one of near-continuous military expansion.

In the first dozen years of Aztec ascendancy, Tenochtitlán was enlarged, and a new temple pyramid bearing twin shrines to Huitzilopochtli and Tlaloc, the ancient Mexican rain god, was built and decorated with multicolored murals painted on mud plaster. Skilled engineers from Texcoco, an allied neighboring state that had assisted the Aztecs in toppling their overlords, subsequently helped design a ten-mile-long dike that prevented the brackish waters of the eastern end of the lake from contaminating the freshwater zone where chinampa cultivation flourished. Other major hydraulic engineering schemes included canals, dams, and a double-channeled stone aqueduct three miles long, which ran into the center of the Aztec capital.

All these public works were completed during the twenty-nine-year reign of Motecuhzoma Ilhuicamina, who, ten years after his accession in 1440, had to face the biggest natural disaster to befall Aztec Mexico. An appalling drought began in 1450 and lasted for two years, bringing terrible privation and hunger to his people. Wild beasts prowled the city streets looking for human prey, and many Aztecs sold themselves into slavery in the Gulf Coast area of present-day Veracruz, where rainfall was plentiful, in order to escape starvation.

Priests assured the king that the drought was a punishment sent by the gods, who were dissatisfied with the number and quality of the human sacrifices offered to them. More victims were needed, the priests insisted, and the traditional Aztec way of obtaining these was through war. An arrangement was therefore made for battles to be staged by appointment between the Aztecs and the independent states of Tlaxcala and Huexotzinco, which also needed living captives for sacrifices. Thus began the Flowery Wars, in which prisoners were taken for that purpose but no territory changed hands. When the drought ended, it was believed that the increased bloodshed had assuaged the thirst of the gods.

SYMBOLS OF DISTINCTION

Personal adornment was a clear sign of status in Aztec society; what men and women wore was strictly controlled by the state. Ordinary people went unornamented, while aristocrats were allowed to flaunt gold, gems, jaguar and ocelot pelts, and tropical bird plumes.

Members of the ruling class perforated the flesh of their heads in order to insert beautifying ornaments that proclaimed their standing. Holes in earlobes were gradually enlarged until disks up to two inches across could be worn in them by adults. A lord was entitled to have the septum of his nose perforated, in order to hang from it a large pendant that in some cases almost covered the mouth. Noblemen also wore elaborate labrets, or lip plugs *(below).*

The prestige associated with facial decoration was such that similar markings were featured regularly on images of the gods. Large ear and nose ornaments, for example, adorn a head of the moon goddess, Coyolxauhqui *(right),* standing two and one-half feet high and made of greenstone, the most highly prized material in the Aztec world. The decorations on her cheeks—stylized bells and the Aztec symbol for gold (a cross with four dots)—were especially for the goddess, whose name meant "She of the Golden Bells."

This bird-headed labret *(above)* was made from rock crystal and gold by Mixtec craftsworkers, the most skilled jewelers in the Aztec empire. As shown at right, it was worn below the lower lip, projecting more than two inches out. It was held in place by a gold flange that fit inside the mouth.

In the meantime, the exiles in Veracruz had been sending home valuable military intelligence about the tropical coastal region. The information would help the Aztecs win their first campaign outside the Valley of Mexico. Aztec ambitions next lay to the west, but there Motecuhzoma's grandson, Axayacatl, was unsuccessful. His army was defeated by the warriors of the kingdom of Michoacán, who prevented any growth in that direction. Axayacatl did, however, manage to remove a small but irritating thorn in Tenochtitlán's side: He attacked the trading city of Tlatelolco, which was located on an island only a few hundred yards to the north of the Aztec capital. Trumped-up charges of insulting behavior by Tlatelolco market women—who were reported to have bared their buttocks in a gesture of contempt for their neighbors from the more powerful state—provided Axayacatl with the necessary pretext for going to war; victory for Tenochtitlán ended a 128-year-long rivalry between the two cities, which were then merged.

Over the course of the century, the Aztecs were almost undefeated in a series of campaigns against rival city-states; Michoacán in the west was their only failure. By the year 1500, they had won control of almost all of central Mexico and the Gulf Coast, as well as much of the southern area of the country and a portion of the Pacific coastal territory.

The empire they constructed was not tightly controlled, and Aztec rulers spent much of their time suppressing revolts. Their last king, Motecuhzoma Xocoyotzin—better known as Montezuma, the name bestowed on him by the Spaniards—was more of a philosopher than a warlord. He might well have made the empire more bureaucratic and less warlike had his rule not been abruptly ended in 1520 after the arrival of Spanish soldiers under Hernán Cortés, whose coming was to spell the destruction of Aztec civilization. As it was, Montezuma did manage to transform Tenochtitlán into a beautiful and well-run city.

By the time of the Spanish conquest, the Aztec capital was the home of as many as 200,000 people. Nobles, priests, warriors, traders, artisans, laborers, porters, and serfs lived in a city that was five times as populous as the London of Henry VIII, Montezuma's contemporary. The Spaniards compared it to Venice, because Tenochtitlán was a city of canals. Thousands of canoes thronged the grid of waterways that formed its streets, and the surrounding lake bustled with small craft shuttling between the island and the shore.

Three causeways linked Tenochtitlán to the mainland. They were pierced at intervals by channels that allowed currents to circulate; the wooden bridges spanning the gaps could be raised if the city was threatened. The approaches to the city were always busy with pedestrians and porters: The Aztecs had no beasts of burden and no wheeled vehicles, and everything that could not be transported by water had to be carried on human backs.

The city itself was divided into four parts by the major thoroughfares, each quarter having its own temple and military leader. Within the quarters, the city was subdivided into eighty or ninety local wards, the residential areas of the city. Here, white, single-story, flat-roofed houses presented windowless facades to the streets and canals. Gateways in the walls led to inner patios, often adorned with carefully tended flower gardens, onto which the rooms opened. The streets were kept spotlessly clean; rubbish was dumped on the city outskirts, and sewage from the reed-walled public latrines was either flushed away by the lake currents or else collected and sold by the boatload as fertilizer for the chinampas.

The principal marketplace was in the northern part of the city—the former Tlatelolco. On an average day, 25,000 buyers and sellers thronged the town square, increasing to 50,000 for the special markets held at five-day intervals. "We were astounded," wrote Díaz, a companion of Cortés's, "at the great number of people and quantities of merchandise, and at the orderliness and good arrangements that prevailed. . . . Every kind of merchandise was kept separate and had a fixed place marked for it." Luxury items such as gold, silver, precious stones, and feather cloaks were for sale, as were those unfortunate citizens who, due to poverty, had contracted themselves into lifelong servitude as slaves. Cotton and sisal clothing was available, together with sisal rope and sandals. Pelts of puma, jaguar, deer, and otter were displayed, alongside live animals for the pot: turkeys, ducks, and rabbits, as well as plump little dogs bred especially for the table.

The Aztecs had no coinage, so all transactions in the market took the form of barter. Cacao beans—scarce, and therefore precious—were sometimes used as a standard unit of value, as were goose quills filled with gold dust. According to Díaz, "they used to reckon their accounts with one another by the length and thickness of these little quills, how much so many cloaks or so many gourds of chocolate, or so many slaves, were worth, or anything else they were bartering." Three market inspectors were always on duty to regulate prices and to check the honesty of the dealers, all of whom were taxed, primarily in corn to keep the army provided with food.

Towering over the streets, their tops so high that the commotion of the marketplace was but a murmur, loomed the massive temple pyramids bearing the brightly painted sanctuaries of the gods. Each quarter had its own temple, but the national shrine, the most important in the empire, lay at the very center of the city. This was the white-paved Sacred Precinct, dominated by the 130-foot-high pyramid with the twin shrines of Huitzilopochtli and Tlaloc. Steep staircases, stained with the blood of sacrificial victims, led to the holy places of the gods, where their images, encrusted with gold and precious stones, were served by priests garbed in black, their hair matted with blood and their tongues and ears shredded by continual rituals of self-mutilation. In front of the images stood stone blocks on which human sacrifices were offered up to the gods. Díaz, who was taken to the shrines by Montezuma himself, also noted "some smoking braziers of their incense, which they call copal, in which they were burning the hearts of three Indians they had sacrificed that day." He added that "all the walls of that shrine were so splashed and caked with blood that they, and the floor too, were black. Indeed, the whole place stank abominably."

The Great Temple may have disgusted the Spaniards, but to the Aztecs it was both beautiful and awesome. It was rebuilt at least seven times, ever larger and ever more lavishly decorated with painting and sculpture. The Aztec kings transferred to the Great Temple carvings from ancient temples in the old Toltec capital of Tula, fifty miles to the northwest, as well as masks made of jade and

146

hardstone that had survived from earlier Mexican civilizations, to add the authority of antiquity to their work. The shrines also incorporated dedicatory caches of rare and valuable objects, including crocodile and jaguar heads, along with coral and conch shells from the Gulf Coast.

Other temples were dedicated to lesser divinities: Xipe Totec, the "Flayed One"; Coatlicue, "She of the Serpent Skirt"; Tezcatlipoca, "Smoking Mirror"; and Quetzalcoatl, "Plumed Serpent." In the center of the Sacred Precinct, near the foot of the great pyramid, was placed a low platform on which stood a rack. On it, tens of thousands of human heads were skewered as a macabre record of all the sacrifices made in the precinct.

Near the Sacred Precinct was another site of great symbolic and divinatory significance. The Ball Court was an arena shaped like a capital letter "i," with walls inclining at an angle of roughly forty-five degrees, on which a ritual game was played before ranks of spectators. The details of the game have been lost, but it is known that the players formed teams and wore padded clothing; their aim was to hit a ball of solid rubber with their elbows, hips, shoulders, or knees, but apparently not with their hands or feet, toward stone rings set high on the walls of the court. A goal was a great event; the watchers celebrated it by giving jewelry and clothing to the scorer. Points could be scored by means other than goals, but the system on which they were awarded is no longer understood. It is believed that the game owed its ritual significance to an identification of the ball with the sun. The game had been played by the Toltecs, who regularly sacrificed players; the Aztecs, it seems, did so rarely, if at all.

The imperial palace stood beyond the Snake Wall to the south of the Sacred Precinct. Two stories high, its buildings were grouped around central gardens fragrant with the scent of exotic flowers and medicinal plants. It was so vast that one visitor described it as being like a small town. Cortés wrote that it was "almost impossible to describe its beauty and magnificence."

The emperor, whose palace this was, was selected from the royal line by a council of nobles, senior warriors, and priests, the succession normally passing from brother to brother before descending to the next generation. His power was nearly absolute. Advised by four principal lords, he concerned himself with foreign diplomacy, war, and tribute. As the highest legal authority in the land, he presided in the most difficult law cases. Internal affairs of state were handled by a close relative, who served as a kind of grand vizier.

Surrounded by 3,000 servants, two wives, and many concubines, the king lived in the upper story of the palace. On the ground floor was kept much of the state's wealth, in the form of gold, jade, clothing, corn, beans, and other foodstuffs. Here, too, were the most secure prisons, the high courts of justice, and the meeting places of the Council of War, responsible for military planning. Visiting foreign rulers and other dignitaries were lavishly entertained in luxurious halls where midday banquets were served on finely painted multicolored pottery. Guests chose from among some thirty dishes, including delicacies such as axolotl (a kind of salamander lacking hard bones) served with yellow peppers, fish garnished with cherrylike fruits, and winged ants. The emperor sat alone at a table covered with a cloth, shielded from sight because no one was supposed to see him eat. During the banquets, singers, dancers, and musicians performed, along with acrobats, jugglers, and dwarfs, retained as curiosities in the royal household.

Like many monarchs, the Aztec rulers also kept a menagerie. Birds of prey, pumas,

BLOODY RITES TO NOURISH THE SUN

The four-tiered Great Temple at Tenochtitlán was crowned with two shrines. One, decorated in blue, was dedicated to Tlaloc, the rain god. A chacmool figure outside received the hearts of his victims. The other sanctuary was painted red and had a frieze of human skulls. It belonged to the sun god Huitzilopochtli, whose victims were sacrificed on a stone block.

Human sacrifice was central to Aztec civilization. Each year between 10,000 and 20,000 victims met their ends in religious rituals, usually conducted on the top of temple pyramids *(left)*. The Aztecs regarded such ceremonies as essential to their survival; without the spilling of human blood and the offering of human hearts to nourish the sun and other gods, the world, they believed, would be destroyed.

Most of those chosen for sacrifice were men, usually prisoners of war. Methods of killing varied according to which god was being honored. Victims for Xipe Totec, the god of springtime and the patron of goldsmiths, were ritually killed by warriors and then flayed. Their skins were then worn by priests for twenty days.

The most common form of sacrifice, however, was employed in honor of the sun god Huitzilopochtli. Wearing only a loincloth, the victim was usually painted with vertical red and white stripes. He climbed the steep stairway that adorned the front of the temple, ascending to the platform in front of the god's shrine, where he was seized by four long-haired priests. Taking one limb each, they stretched their prey over a stone block twenty inches high. A fifth priest, wielding a razor-sharp stone knife, made a swift sideways stroke across the exposed chest, cutting through the breastbone and ribs. The still-beating heart was wrenched out and held aloft to the sun, and the god's image was anointed with fresh, warm blood.

Usually the hearts were placed in stone vases, but those offered to the rain god, Tlaloc, were placed in vessels held by *chac-*

mools, stone carvings of reclining male figures, their heads averted, holding receptacles on their bellies. The victim's body was allowed to roll down the pyramid steps to the plaza, where it was decapitated and its head skewered on a wooden framework known as the skull rack.

A very few important victims were chosen to impersonate the gods. For example, a physically perfect youth was selected annually to become the incarnation of Tezcatlipoca. Throughout the year, he lived a life of pleasure; he was taught to play the flute, wore gold jewelry and priceless clothes, smoked tobacco, and was revered by all. Twenty days before the sacrifice, he was married to four young women. When the day itself dawned, he mounted the temple steps, breaking a clay flute on each step until, at the top, he was seized and his heart ripped out. Young women were similarly chosen to impersonate the corn goddess; they were eventually decapitated to symbolize the harvest of ears of corn.

Shown from three different angles, a statuette portrays Xipe Totec wearing skin flayed from the face, torso, and arms of a sacrificial victim.

jaguars, coyotes, foxes, and wildcats filled its cages. Díaz, who visited the zoo, was particularly impressed by the emperor's rattlesnakes—previously unknown to Europeans—which, he reported, "are kept in jars and large pots, with a great many feathers, and it is there that they lay their eggs and bring up their little serpents." On the whole he found the place alarming: "When the tigers and lions roared, and the wolves and foxes howled and the serpents hissed, it was dreadful to hear and one would have thought oneself in hell."

The palace and its attendant marvels all served to emphasize the power and magnificence of the reigning monarch, which his subjects were never allowed to forget. In public appearances he was a splendid sight, carried in a litter and wearing a cloak of dyed cotton, embroidered and decorated with feathers, and sandals heavily ornamented with gold. Gold, jade, turquoise, and feather jewelry adorned him, and he was crowned with a breathtakingly elaborate feather headdress.

Although no other individual cut as fine a figure as the king, dress immediately signaled the rank of the wearer throughout Aztec society. It was easy to pick out commoners, the bulk of the population, who wore cloaks of coarse sisal over the loincloths that were their only other garments. The grades of warriors and nobles could be identified by the degree of sumptuousness in their costumes and insignia. Some displayed their status and wealth by wearing several brilliantly colored cloaks on top of one another, carefully tied so as to display the underlying layers.

In the early days of the Aztec empire, the nobility was a nonhereditary caste whose members drew their position directly from the king, who provided them with the great agricultural estates that were the source of their wealth; the estates reverted to the king on their deaths. As time passed, however, the king more often granted titles to such estates to the holders' heirs, and by the latter part of the fifteenth century, hereditary landowning at the king's discretion was the norm among the noble classes.

There were two ways for a man to achieve high position in Aztec society. One way required education at one of the half-dozen elite schools attached to the temples at Tenochtitlán; the prerequisite for gaining entrance to the schools was usually noble birth, because they were open primarily to the children of the ruling class. Youngsters began their studies when they were about six years old, being taught the manners of polite society and how to speak well in the elliptical manner favored for public oratory. They also learned the sacred songs, astrology, calendrical computation, and how to interpret dreams. The boys spent much time in prayer and fasting, enduring nightlong vigils and offering blood sacrifices to the gods by piercing their tongues and ears. Through these activities—and through punishments such as being forced to inhale the choking fumes of fires that contained fiercely hot red chili peppers—students learned self-control and self-discipline, traits highly valued in Aztec society. They then were virtually guaranteed a secure future in the upper ranks of government or the priesthood.

The second way of rising in rank was open to commoners as well as to nobles: through excellence as a warrior. All Aztec men were trained for war from childhood; indeed, when the midwife cut the umbilical cord on a newborn boy, the ritual phrases she intoned included: "Dear son . . . you must understand that your home is not where you have been born, for you are a warrior . . . your mission is to give the sun the blood of enemies to drink." It was traditional for a boy to have his hair cut short at about his tenth birthday, but a lock of hair on the nape of the neck was left long; it could be cut only when he had taken a prisoner on the battlefield, after

This ceramic stamp in the form of a dancing monkey was coated with paint and used to imprint an image either on textiles or on the body as decoration. In its vigorous high spirits, the animal symbolized for the Aztecs the pleasures of life and the associated dangers of sensual indulgence.

which he was entitled to wear dyed and embroidered clothes. The capture or slaughter of four enemies promoted a soldier to the rank of commander, with the privileges of wearing a feather headdress and leather bracelets and of occupying a seat on the Council of War.

The pinnacle of a military career was to become a member of one of two exclusive military orders. A successful warrior might become an Eagle Knight, a soldier of the sun entitled to wear a helmet in the form of an eagle's head; or he might join the Jaguar Knights, becoming one of the god of war's soldiers, who wore jaguar skins as their insignia. Promotions to the orders were conferred by the emperor at an annual parade, at which he also awarded other tokens of distinction, including plugs that could be inserted into perforations in the lower lip, disk-shaped shields covered in heraldic featherwork, wooden sword-clubs with razor-sharp obsidian blades, piles of cloaks and loincloths, and the revenues of estates.

There was one other way, besides engaging in war or gaining an education, to amass great wealth, though not government position. Beginning in the early 1400s, guilds of long-distance traders called *pochteca* started to take charge of a monopoly that controlled the importation of cotton from the Gulf Coast and elsewhere to Tenochtitlán, and although they were commoners, the members of the guild became wealthy. These merchants formed a distinct class in the cities, living together in special districts, passing on the profession from father to son, and marrying only into other pochteca families. They enjoyed the privileges of having their own courts and of sending their sons to the temple schools. These merchants were careful not to flaunt their wealth and offend the emperor: After a profitable trading expedition, they would discreetly slip back into the capital by night, so that darkness might conceal their treasures.

During the course of the fifteenth century, their markets expanded, and caravans of porters led by intrepid pochteca traveled hundreds of miles from the capital carrying stocks of city-manufactured goods: knives wrought of obsidian, rabbit-fur blankets, cochineal dye, medicinal herbs, and finely made clothes. In exchange, they sought luxurious foreign commodities such as jade, seashells, jaguar skins and puma pelts, and lustrous green tail feathers from the forest bird known as the quetzal.

Trading missions could last for months, even years, and they were dangerous. Often disguised in native costume and speaking the local language, the pochteca gathered not only luxuries for the royal palaces but military intelligence. Sometimes they acted as agents provocateurs, for the Aztecs frequently used attacks on pochteca

Some of the finest Aztec sculptures represented animals, usually with symbolic religious associations. The coiled rattlesnake *(top)*, for example, was linked with Coatlicue, an earth-mother goddess who wore a skirt of braided snakes. Dogs *(middle)* were thought to help the spirits of the dead pass through the underworld and were often sacrificed at funerals. Grasshoppers *(bottom)* were less frequently portrayed; this one may represent Chapultepec, the Hill of the Green Grasshopper, the first area of settlement near Lake Texcoco.

as an excuse for declaring war on other states. Conquest thus followed the merchants' caravans, and trade became tribute.

Warfare was inextricably built into the structure of Aztec society. The upper classes were convinced that they had a divine mandate to conquer and exact tribute from lesser peoples. In the words of an Aztec poet, "You have been sent into warfare. War is your reward, your task."

Aztec warfare was formalized. Before battle began, at least three attempts were made to negotiate the enemy's surrender and the terms of tribute that would be paid. If these failed, the army took to the field on foot. Díaz reported that warriors were gorgeously dressed in "cotton armor richly worked on the outside with different-colored feathers, which they used as devices and distinguishing marks, and they had casques and helmets made of wood and bone, which were also highly decorated with feathers on the outside." For arms, the Aztecs used small swords set with obsidian blades, bows and arrows, javelins, throwing sticks, and slings.

There was usually no attempt at a surprise attack. Priests would blow blasts on conch-shell trumpets and shrill whistles, then veterans would lead the warriors forward, shouting battle cries. Engagements consisted of many skirmishes between individual warriors seeking only to incapacitate each other, since the aim was less to kill the enemy than to return home with as many prisoners as possible. Behind the ranks of soldiers came special units whose job was to tie up the wounded before they regained consciousness. The enemy acknowledged defeat when their city temple had been taken and burned; indeed, the sign for "conquest" in Aztec picture writing was a blazing, toppled temple.

Conquered peoples were forced to recognize the Aztecs as overlords and to pay taxes. Tribute demands were heavy: The province of Soconusco, about 800 miles away, had to send five and one-half tons of cacao beans every six months, together with such luxury items as ocelot skins and live eagles. The Aztecs depended on these deliveries for their very survival; records kept by Aztec scribes show that Tenochtitlán, despite the fecundity of its chinampas, still found it necessary to import food as well as luxuries. Each year more than 7,500 tons of corn and almost 4,500 tons of beans were sent in as tribute, along with about two million cotton cloaks.

It was, therefore, not surprising that rebellions frequently broke out in provinces suffering such penal taxation. Insurrection was made easier because the Aztecs made no attempt to assimilate newly won territories, imposing neither their language nor their customs on defeated states. Local ruling dynasties were frequently allowed to remain in power, a practice that provided new leaders for later revolts. The Aztec empire exercised, in fact, little more than hegemony over the

The Aztecs adorned images of their gods with stone masks that served to give the figures their identities. The gaping visage below represented Xipe Topec, the deity of spring and new growth and the patron of goldsmiths, while the staring face opposite was that of Tezcatlipoca, the evil magician who was the god of war. Carved above his temple are glyphs spelling out his name, which means "Smoking Mirror"—possibly a reference to techniques of divination associated with his cult.

defeated city-states, which needed frequent reconquest to keep them securely under the thumb of the imperial overlord.

The fact was that warfare was less a political instrument for the Aztecs than a religious rite. Death on the battlefield was considered honorable, something to be sought. In the words of an Aztec song:

> There is nothing like death in war,
> Nothing like the Flowery Death,
> So precious to him who gives life.
> Far off I see it: My heart yearns for it.

Every Aztec fighter believed that the spirits of warriors killed in battle went directly to the paradise of the sun god, to accompany him through the sky in the form of hummingbirds. This was infinitely preferable to the fate awaiting almost everyone else, since the Aztecs conceived of the universe as a series of vertically stacked disks, to the very lowest of which the great majority of civilians could expect to descend in the afterlife. This realm was known as the Region of the Dead, Where the Streets Are on the Left, the left being associated by the Aztecs with bad luck; its rulers were the Lord and Lady of the Dead, hellish counterparts of the creator god, Ometeotl.

One of the convictions central to the faith of the Aztecs was a solar myth that fueled the attitude toward warfare—and, as a matter of fact, made the waging of war a necessity. The Aztecs believed that the mother of the sun god Huitzilopochtli first gave birth to the moon and 400 stars. She then became pregnant with the sun, who was sired by a ball of feathers. Jealous of their unborn brother, the stars, egged on by their sister, the moon, cut off their mother's head. Huitzilopochtli then emerged from her womb fully grown and fully armed, slew his half brothers and cut his half sister into little pieces.

This mythical drama was, to Aztec eyes, reenacted daily with the rising of the sun. Huitzilopochtli needed food if he was to beat his enemies and continue to nourish the earth. Unless he was fed with the hearts and blood of brave captives, he would fail to rise and the human race would perish. Hence the Aztecs' constant need for large numbers of prisoners of war. It has been estimated that 10,000 people were sacrificed every year; and on one special occasion, the rededication of the newly enlarged Great Temple, as many as 20,000 people died in the course of a four-day celebration.

The most common method of sacrifice was for the victim to be held by four priests, who stretched him

 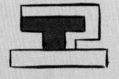  

| ALLIGATOR | WIND | HOUSE | LIZARD | SERPENT |

TIME CHARTS OF THE APOCALYPSE

The Aztecs had two separate systems for measuring the passage of time, both based on the ideas of earlier Mexican civilizations. One was the solar year, divided into eighteen months of twenty days, with an additional five "unlucky" days added on at the end to bring the total to 365. The other was the Sacred Almanac, a 260-day cycle based on a combination of the numbers 1 to 13 with twenty named days *(below)*. This calendar was used only for divination and astrology, and for the most part it operated independently of the solar year system.

Once every fifty-two years, however, the start of the two cycles coincided. The Aztecs believed it to be an occasion of ill omen and cosmic danger, during which the universe was at risk of destruction and elaborate precautions had to be taken in order to avert catastrophe. A page from an Aztec manuscript *(right),* later annotated by a Spanish scholar, shows some of the safeguards and preventive measures that were regarded as necessary.

The Sacred Almanac system can be pictured as two interlocking cogwheels. One bore numerals from 1 to 13, indicated as dots. The other had the name-signs of the twenty days, seen at the top and bottom of these pages. Here, the date shown where the wheels connect is *1 Alligator;* the next would be *2 Wind.* Names and numbers had special qualities: *2 Rabbit,* for example, was unlucky, as was any date with the numbers 4, 5, 6, 8, or 9.

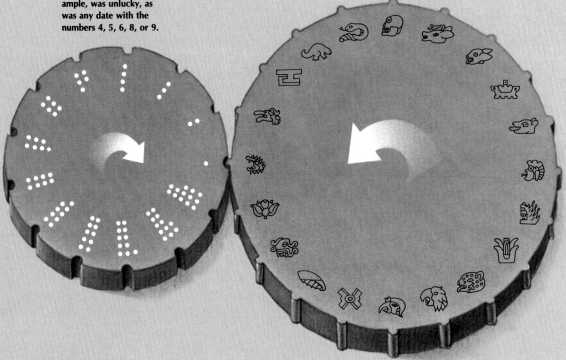

| MONKEY | GRASS | REED | JAGUAR | EAGLE |

DEATH

DEER

RABBIT

WATER

DOG

Footprints from a green mound representing the Hill of the Star, south of Tenochtitlán near Colhuacán, indicate the route to the site of the rekindling fires *(center)*.

Pregnant women were considered especially at risk at the end of a cycle, and particular care was taken to protect them. Here, an expectant mother is shown taking shelter inside a large grain pot, guarded by a warrior bearing a shield and a wooden club set with razor-sharp obsidian blades.

All fires were extinguished in the danger period and then ritually relighted. Four priests, one for each point of the compass, are shown rekindling fagots that will light fires anew in temples across the empire.

Aztec legend claimed that children could be transformed into rats in the danger period and might then attack people. Here, an armed soldier protects women carrying masks to hide their identities against such an assault.

VULTURE

MOVEMENT

FLINT KNIFE

RAIN

FLOWER

over the sacrificial block at the summit of the temple pyramid. A fifth then took a flint knife and cut out the man's heart, throwing it into a brazier where it burned for the nourishment of the god. Victims met their deaths in silence or, sometimes, with rejoicing, as they, like warriors killed in war, were assured of a place in the sun god's heaven. Some prisoners even declined an offer of clemency, preferring the fate known as the Flowery Death.

Other gods also received sacrifices, usually by methods appropriate to their attributes: Children were drowned as offerings to the rain god, and the fire god's victims were made insensible with intoxicating drugs and thrown alive onto pyres. Those singled out as offerings to Xipe Totec, the Flayed One and god of spring, were, like King Coxcox's daughter, tied to a frame, shot with arrows, and finally flayed; the priests then wore the skins for twenty days, by which time, Díaz noted, "they smelled like dead dogs."

The Aztecs were haunted by a fear that the sun would not rise; and they also lived in dread of the cataclysmic ending of the world they knew. According to their cosmology, such an event would not have been unprecedented. They believed, in fact, that four previous epochs of creation had all ended in disaster, each one as a result of a natural catastrophe at the culmination of a fifty-two-year cycle calculated by their astronomers. Fifteenth-century Aztec priests claimed that the world would be destroyed by an earthquake; the only hope of mitigating or delaying the cataclysm lay in appeasing the wrath of the fire god.

The danger period at the end of the then-current fifty-two-year cycle, calculated to occur in 1507 of the Christian calendar, naturally aroused terrible apprehension. The priests prepared instructions for the dreaded day: Fires were to be put out, pregnant women locked in granaries so they wouldn't turn into wild animals, and children kept awake because, if they slept, they might be transformed into rats. Priests waited to see a star or stars—possibly Aldebaran or the Pleiades—pass the zenith, indicating that the world would continue. The priests' prescriptions were followed, and on the top of the Hill of the Star, near Colhuacán, a victim was sacrificed, fire kindled in the cavity where his heart had been, and embers taken from there to relight all other hearths. Such cycles of cosmic threats and narrow escapes were central to the Aztec view of the world.

Worship of a creator god, the sun, moon, and stars was also central to the beliefs of the other great fifteenth-century American state, that of the Inca, which like the Aztec kingdom, developed in isolation. The two American cultures had much in common: Although the Aztecs and the Incas lacked wheeled transport and draft animals, both peoples were skilled engineers and carried out vast public works; and both increased their territory through well-organized military campaigns. The Incas ate corn, beans, and chili peppers, as did the Aztecs, although the Incas also grew potatoes and other tubers. There was, however, one profound difference between the civilizations: While Aztec society was geared primarily to warfare to provide sacrificial victims for the ever-hungry sun, the Inca realm revolved around duty and obligation to the state.

At its height in the early sixteenth century, the Inca empire covered more than 375,000 square miles. It extended along the Andean mountain chain from the southern frontier of present-day Colombia, taking in Ecuador, Peru, Bolivia, and parts of Chile and Argentina. It incorporated about 100 ethnic groups, ranging from the highly civilized Chimu of north Peru to the savage Canari of Ecuador. To hold together this vast empire and to control its mixed population of 32 million people, the Incas created a totalitarian state in which the smallest detail of everyday life, from the sanitary condition of peasants' huts to the work allocated to the blind, was closely controlled by a multitude of bureaucrats.

The founders and rulers of this state probably existed as a distinct people as early as the twelfth century; legend told that they had been taken to their homeland in the Cuzco area of present-day Peru by their first king, or *inca*, Manco Capac. They were then only one of a number of warring tribes in the region, but over the centuries, they seized more territory by force of arms.

The Inca empire properly so called, however, was both created and destroyed in a period of time that spanned less than ninety years. The empire began when a warrior-king named Pachacuti seized the throne from his father in 1438, vanquished the neighboring Chanca people, and set in motion a program of military expansion. His two successors brought vast territories under Inca control. The most important achievement of the first of these, Tupac Yupanqui (who reigned from 1471 to 1493), was the conquest, in 1476, of the highly developed Chimu state of northern coastal Peru. From this campaign, Tupac Yupanqui brought to his capital of Cuzco vast quantities of gold and other riches and large numbers of highly skilled artisans: goldsmiths and silversmiths, weavers and potters. More important, the Incas seem to have adopted some elements of the advanced administrative and communications structure the Chimu had developed to run their own state.

Tupac Yupanqui's son, Huayna Capac, pushed the bounds of the empire even farther north and east. Huayna Capac also invaded the rain forest of the upper Amazon—much to the disgust of his generals and officials, who were used to the drier highland zones of the Andes and to more formal methods of warfare. Thousands perished fruitlessly in the campaign, and in the end, the Incas abandoned the attempt to incorporatè stateless "savages" into their tightly controlled realm. Despite such setbacks, the empire continued to grow until rapidly destroyed, early in the sixteenth century, by civil war, new diseases, and Spanish invaders.

At the center of the empire was the Inca himself, whose role was described by the grandiose titles he assumed: "Unique Inca, Emperor Rich and Powerful in War, Son of the Sun, Liberal and Powerful Lord, Lover and Benefactor of the Poor." Each Inca was seen as the temporary embodiment of a continuing, unending principle of divine kingship. When a reigning Inca died, his body was preserved by mummification and remained in the royal palace, where it was tended, as the Inca had been in life, by numerous servants. Food and drink were regularly offered to the remains. All the wealth and possessions the ruler had enjoyed remained his, only his office passing to his successor. The mummified bodies even continued to play a public role. According to a Spanish chronicler, high officials "brought the royal mummies, lavishly escorted, to all their most important ceremonies. They sat them all down in the plaza in a row, in order of seniority. . . . It was customary for the dead rulers to visit one another, and they held great dances and revelries." Each Inca could go to consult his deceased peers for advice.

Since his predecessor continued to "live" in his original palace, each Inca on his succession had a new one constructed. Often, he was also obliged to acquire new territories to meet the expense of

Stretching from present-day Ecuador to central Chile, the empire of the Incas encompassed extremes of climate and terrain that included rain forest, scorching desert, bleak high-altitude grassland, and snow-covered Andean peaks. A correspondingly large variety of crops were grown, each suiting its environment, but few animals were domesticated. Perhaps the most important was the llama, which provided meat, hides, sinews, and coarse wool, as well as being the only available beast of burden. Small gold llamas like the one below were buried in the graves of nobles.

Quito
CANARI
CHIMU
Amazon, River
Huánuco Pampa
Machu Picchu COLLA
Cuzco
CHANCA
ANDES MOUNTAINS
Pacific Ocean

159

erecting and running it and of supporting his large household. The imperial palace was built of the finest masonry and was decorated with sheets of gold and silver that were hammered onto the stone blocks. The emperor lived in the most secure quarters at the palace center where, each day, he received a constant stream of emissaries and officials reporting from all parts of his vast realm.

The ruler's daily schedule was regimented. He rose early to start on government business, then ate the main meal of the day between eight and nine in the morning; his only other repast was a light supper taken shortly before sunset. Although the Inca did not drink with meals, he imbibed beer made from fermented corn, the nation's favorite alcoholic beverage, after dinner, and he continued to drink until darkness had fallen. He went to bed soon after, sleeping on blankets made of fine vicuna; mattresses were unknown.

The monarch was more extravagant in the matter of dress, since he never wore a garment twice, presenting it to a kinsman after use. The Inca's main symbol of kingship was a fringe of red-dyed vicuna tassels worn around his forehead; his clothes were made of the finest fabrics, and they were woven in exclusive designs. When he appeared in public, he was carried on a litter of fifteen-karat gold borne by twenty specially trained bearers. Periodically, he would go forth from his capital, traveling on imperial tours of the provinces. To carry out the business of the visit, he would sit in state on a red-painted stool placed at the top of a stone platform constructed for him in the square of the provincial capital.

On his accession, each Inca married one of his full sisters, to stress and maintain the exclusiveness of the royal line and to show he was not bound by the rules governing ordinary men, who were forbidden incest. Only children born of this union were legitimate heirs—a situation that might in time have led to the ill effects of inbreeding had Inca rule not been cut short.

The Inca stood at the pinnacle of an enormous social pyramid. Directly under him were the nobles of the royal blood. From them were chosen his most senior counselors—the Prefects of the Four Quarters of the Empire—and the governors of the provinces within each quarter. This was a small and exclusive group, numbering perhaps 500 at the end of the fifteenth century. They were too few to fill all the high posts in the empire, so a class of "Incas by Privilege," appointed by royal mandate, was created to make good the labor shortage.

Both groups received many benefits from the state they served: They paid no taxes; they were subject to their own legal codes; they had the right to wear vicuna and cotton clothing and, most evident, to adorn themselves with large, ornate gold and silver disk-shaped plugs, worn in the pierced and stretched lobes of their ears. Their sons were also assimilated into the ruling system: They were obliged to go for their education to the House of Teaching in Cuzco, as were the sons of provincial chiefs whose territories had been absorbed into the empire. The latter were sent there as much as hostages as to absorb the state-ordered teaching of Inca history and religion and the Quechua language, spoken by the Incas themselves and consequently the official tongue of the empire.

Farther down the social pyramid, an almost endlessly subdivided hierarchy of bureaucrats burgeoned in each province, usually recruited from the ranks of the leading families of the region. At the top were those held responsible to the central government for the supervision of a group of 10,000 households. The next rank of officials was responsible for 5,000 households. To these, in turn, reported the officals

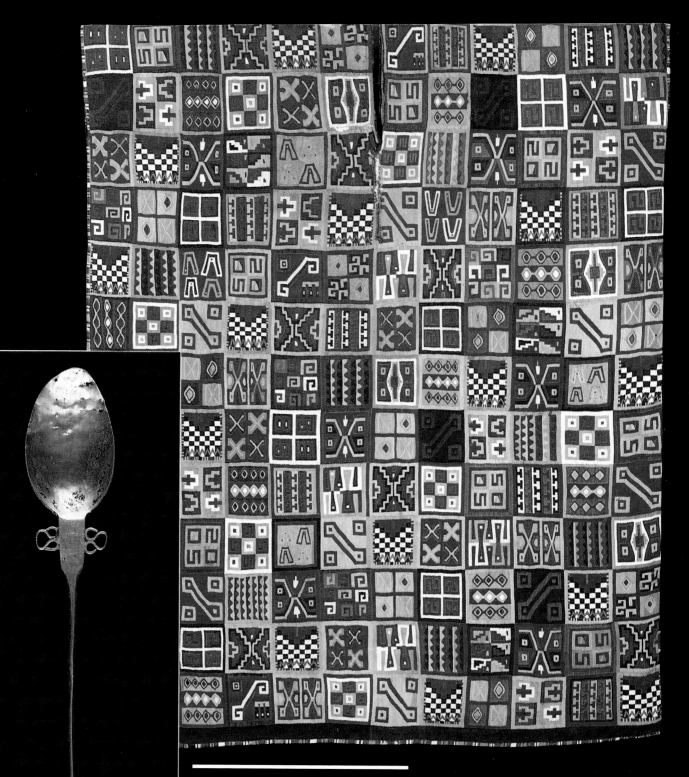

A luxurious tapestry poncholike shirt features a checkerboard pattern of twenty-four textile designs. Only nobles and other privileged members of Inca society were permitted to wear such finery or to possess precious jewelry such as the hammered-gold pin *(left)*.

charged with the care of 1,000 households; below these, Inca society was still further subdivided and administered in units of 500, 100, 50, and finally, 10 households. In all, there were probably about 300,000 bureaucrats, each one answerable to the emperor himself through his representative in the rank immediately above.

Through these officials, the influence of the state reached into every corner of people's lives. The population was carefully counted in regular censuses, and every person was allocated for tax purposes to an appropriate age grade. Young adults had to make the largest contribution, either in goods or in labor, since cash was not used; the old were spared taxes altogether and required to perform only light tasks. Most tax revenues were paid in foodstuffs: Two-thirds of all agricultural crops went to the state. Throughout the empire, the cultivated land was divided into three parts. One-third of the produce was grown for the gods, and one-third for the Inca. Only the final one-third, the last to be planted and harvested, was retained for the direct use of the cultivators themselves.

The land of the gods and of the Inca was planted with great ceremony. According to one Spanish account, "If the Inca himself, or some other high official, happened to be present, he started the work with a golden foot plow . . . and following his example, all did the same. However, the Inca soon stopped working, and after him the other officials and nobles stopped also and sat down with the king to their banquets and festivals, which were especially notable on such days. The common people remained at work. Each man put into his section his children, and wives, and all the people of his house to help him."

Huge quantities of foodstuffs, including corn, beans, potatoes naturally freeze-dried in the icy highlands, and high-altitude grains such as the milletlike quinoa, were kept in state and temple storehouses constructed at the centers of regional government. One warehouse complex at Huanuco Pampa, for example, could hold more than one million bushels of grain. Some of this officially collected produce was sent to Cuzco to support the court and temple officials. The rest was kept in the provinces as a reserve for distribution during famines and for use by the old and disabled, whom the state supported.

Able-bodied commoners also contributed their labor to the state by assisting in public-works programs that included road making, canal digging, constructing agricultural terraces on precipitous mountainsides, and building bridges and temples. Some were sent with their families, often over long distances, to the state-owned gold, silver, tin, and copper mines. There, at high altitudes and in poor conditions, they worked from noon to sunset for four months at a time. Here too, however, the state was mindful of its subjects' welfare. According to one account, "If one of the Indians in the mines got sick, he was allowed to return home at once, and another came to take his place; but none was assigned to the mines unless he was married, so that his wives could look after his food and drink. . . . Besides this, they were permitted to stop several days in the month for their feasts and recreation."

Everyone in the Inca world was expected to make a productive contribution to society, but care was taken to give all men and women work appropriate to their skills and health. Blind people, for example, were kept occupied in the coastal regions picking seeds from cotton bolls; in the highlands, they husked corncobs.

Adult males aged between twenty and fifty could be drafted into the army as part of their labor tax. They were grouped in units of 10 under a sergeant who supervised their training; equipment and supplies came from government stocks. Units of 100 or more were commanded by professional soldiers. Such organization helped the empire grow; assured of supplies, the Incas could field extremely large armies to conquer new territories. Tupac Yupanqui had an army of a quarter of a million troops in the field when he subjugated the Chimu.

Soldiers were equipped with quilted cotton tunics and helmets, and most fought with slings, clubs, maces, and halberds. Some regional detachments used their traditional weapons, as in the case of the forest Indians, who fought with bows and arrows, or the Colla, who used bolas, whirling lengths of rope with stones on the ends thrown to stun and entangle the enemy. Inca armies were no better armed than those of their enemies; their success was based on the security of supplies and their ability to move with great rapidity along the superb network of highways constructed by the state.

There were more than 15,000 miles of these highways, which were reserved for the use of those traveling on official business. This was a land of pack animals and foot travelers, and so each length of road was carefully designed to suit the volume of pedestrian traffic it would bear. Lesser-used thoroughfares, or those constructed through difficult terrain, might be little more than three feet wide, while more-used roads measured more than fifty feet across. The Inca engineers tried, where possible, to build on solid ground but, if required, would build causeways and drainage canals in swampy districts and construct suspension bridges over deep river chasms.

The protruding stone pegs on this wall in the Andean town of Machu Picchu would have served to secure a steeply pitched roof frame, which would then have been thatched over with grass. Niches such as the ones shown here are a common feature of Inca buildings, and seem to have been decorative. Doorways and windows were made in the same shape and design as the niches and, like them, were capped by a single block of stone. Inca masons used hard stone hammers to shape the blocks, working by trial and error to achieve a close fit. The results were so perfectly keyed together that walls would generally settle back into position even after being shaken by earthquakes.

The main routes ran on a north-south axis. The principal coastal road ran wide and straight through the desert that backs the shoreline in Peru, with stone or clay walls on each side to prevent it from being obliterated by the perpetually drifting sand. The second main road lay parallel to it along the Andean chain from Cuzco to Quito, and the two were linked by lesser roads along their entire extent. Rest houses and stores for the use of official travelers were built a day's journey apart along the highways.

To speed the flow of government information, the Inca created a corps of special messengers. It was their job to run in relays along the state roads. Every mile or two, there were stations where a runner passed the message to the next, first announcing his approach by blowing a blast on a conch-shell trumpet. The system worked superbly: A message could travel 150 miles in a day.

Cuzco, where so many of the relayed messages were dispatched or received, was the heart of the empire; its name translates as the "Navel of the World." The social makeup of the city was unusual, since, as the religious and governmental center of the empire, it was inhabited only by the Inca, his nobles, and their servants. Besides the imperial palace, there were at least three major temples serving the state religion.

Arteries of the Incas

To link their far-flung domains, the Incas relied on a network of superbly engineered roads. More than 15,000 miles of highway, used only by travelers on official business, allowed speedy, reliable communications with the central government at Cuzco and the movement of troops and supplies wherever they were needed. Without this infrastructure, the huge and complex Inca state would have collapsed.

The roads were designed for use by foot travelers and llama caravans. State lodgings were located about every ten miles or so, and staging posts were placed every one to two miles. State couriers were assigned to these posts for fifteen-day periods, waiting for runners to arrive with messages, which they would then carry on to the next base.

As there were no wheeled vehicles, the roads were sometimes constructed as zigzag stairways up mountainsides, and precipitous gorges were crossed by the world's earliest suspension bridges. These were made by slinging two twisted sisal cables, each the thickness of a man's thigh, over a pair of stone towers on either side of the chasm and burying the cable ends deep in the ground. The wickerwork or plank bridge floor was suspended by smaller cables, swaying above the torrent.

When Inca Pachacuti transformed Cuzco from a village of mud huts into a stone-built capital city, he gave its groundplan the shape of a gigantic puma. Serving as the head of the beast was a rocky outcrop topped by an enormous fortress that was large enough to shelter all the city's population of about 10,000 people. The tail of the puma was formed by two rivers joining at a narrow angle; the body was filled with great palaces and temples.

In Cuzco, as in other great cities of the empire, the Inca skill in stone construction was proudly displayed. Using only hard stone hammers and such simple abrasives as sand and water, the city's stonemasons cut huge blocks of granite and other stones to size, fitting them so tightly that, even without mortar to secure them, not even a thin knife blade could be pushed between them. Inca stonemasons took pride in the excellence of their work and beveled the exposed edges of blocks to emphasize the closeness of their fit.

Buildings rarely had windows. They were entered through doorways narrowing toward the top, and all, however prestigious, were roofed with grass thatch. The designs for such buildings, and even for whole towns, were worked out in small models, sometimes made of stone, sometimes of clay.

The Inca himself, on whom the life of Cuzco turned, was believed to be descended from the sun, and he therefore played a crucial part in all major religious ceremonies. These took place in the main public square, occupying the space beneath the puma's belly in the city's groundplan. Here, sacrifices of brown llamas to the creator god Viracocha and white llamas to the sun were made each day. Citizens of lesser rank left offerings of cornmeal, guinea pigs, llama fat, and coca leaves. At crucial moments in the empire's history—after a great defeat, an earthquake, during famine or plague—human sacrifices were made. And when a new Inca ascended the throne, as many as 200 physically perfect young boys and girls were feasted, made drunk, and then were strangled or had their throats cut.

Cuzco played a key role in the political control of the empire. The chief noble of each province incorporated into the Inca empire was required to keep a house in the capital and to live there for four months of each year. He also had to staff it with servants from his own land, so the capital became an ethnic microcosm of the entire kingdom. So as to echo the four-part division of the empire, Cuzco was divided into quarters by its major thoroughfares.

The Inca lived in great splendor, surrounded by accouterments befitting his wealth and political preeminence. In addition to the sweet-smelling plants, flowers, and beautiful trees in his palace garden were their replicas fashioned out of gold and silver. One chronicler reported that the models "were done in natural size and style with their leaves, blossoms, and fruits, some beginning to sprout, others half-grown, others in full bloom. Among these and other splendors, they made fields of corn, copying the leaves, cob, stalk, roots, and flowers from life. The beard of the corn husk was done in gold and the rest in silver, the two being soldered together. They made the same distinction in dealing with other plants, using gold to copy the flower or anything else of a yellow tint and silver for the rest."

Some goldwork and silverwork was made by captured Chimu smiths and their descendants, who were kept in the capital and, like all other incorporated groups, obliged to wear their distinctive native dress. The Chimu were probably the most creative craftworkers of the empire. The Inca people themselves had developed a more standardized approach; many of the woven textiles, the handmade pottery vessels, the metal and stone tools, and even the gold and silver figures they made as offerings to the gods were mass-produced by state-supervised workers.

The glories of the monarch's gold-and-silver garden in Cuzco were far removed, in every sense, from the lives of the vast number of commoners who made up the majority of his subjects. Although the common folk could rely on the state to support them in time of need, throughout their lives they were not allowed to own more than was necessary for survival unless permitted to do so by a special license from the emperor. Their daily diet was monotonous: They ate primarily soups and stews made of corn and potatoes and other tubers; and on very rare occasions, they were able to supplement their menus with small quantities of guinea-pig meat or dried llama flesh. Most illuminating of all is the fact that in the Inca legal system there were no fines, because the peasants had nothing with which they could have paid them.

In the year 1500, the Inca monarchy, like the Aztec empire, seemed to be at its height. The appearance of security was to prove illusory. Within thirty-five years, both realms were to fall to conquistadors vastly outnumbered in fighting strength by the indigenous population.

The destruction of the two great civilizations of the Americas was perhaps partly a result of overconfidence; in each case, the rulers apparently came to believe in the myth of their own divine power, and when the Spaniards challenged that belief, both declined into a state of uncomprehending passive resignation. It would, however, be unfair to blame them for that failing; because it was a product of the extraordinary isolation of the two civilizations—isolation from each other and from the rest of the world. Mastery of their own political environment first allowed them to flower in exotic and baroque splendor; then, when the outside world came calling, the limitations of their knowledge and experience left them exposed and at the mercy of imported disease to which they had no immunity, as well as to the swords and guns of a few battle-hardened adventurers. ▬

1400-1410	1410-1420	1420-1430	1430-1440	1440-1450

Aztec warriors under Itzcoatl sack the city of Azcapotzalco, which they had formerly served as mercenaries. The victory marks the emergence of the Aztecs as the greatest power in the Valley of Mexico (1428).

Seizing power from his father, Pachacuti embarks on a career of conquest that lays the foundation of the Inca empire (1438).

Montezuma I ascends the throne. In the course of a twenty-eight-year reign, he stantially enlarges the emp (1440).

THE AMERICAS

Jan Hus is burned at the stake as a heretic (1415).

A Portuguese fleet seizes the North African port of Ceuta (1415).

The Council of Constance ends the Great Schism in the Church with the election of a new, generally accepted pope (1417).

In the First Defenestration of Prague, Hussite rebels throw loyalist councilors to their death, marking the start of the Hussite wars (1419).

The reforming minister Jan Hus is appointed rector of Prague's Bethlehem Chapel (1402).

The *Geography* of Claudius Ptolemaeus (Ptolemy) is translated into Latin (c. 1406).

The forces of Emperor Sigismund I are defeated by Jan Žižka outside Prague, saving the Bohemian capital from capture (1420).

Jan Žižka achieves another decisive victory over the emperor at the Battle of Kutná Hora (1421).

Jan Žižka dies (1424).

Gil Eanes successfully sails past Cape Bojador on the coast of West Africa (1434).

An agreement known as the Compacts, signed by representatives of the Catholic Church and the Bohemian nobility, ends the Hussite wars (1436).

Filippo Brunelleschi completes Florence's cathedral (1436).

WESTERN EUROPE

The Ottoman sultan, Bajazet, threatens an assault on the city of Constantinople but is distracted by an invasion of his lands by the Mongol forces of Tamerlane. At the Battle of Ankara, Tamerlane defeats the Ottoman army and Bajazet is captured (1402).

Civil war divides the remnants of the Ottoman Empire (1403).

Mehmet I defeats and kills a rival claimant to reunite the Ottoman Empire (1413).

Constantinople is besieged unsuccessfully, by an Ottoman army led by Sultan Murad II (1422).

At the Council of Florence, a document is signed whose purpose is to end the schism between the Orthodox and Roman Catholic branches of Christianity (1439).

The Turks unsuccessfully b Belgrade (1440).

The Ottomans gain a decis victory over Vladislav I of gary and an army of Weste crusaders at the Battle of (1444).

Constantine XI is crowned emperor of Byzantium (14

THE MIDDLE EAST AND THE BALKANS

The death of Harihara II unleashes a succession struggle for control of the Vijayanagar empire (1404). Deva Raya I emerges two years later as undisputed ruler.

Ahmad I moves the Bahmani capital to Bidar (1422).

Vijayanagar clashes with the kingdom of Orissa, starting a rivalry that lasts for over 100 years (c. 1430).

The death of Deva Raya II to a period of factionalism civil strife in Vijayanagar (

INDIA

TimeFrame AD 1400-1500

-1460	1460-1470	1470-1480	1480-1490	1490-1500

Christopher Columbus sails across the Atlantic, reaching the Bahamas, Cuba, and Hispaniola (1492).

The Genoese explorer John Cabot, sailing from Britain, reaches the coast of Canada (1497).

The Aztecs under Axayacatl declare war on the independent city-state of Tlatelolco near their capital city of Tenochtitlán and bring it under their control (1473).

Under Tupac Yupanqi, Inca soldiers conquer the highly developed Chimu state of northern Peru (1476).

The Aztec ruler Tizoc dies suddenly—perhaps from poison—and is replaced by the warlike Ahuitzotl (1486).

Christopher Columbus, on his third transatlantic voyage, makes his first landfall on the American mainland, near the mouth of the Orinoco River (1498).

...brings two years of ...n and suffering to the ...ople (1450-1452).

The Treaty of Tordesillas divides the undiscovered world into Spanish and Portuguese spheres of influence (1494).

Charles VIII of France invades Italy (1494).

Prince Henry the Navigator dies (1460).

Pope Pius II repudiates the Bohemian Compacts (1462).

Afonso V of Portugal leases exploration rights in Africa to the entrepreneur Fernão Gomes (1469).

Christopher Columbus submits a plan to Ferdinand and Isabella, rulers of Spain, for reaching Asia by sailing westward across the Atlantic Ocean (1486).

The monk Girolamo Savonarola takes over the government of Florence (1494).

Savonarola is burned at the stake (1498).

...o da Vinci is born in a ...utside Florence (1452).

...of Podebrady, a Hussite ...izer, ascends the throne ...mia (1458).

Lorenzo the Magnificent and his brother Giuliano preside over the Medici family and, in effect, rule Florence (1469).

George of Podebrady dies (1471).

The Portuguese mariner Bartolomeu Dias sails around the southernmost tip of Africa, discovering the Cape of Good Hope (1488).

A more ambitious invasion of Italy is mounted by the new French king, Louis XII (1499).

...II becomes Ottoman ...451).

...inople falls to Sultan ...II. Its capture marks ...of the 1,000-year-old ...e Empire (1453).

...garian general János ...turns the Ottomans ...r a further siege of Bel-...456).

...Corvinus, János Hun-...on, ascends the Hungar-...e. In the course of his ...o-year reign, Hungary ...the dominant state in ...urope (1458).

The Ottomans conquer Trebizond, on the Black Sea—the last remaining Byzantine outpost (1461).

The Ottomans conquer Bosnia (1464).

Mehmet II occupies the fortress of Otranto in southern Italy—recaptured the following year—but fails to capture Rhodes in a three-month siege (1480).

Mehmet II, the Conqueror, dies (1481).

Vijayanagar's first dynasty, the Sangama, comes to an end amid a welter of assassinations. The throne passes to a victorious general, Narasimha Saluva (1485).

The sultan of Delhi, Sikandar II Lodi, annexes Bihar (1492).

The Persian émigré Mahmud Ghawan becomes chief minister of the Bahmani sultanate (1463).

Vasco da Gama's Portuguese fleet arrives at the port of Calicut (1498).

ACKNOWLEDGMENTS

The following materials have been reprinted with the kind permission of the publishers: Page 93: "When they tried to scale . . .," quoted in *John Žižka and the Hussite Revolution*, by Frederick G. Heymann, Princeton, N.J.: Princeton University Press, 1955. Page 101: " . . .convivial together in brotherly love . . ." and page 106: " . . .some of them fell into such insanity . . .," both quoted in *A History of the Hussite Revolution*, by Howard Kaminsky, Berkeley: University of California Press, 1967. Page 141: " . . .these great towns . . ." and subsequent quotations from Bernal Díaz del Castillo are taken from *The Conquest of New Spain*, by Bernal Díaz del Castillo, translated by John M. Cohen, London: Penguin Books, 1963. Page 155: "There is nothing like death in war . . .," quoted from *Mexico*, by Michael D. Coe, London: Thames and Hudson, 1984. Page 159: "They brought the royal mummies . . .," quoted from *Religion and Empire*, by Geoffrey W. Conrad and Arthur A. Demarest, Cambridge: Cambridge University Press, 1984. Page 162: "If the Inca himself . . .," quoted from *Handbook of South American Indians*, by John Howland Rowe, Washington, D.C., Smithsonian Institution Bureau of American Ethnology, Bulletin 143, 1946. Page 166: " . . .were done in natural size and style . . .," quoted from *Royal Commentaries of the Incas*, by Garcilaso de la Vega, translated by Harold V. Livermore, Austin: University of Texas Press, 1966.

The editors also wish to thank the following individuals and institutions for their valuable assistance in the preparation of this volume:
Austria: Vienna—Eva Irblich, Handschriftensammlung der Österreichische Nationalbibliothek.
England: Havant—Ian Friel, Mary Rose Trust. Ipswich—Roger Finch. London—Tony Campbell, Map Librarian, British Library; James Chambers; Jeremy Davies; Christopher Gravett, Department of Western Asiatic Antiquities, British Museum; Lotte Hellinga, Deputy Keeper, Collection Development, British Library, Humanities and Social Services; Stuart Laidlow; James Mosley, Librarian, St. Bride Printing Library; Sarah Posey, Department of Ethnography, British Museum; Anthony Shelton, Curator (American Collections), Department of Ethnography, British Museum; Deborah Thompson; Richard Watson. Northampton—Jane Swann, MBE. Saltash—Basil Greenwood, Fellow of the University of Exeter, formerly Director, The National Maritime Museum.
France: Paris—François Avril, Curateur, Département des Manuscrits, Bibliothèque Nationale; Béatrice Coti, Directrice du Service Iconographique, Éditions Mazenod; Marie Montembault, Documentaliste, Département des Antiquités Grecques et Romaines, Musée du Louvre.
Italy: Florence—Brigitte Baumbusch. Rome—Bruno Brizzi; Marta Corsangeo, Biblioteca Casanatense.
Mexico: Mexico City—Salvador Guil'liam, Museo Templo Mayor. Tabasco—Instituto de Cultura de Tabasco Carlos Pellicer Camara.

PICTURE CREDITS

The sources for the illustrations that appear in this book are listed below. Credits from left to right are separated by semicolons; from top to bottom they are separated by dashes.

Cover: Charles Thompson. **2, 3:** Maps by Allan Hollingbery. **8:** Roger Viollet, Paris. **10, 11:** Map by Allan Hollingbery. **12, 13:** Sociedade de Geografia de Lisboa, Lisbon. **14, 15:** Museu Nacional de Arte Antiga, Lisbon. **18, 19:** Art by Lionel Jeans. **22, 23:** John Freeman, London; Werner Forman Archive, London / British Museum, London. **24, 25:** Courtesy Board of Trustees of the Victoria and Albert Museum, London. **27:** Robert Harding Picture Library, London, courtesy Museo Civico, Como; Agosto, Genoa, courtesy Palazzo Tursi, Genoa—Augusto Meneses, courtesy Capilla Real, Granada. **31:** Philadelphia Museum of Art: gift of John T. Dorrance—map by Allan Hollingbery. **32, 33:** Art by Jonothan Potter. **35:** Bibliothèque Royale Albert ler, Brussels, MS. 9231. fol. 281v. **36, 37:** Biblioteca Estense Universitaria, Modena. **38, 39:** Michael Holford, Loughton, Essex, England, courtesy National Maritime Museum, Greenwich. **40, 41:** David Lees, courtesy Biblioteca Estense Universitaria, Modena; Germanisches Nationalmuseum, Nuremburg. **42:** Museo di Firenze com'era, Florence / Scala, Florence. **44:** Map by Allan Hollingbery. **46:** Detail from *The Journey of the Magi* by Benozzo Gozzoli, from the Medici Chapel in the Palazzo Medici-Riccardi, Florence / Scala, Florence; Museo Nazionale di Bargello / Scala, Florence. **47:** *Lorenzo de Medici (1449-1492), Il Magnifico*, Andrea del Verrocchio, National Gallery of Art, Washington, D.C., Samuel H. Kress Collection. **51:** S. Francesco, Prato / Scala, Florence. **52:** Biblioteca Trivulziana, Milan / Scala, Florence. **53:** Palazzo Ducale, Urbino / Scala, Florence. **54:** Italfotogieffe, Florence. **56, 57:** Background and top left, Biblioteca Ambrosiana, Milan; Casa Buonarroti, Florence / Scala, Florence; Rampazzi, Torino. **58, 59:** Museo di Firenze com'era, Florence / Scala, Florence. **60, 61:** Art by Malcolm Chandler; Accademia, Venice / Scala, Florence; Musée Conde, Chantilly / Scala, Florence—courtesy Board of Trustees of the Victoria and Albert Museum, London. **63:** Bibliothèque Nationale, Paris, MS. Fr. 5091, fol. 15v. **65:** Windsor Castle, Royal Library, © 1988 Her Majesty The Queen. **66, 67:** Art by Andrew Robinson; Donato Pineider, Florence, courtesy Biblioteca Nazionale Centrale, Florence. **68, 69:** Palazzo Ducale, Urbino / Scala, Florence. **70:** Windsor Royal Library, © 1988 Her Majesty The Queen; Réunion des Musées Nationaux, Paris. **71:** Edimedia / CDA / Guillemot, Paris, courtesy Musée du Louvre, Paris. **72, 73:** Museo Nazionale di Bargello, Florence / Scala, Florence. **74:** Detail from MS. Fr. 9087, fol. 207, Bibliothèque Nationale, Paris / Sonia Halliday Photographs, Weston Turville, Buckinghamshire, England. **76:** Map by Allan Hollingbery. **79:** Detail from *The Journey of the Magi* by Benozzo Gozzoli, from the Medici Chapel in the Palazzo Medici-Riccardi, Florence / Scala, Florence. **80, 81:** Sonia Halliday Photographs, Weston Turville, Buckinghamshire, England. **82, 83:** Map by Allan Hollingbery; art by Jonothan Potter. **84:** Istanbul University Library, no. F 145, fol. 27 / Axia Art Consultants

BIBLIOGRAPHY

THE AMERICAS

Ascher, Marcia, and Robert Ascher, Code of the Quipu. Ann Arbor, Michigan: University of Michigan Press, 1981.

Baquedano, Elizabeth, Aztec Sculpture. London: British Museum Publications, 1984.

Berdan, Frances, The Aztecs of Central Mexico. New York: Holt, Rinehart and Winston, 1982.

Boone, Elizabeth, ed., Ritual Human Sacrifice. Washington, D.C.: Dumbarton Oaks, 1984.

Bray, Warwick, Everyday Life of the Aztecs. New York: G. P. Putnam's Sons, 1968.

Broda, J., D. Carrasco, and E. Matos, The Great Temple of Tenochtitlan. Berkeley, California: University of California Press, 1987.

Burland, Cottie, The Aztecs: Gods and Fate in Ancient Mexico. London: Orbis, 1980.

Coe, Michael D., Mexico. London: Thames and Hudson, 1984.

Collier, G., R. Rosaldo, and J. Wirth, eds., The Inca and Aztec States, 1400-1800. New York: Harcourt Brace Jovanovich, 1982.

Conrad, Geoffrey W., and Arthur A. Demarest, Religion and Empire. Cambridge, England: Cambridge University Press, 1984.

Davies, Nigel, Human Sacrifice in History and Today. New York: Morrow, 1981.

de la Vega, Garcilasco, Royal Commentaries of the Incas. Transl. by Harold V. Livermore. Austin, Texas: University of Texas Press, 1966.

del Paso y Troncoso, Francisco, Descripción, Historia y Exposición del Códice Borbónico. Mexico City: Siglo Veintiuno, 1981.

Díaz del Castillo, Bernal, The Conquest of New Spain. Transl. by John M. Cohen. London: Penguin Books, 1963.

Gasparini, Graziano, and Luise Margolies, Inca Architecture. Transl. by Patricia J. Lyon. Bloomington, Indiana: Indiana University Press, 1980.

González Torres, Yolotl, El Sacrificio Humano entre los Mexicas. Mexico City: Fondo de Cultura Económica, 1985.

Graulich, Michel, "Double Immolations in Ancient Mexican Sacrificial Ritual." History of Religions (Chicago), 1988.

Hemming, John, Monuments of the Incas. Boston: Little, Brown, 1982.

Hyslop, John, The Inka Road System. Orlando, Florida: Harcourt Brace Jovanovich, 1984.

Kendall, Ann, Everyday Life of the Incas. New York: G. P. Putnam's Sons, 1973.

Lothrop, S. K., W. F. Foshag, and Joy Mahler, Pre-Columbian Art. London: Phaidon Press, 1957.

Marquina, Ignacio, Arquitectura Prehispánica. Mexico City: Instituto Nacional de Antropología e Historia Secretaria de Educación Pública, 1951.

Matos Moctezuma, Eduardo:
The Great Temple of the Aztecs. Transl. by Doris Heyden. London: Thames and Hudson, 1988.
"The Great Temple of Tenochtitlán." Scientific American, August 1984.

Matos Moctezuma, Eduardo, and M. León-Portilla, El Templo Mayor. Mexico City: Beatrice Trueblood, 1981.

Nicholson, H. B., with Eloise Quiñones Keber, Art of Aztec Mexico. Washington, D.C.: National Gallery of Art, 1983.

Pasztory, Esther, Aztec Art. New York: Harry N. Abrams, 1983.

Pollard Rowe, Ann, Elizabeth P. Benson, and Anne-Louise Schaffer, eds., The Junius B. Bird Pre-Columbian Textile Conference: May 19th and 20th, 1973. Washington, D.C.: The Textile Museum and Dumbarton Oaks, Trustees for Harvard University, 1979.

Rowe, John Howland, Handbook of the South American Indians. Washington, D.C.: Smithsonian Institution, 1946.

Stuart, Gene S., The Mighty Aztecs. Washington, D.C.: National Geographic Society, 1981.

Von Hagen, Victor Wolfgang, The Royal Road of the Inca. London: Gordon-Cremonesi, 1976.

INDIA

Barrett, Douglas:
Painting of the Deccan. C XVI-XVII. London: Faber Gallery of Oriental Art, 1958.
Painting of India. Bombay: Taraporevala, 1968.

Barrett, Douglas, and Basil Gray, Indian Painting. London: Macmillan, 1978.

Braudel, Fernand, Gianni Guadelupe, and Francesco Carletti, "Gao Dourado." FMR (Milan), December 1984.

Devakunjuri, D., Hampi. New Delhi: Archeological Survey of India, 1983.

Edwardes, Michael, Indian Temples and Palaces. London: Paul Hamlyn, 1969.

Filliozat, V., ed., The Vijayanagar Empire as Seen by Domingo Paez and Fernao Nuniz. Transl. by Robert Sewell. New Delhi: National Book Trust, 1977.

Fritz, John, George Michell, and M. S. Nagaraja Rao, Where Kings and Gods Meet. Tucson, Arizona: University of Arizona, 1984.

Heras, F. V., Aravidu Dynasty of Vijayanagar. Madras: B. G. Paul, 1927.

Hurlimann, Martin, India. Transl. by D. J. S. Thomson. London: Thames and Hudson, 1967.

Longhurst, A. H., Hampi Ruins. New Delhi: Asian Educational Services, 1987.

Mahalingam, T. V., *Administration and Social Life under Vijayanagar*. Madras: University of Madras, 1969-1975.

Michell, George:
The Hindu Temple. London: Elek, 1977.
Homage to Hampi. Bombay: Marg, 1980.
Temples of South India. Delhi: Ministry of Information, 1960.
Vijayanagara: City of Victory. London: Trueword, 1982.

Michell, George, and Vasundhaia Filliozat, *Splendours of the Vijayanagara Empire.* Bombay: Marg, 1981.

Michell, George, Catherine Lampert, and Tristam Holland, eds., *The Image of Man: The Indian Perception of the Universe through 2000 Years of Painting and Sculpture.* Hayward Gallery catalog. London: Arts Council of Great Britain / Weidenfeld and Nicolson, 1982.

Rajasekhara, Sindigi, *Masterpieces of Vijayanagara Art.* Bombay: Tarpole, 1983.

Salatore, R. N., *Vijayanagara Art.* Delhi: Sundeep Prakashan, 1982.

Sastri, Nilakanta, *A History of South India.* Madras: R. Dayal / OUP, 1987.

Sewell, R. A., *A Forgotten Empire.* New Delhi: National Book Trust / George Allen and Unwin, 1970.

Sivaramamurti, C.:
An Album of Indian Sculpture. Delhi: National Book Trust, 1975.
L'Art en Inde. Paris: Éditions d'Art Lucien Mazenod, 1977.
Indian Painting. New Delhi: National Book Trust, 1970.
Indian Sculpture. New Delhi: Allied Publishers / Indian Council for Cultural Relations, 1961.
South Indian Bronzes. New Delhi: Lalit Kala Akademi Series of Indian Art, 1963.
South Indian Painting. Delhi: National Museum of Delhi, 1968.

THE MIDDLE EAST AND THE BALKANS
The Arts of Islam. London: Arts Council of Great Britain, 1976.

Babinger, Franz, *Mehmed the Conqueror and His Time.* Princeton, New Jersey: Princeton University Press, 1978.

Betts, R. R., *Essays in Czech History.* London: University of London, 1969.

Browning, Robert, *The Byzantine Empire.* London: Weidenfeld and Nicolson, 1980.

Geanakoplos, Deno John, *Byzantium: Church, Society and Civilization Seen through Contemporary Eyes.* Chicago: University of Chicago Press, 1984.

Gravett, Christopher, *German Medieval Armies: 1300-1500.* London: Osprey, 1985.

Heymann, Frederick G., *John Žižka and the Hussite Revolution.* Princeton, New Jersey: Princeton University Press, 1955.

Horejsi, Jirina, et al., *Renaissance Art in Bohemia.* London: Hamlyn, 1979.

Inalcik, Halil, *The Ottoman Empire: The Classical Age, 1300-1600.* London: Weidenfeld and Nicolson, 1973.

Kaminsky, Howard, *A History of the Hussite Revolution.* Berkeley, California: University of California Press, 1967.

Krischen, Fritz, *Die Landmauer von Konstantinopel.* Berlin: Walter de Gruyter, 1938.

Kritoboulos, *History of Mehmed the Conqueror.* Transl. by Charles T. Riggs. Princeton, New Jersey: Princeton University Press, 1954.

Lane, Arthur, *Later Islamic Pottery.* London: Faber and Faber, 1971.

Lutzow, The Count, *The Hussite Wars.* New York: E. P. Dutton & Co., 1914.

Macek, Josef, *The Hussite Movement in Bohemia.* Prague: Orbis, 1958.

Monroe, Will S., *Bohemia and the Czechs.* Boston: L. C. Page, 1910.

Moorhouse, Geoffrey, and the Editors of Time-Life Books, *Prague* (The Great Cities series). Amsterdam: Time-Life Books, 1980.

Mullett, Michael A., *Radical Religious Movements in Early Modern Europe.* London: George Allen and Unwin, 1980.

Nicol, Donald M., *The Last Centuries of Byzantium: 1261-1453.* London: Rupert Hart-Davis, 1972.

Petsopoulos, Yanni, ed., *Tulips, Arabesques & Turbans: Decorative Arts from the Ottoman Empire.* London: Alexandria Press, 1982.

Portal, Roger, *The Slavs.* London: Weidenfeld and Nicolson, 1969.

Runciman, Steven, *The Fall of Constantinople: 1453.* Cambridge: Cambridge University Press, 1965.

Setton, Kenneth M., ed., *A History of the Crusades.* Vol. 17. Madison, Wisconsin: University of Wisconsin Press, 1975.

Spinka, Matthew:
John Hus. Princeton, New Jersey: Princeton University Press, 1968.
John Hus at the Council of Constance. New York: Columbia University Press, 1965.

Stylianou, Andreas, and Judith A. Stylianou, *The Painted Churches of Cyprus: Treasures of Byzantine Art.* London: Trigraph, for the A. G. Leventis Foundation, 1985.

Van Millingen, Alexander, *Byzantine Constantinople.* London: John Murray, 1899.

WESTERN EUROPE
Aston, Margaret, *The Fifteenth Century: The Prospect of Europe.* London: Thames and Hudson, 1968.

Azurara, Gomes Eanes de, *The Chronicle of the Discovery and Conquest of Guinea.* Ed. and transl. by Raymond Beazley and Edgar Presage. London: The Hakluyt Society, 1896-1899.

Bagrow, Leo, *History of Cartography.* London: C. A. Watts and Co., 1964.

Bertram, Anthony, *Florentine Sculpture.* London: Studio Vista / Dutton Picture-back, 1969.

Bradford, Ernle, *Christopher Columbus.* London: Michael Joseph, 1973.

Brucker, Gene Adam, *Florence: 1138-1737.* London: Sidgwick and Jackson, 1984.

Bühler, Curt F., *The Fifteenth-Century Book: The Scribes, the Printers, the Decorators.* Philadelphia: University of Pennsylvania Press, 1960.

Carter, Victor, Lotte Hellinger, and Tony Parker, "Printing with Gold in the Fifteenth Century." *British Library Journal.* Vol. 9, 1983.

Chrisman, Miriam Usher, *Lay Culture, Learned Culture.* New Haven, Connecticut: Yale University Press, 1982.

Clair, Colin, *A Chronology of Printing.* London: Cassell, 1969.

Crone, G. R., ed. and transl., *The Voyages of Cadamosto and Other Documents on Western Africa in the Second Half of the Fifteenth Century.* London: The Hakluyt Society, 1937.

Destombes, Marcel, ed., *Mappemondes: A.D. 1200-1500.* Amsterdam: Nico Israel, 1964.

Diffie, Bailey W., and George D. Winius, *Foundations of the Portuguese Empire, 1415-1580.* Minneapolis: University of Minnesota Press, 1977.

Divine, David, *The Opening of the World.* London: Collins, 1973.

Febvre, Lucien, and Henri-Jean Martin, *The Coming of the Book: The Impact of Printing, 1450-1800.* London: NLB, 1976.

Greenlee, William B., ed. and transl., *The Voyage of Pedro Alvares Cabral to Brazil and India from Contemporary Documents and Narratives.* London: The Hakluyt Society, 1938.

Harley, J. B., and David Woodward, eds., *The History of Cartography.* Vol. 1. Chicago: University of Chicago Press, 1987.

Hay, Denys, *A General History of Europe in the 14th and 15th Centuries.* New York: Longman, 1966.

Hay, Denys, ed., *The Age of the Renaissance.* London: Thames and Hudson, 1967.

Herrlinger, Robert, *History of Medical Illustration from Antiquity to A.D. 1600.* London: Pitman, 1970.

Holmes, George, *Europe: Hierarchy and Revolt, 1320-1450.* London: Collins, 1975.

Jane, Cecil, transl., *The Journal of Christopher Columbus.* London: Anthony Blond, 1968.

Knecht, Robert, *Renaissance and Reformation.* London: Hamlyn, 1969.

La Roncière, Monique de, and Michael Mollat du Jourdin, *Sea Charts of the Early Explorers.* New York: Thames and Hudson, 1984.

McMurtrie, Douglas C., *The Book: The Story of Printing & Bookmaking.* London: Pitman, 1938.

Masson, Irvine, *The Mainz Psalters and Canon Missae: 1457-1459.* London: The Bibliographical Society, 1954.

Meyer-Baer, Kathi, *Liturgical Music Incunabula.* London: The Bibliographical Society, 1962.

Osborne, Harold, *The Oxford Companion to Art.* Oxford: Clarendon Press, 1970.

Pirenne, Henri, *A History of Europe from the Invasions to the XVI Century.* London: George Allen and Unwin, 1939.

Plumb, J. H., *The Horizon Book of the Renaissance.* New York: American Heritage, 1961.

Ravenstein, E. G., ed. and transl., *The Journal of the First Voyage of Vasco da Gama, 1497-1499.* London: The Hakluyt Society, 1898.

Smith, Robert C., *The Art of Portugal: 1500-1800.* London: Weidenfeld and Nicolson, 1968.

Vervliet, H. D., ed., *The Book through 5000 Years.* London: Phaidon, 1972.

Wallace, Robert, and the Editors of Time-Life Books. *The World of Leonardo: 1452-1519* (Library of Art series). New York: Time-Life Books, 1966.

Wallis, Helen M., and Arthur H. Robinson, eds., *Cartographical Innovations: An International Handbook of Mapping Terms to 1900.* Tring, Hertfordshire: Map Collector Publications / International Cartographic Assoc., 1987.

Wilson, Adrian, *The Making of the Nuremberg Chronicle.* Amsterdam: Nico Israel, 1976.

CHINA

Cotterell, Yong Yap, and Arthur Cotterell, *Chinese Civilization.* London: Weidenfeld and Nicolson, 1977.

May, Julian, "The Eunuch of the Starry Raft." *China Now* (London), spring 1988.

Needham, Joseph, *Science and Civilisation in China.* Vol. 4. Cambridge: Cambridge University Press, 1971.

INDEX